VICTORIAN CRITICAL INTERVENTIONS
Donald E. Hall, Series Editor

Frontispiece: John Ruskin, *Works* (29.ii)

PERFORMING THE VICTORIAN
John Ruskin and Identity in Theater, Science, and Education

SHARON ARONOFSKY WELTMAN

The Ohio State University Press
Columbus

Library of Congress Cataloging-in-Publication Data
Weltman, Sharon Aronofsky, 1957–
    Performing the Victorian : John Ruskin and identity in theater, science,
and education / Sharon Aronofsky Weltman.
        p. cm. — (Victorian critical interventions)
    Includes bibliographical references and index.
    ISBN-13: 978-0-8142-1055-0 (cloth : alk. paper)
    ISBN-10: 0-8142-1055-4 (cloth : alk. paper)
    ISBN-13: 978-0-8142-5760-9 (paper)
    ISBN-10: 0-814-25760-7 (paper)
    1.   Ruskin, John, 1819–1900—Criticism and interpretation. 2.
Identity (Psychology) in literature. 3. Self in literature. 4. Role playing. 5.
Feminism in literature. 6.   Ruskin, John, 1819–1900—Knowledge—
Performing arts. 7. Ruskin, John, 1819–1900—Knowledge—Science. 8.
Ruskin, John, 1819–1900—Knowledge—Education. 9.   Ruskin, John,
1819–1900—Political and social views. I. Title.
    PR5267.I35W46 2007
    828'.809—dc22
                                                            2006029116

    Cover design by Dan O'Dair
    Type set in Adobe Garamond
    Cover photograph by the author from her collection

For George Levine,
Upon your retirement,
With great affection and admiration

CONTENTS

LIST OF ILLUSTRATIONS

ACKNOWLEDGMENTS

This is my second book on John Ruskin. As a PhD candidate at Rutgers long ago when I decided I wanted to do a dissertation on Ruskin, I went to my favorite professor, George Levine. I had arrived at graduate school a few years earlier already knowing how to write about poetry and novels; it was George who set my mind ablaze with the realization that one could read non-fiction in the same way. Naturally, I assumed that George would be pleased.

"Ruskin!" He paused, concerned. "Ruskin is a quagmire."

Undeterred, I went to Daniel Harris, another prominent Victorianist at Rutgers. George and Daniel generally disagreed on intellectual matters. I assumed that this would be no exception.

"Ruskin!" he said, surprised. "Ruskin is a morass."

I suppose that they were right. Sixteen years and a dissertation, multiple articles, and two books later, I'm still stuck on Ruskin. No doubt what worried my professors was that in trying to write about someone so prolific and contradictory, I might never finish the degree. Happily, I didn't get bogged down, then or since. Nevertheless, it's true that I have not yet and may never extricate myself. Ruskin still fascinates me.

So my first thanks go to George Levine, who directed the dissertation anyway. Accessible and astonishingly generous, George has continued all these years a caring and inspiring teacher, advisor, and friend. His suggestions for this book have proven as sagacious as all that have gone before.

I have been very lucky in benefiting from the assistance of many other people and institutions in bringing *Performing the Victorian* to print. I want foremost to thank Donald Hall, series editor for Victorian Critical Interventions, not only for his enthusiasm for this project from the first moment I sent him anything, but also for his wisely steering me to expand my discussion of Oscar Wilde. Thanks are due as well to the staff of Ohio State University Press: Senior Editor Sandy Crooms, Managing Editor Eugene O'Connor, copyeditor Stephanie Gilmore, and others.

Several magnificent scholars have offered invaluable advice on revising

Performing the Victorian. Among these most notably are George Landow, Elizabeth Helsinger, Dinah Birch, Francis O'Gorman, and Christine Krueger. Each read the whole book or large portions of it, several in more than one form. They have earned immense appreciation from me for their hard work and brilliant suggestions. To each of these five critics and friends—thoughtful, knowledgeable, and full of excellent counsel—go my heartfelt thanks. This book simply would not exist without their critique and encouragement. In particular, Dinah Birch, Elizabeth Helsinger, and George Landow (a powerhouse of Victorian studies) will find themselves cited and thanked for specific points throughout this book.

To David Hanson, whose presence forty-five minutes away makes south Louisiana a hotbed of Ruskin studies, goes special acknowledgment for delightful Ruskin consultations and a vibrant sense of community. I must also thank the many scholars whose questions and comments at conferences have helped me clarify my thoughts as this book developed. I will never succeed in recognizing them all here, but a few stand out: John Rosenberg, Linda Austin, Kate Newey, Jeffrey Richards, Robert Hewison, James Dearden, Kristine Garrigan, Michael Wheeler, Vince Lankewish, Jeffrey Spear, Sheila Emerson, Julie Codell, Barry Qualls, Keith Hanley, Rachel Dickinson, Robert Parks, Stephen Finley, Martin Danahay, Van Aken Burd, James Spates, and Carolyn Williams. Additional thanks go to Carolyn Williams and Harriet Davidon for specific improvements to portions of chapter 3 at a very early stage. Finally, thanks to everyone who contributes to Patrick Leary's VICTORIA listserve, an essential resource.

My various writing group colleagues know how much I rely on them for help with revision, research, and deadlines. Les Wade and Jennifer Jones Cavanaugh have kept me on solid ground as I moved into scholarship on theater. Carolyn Ware has offered astute commentary, while Robin Roberts has remained throughout a supremely dedicated and effective mentor in every way. (Here I must quickly digress to thank Robin Roberts and Bill Katz for giving me Ruskin cigar boxes.) For renewed intellectual excitement, I will be forever grateful to my current writing group, Daniel Novak, Pallavi Rastogi, and especially Elsie Michie, the most focused and stimulating editor of all. Each of these colleagues has read at least one draft of *Performing the Victorian;* most have read several. I depend more than they can know upon their motivation, keen analyses, and brainy dynamism.

Louisiana State University has provided considerable support for this book, including a 1999–2000 Sabbatical, a 2002 Regents' Summer Research Grant, a 2003 Manship Summer Research Grant, a 2004 Council on Research Summer Research Grant, and a 2006 departmental imaging grant. Three important travel awards also proved most beneficial: 2004 and 2005 Council on Research Travel Grants and a 2005 College of Arts and Sciences International Travel Grant. Anna Nardo and Malcolm Richardson, my department chairs over the past few years, have vigorously supported my work, and I thank them sincerely. For research assistance, thanks go to my graduate assistant, Ilana Xinos, for a semester summarizing many difficult articles, and to my undergraduate assistants, Katie May, for four years of diligent library and office work, and Zach Keller, already a great help. My students in Victorian literature courses have studied Ruskin and theater along with me; thanks to all of them for unstinting enthusiasm, intriguing ideas, and practical assistance, with particular recognition to Mark King, Andrea Adolph, Kris Ross, and Amy Montz.

To Andrea Fellows Walters of the Sante Fe Opera, thanks go for help in obtaining photographs of *Modern Painters,* which the Opera graciously provided; my appreciation extends all the way back to our 1995 symposium, "Giving Voice to *Modern Painters:* John Ruskin—His Life and Times." I would like to express my gratitude Ludovica Villar-Hauser and Beck Lee for so readily sending photographs of the New York and London productions of *The Countess;* their generosity and effort on behalf of this book is most appreciated. My thanks go also to Gregory Murphy for our pleasant and informative breakfast interview. Thanks are due also to Judy Bolton and the Hill Memorial Library at Louisiana State University, by whose courtesy appear the images from *The Illustrated London News.* LSU's Inter-library Loan Research Liaison Suzanne Raether also merits gargantuan thanks for her indefatigable labor on this book's behalf. Stephen Wildman, inestimable Director/Curator of The Ruskin Library at Lancaster University, deserves my gratitude for many kindnesses. Thanks also to Jason Peak and Kevin Duffy at LSU for prompt and careful digital imaging.

Three chapters of *Performing the Victorian* were previously published in different form. Parts of chapter 1, "'Mechanical Sheep' and 'Monstrous Powers': John Ruskin's Pantomime Reality," appeared as "Pantomime Truth and Gender Performance: John Ruskin on Theatre" from *John Ruskin and Gender,* ed. Dinah Birch and Francis O'Gorman (Palgrave, 2002: 159– 76). Chapter 2, "'Pretty Frou-Frou' Goes Demon Dancing: Performing Species and Gender in Ruskin's Science," is a much expanded version of "Myth and Gender in Ruskin's Science," *Ruskin and the Dawn of Modernism,* ed. Dinah Birch (Oxford UP, 1999: 153–73). Portions of chapter 4, "Ruskin and the Wilde Life: Self and Other on the Millennial Stage," were published as "Victorians on Broadway at the Present Time:

Ruskin's Life on Stage" from *Functions of Victorian Culture at the Present Time,* ed. Christine Krueger (Ohio UP, 2002: 79–94).

Finally, I would like to let my family and friends know how much I treasure their steadfast encouragement. Ellen and Brian Cole, Wayne Aronofsky, and Marianne Lichtenstein often ask about the book; it's gratifying to know that they will be pleased to see it in print. I would like to remember most fondly my feisty father-in-law, Abe Lichtenstein, who first told me about the Ruskin cigar and who expressed continual astonishment that one could spend so much of one's career writing about one person. Likewise, the Lichtensteins, Weltmans, Ordiways, Palmers, Rubens, and Shwiffes have for years charitably taken interest in my research, as have Andrea Roosth and Mimi Heintz. To my children, Alex and Elizabeth Weltman, go my heartiest thanks for frequently getting off the computer when asked, for seeming curious about John Ruskin and Victorian culture, and for being proud of their mother. To Jerry Weltman, who puts up with a lot, still reads my work, and knows when to applaud—as always *y para siempre: Gracias, mi amor.*

"Going to the Morning Performance of the Pantomime." *The Illustrated London News* 60 (January 13, 1872): 48.

Introduction
Unstable as Water

On the eve of the twenty-first century, two new hit shows featuring the Victorian author John Ruskin as a major character played to enthusiastic audiences in New York and San Francisco. It was the year 2000, centenary of the nineteenth-century British writer's death. But a fever for anniversary trivia alone could not have triggered Ruskin's sudden theatrical eminence. One of these plays, Greg Murphy's *The Countess,* had opened off Broadway in 1999 to become the longest-running new production of that season. The other, Tom Stoppard's prize-winning *The Invention of Love,* had previously premiered in 1997 at the National Theatre in London.[1] Even an opera based on Ruskin's life had debuted in 1995.[2] Before this, the last puff of general public awareness about Ruskin had been the cheap and ubiquitous Ruskin Cigar, gone since the 1950s. Now, decades of middle-brow neglect abruptly ended. Suddenly, John Ruskin was a star.

But what kind of a star? These entertaining—even excellent—shows still playing regionally all over the United States create for present-day audiences a perverse, ineffectual, repressed effete who exists primarily as a favorable contrast to our currently more liberated selves. The distorted view of Ruskin's life on stage helps us establish our contemporary identities as superior, an ignominious utility he shares with the rest of Victoriana. But in what other ways, beyond providing fodder for theater-going self-complacency, is thinking about Ruskin and performance useful now? *Performing the Victorian* answers this question by examining Ruskin's own ideas about theater, his conflicted understanding of identity as the result of performance rather than essence, and his fascination with all processes of performance and change. In addition to considering how contemporary theater presents Ruskin for us now and how Ruskin viewed theater and performance then, this study reintegrates Ruskin's social and aesthetic critique (including his theater criticism) with the enigma of his sexuality. Unknowable, it can be seen as a dissident force that ruptures our settled concept of identity based on a polarity of sexual orientations.

John Ruskin's radical social criticism helped to establish the English Labour party, famously motivated Gandhi to transform his life,[3] and justified more progressive education for middle-class women and working men. He is even better known as the chief champion of the artist J. M. W. Turner, the most erudite advocate for the Gothic revival in architecture, and the theoretical inspiration for both the Pre-Raphaelite and the Arts and Crafts movements. Throughout these various accomplishments, his influential art and architecture criticism always carries explicit social critique. Perhaps he is best known among writers and critics as a delicious prose stylist whose word paintings were excerpted from weighty treatises for sale in diminutive gilt-edged gift volumes as examples of sheer beauty well into the twentieth century. The once-revered Victorian sage now symbolizes a repressed and outmoded Other to contemporary culture, which defines itself partly in reaction to a mis-remembered Victorian past. This representation of Ruskin appears not only in the theatrical productions mentioned above but also in much Victorian scholarship and the work of second-wave feminist literary critics.[4] Even the unreadable cipher of Ruskin's sexuality has made him easy to stereotype and dismiss. *Performing the Victorian: John Ruskin and Identity in Theater, Science, and Education* counters that popular and scholarly appropriation of Ruskin as the prime example of Victorian stodginess and stultifying patriarchy by showing how fundamentally Ruskin destabilizes categories of identity in much of his writing, but particularly in works on theater, science, and women's education in the second half of his career.[5] This is also the first book on Ruskin and theater in his own day or on theatrical representations of Ruskin in ours.

Performing the Victorian extends the work of my previous book, *Ruskin's Mythic Queen: Gender Subversion in Victorian Culture.* There I argue that, although Ruskin's often-quoted "Of Queens' Gardens" is typically seen as the quintessential statement glorifying Victorian women's constrained domestic sphere, his richly mythopoetic prose offers an alternative discourse that surprisingly yields the tools to escape fixed categories of gender. In contrast to Coventry Patmore's *The Angel in the House,* Ruskin's essay provides an ideal of active queenship (based partly on Queen Victoria) that redefines the domestic sphere much more broadly. Myth, with its cultural cachet and myriad examples of bodily transformation, supplies the opportunity for gender subversion not only in Ruskin's mythography,[6] but also in the works of other nineteenth- century authors.[7] Besides placing Ruskin's use of myth into historical context, *Ruskin's Mythic Queen* shows how he feminizes language by placing it under the control of the Greek goddess Athena.[8]

Performing the Victorian builds on this earlier work, concentrating now on Ruskin's understanding of theater and performance rather than on his ideas about myth; it argues that Ruskin destabilizes all identity classifications, not just the gender divide. While most Victorianists recognize that viewing Ruskin as merely old-fashioned ignores his originality and revolutionary significance, they do not generally go far enough in acknowledging Ruskin's inventive subversion of basic categories, both ontological (such as gender, nation, race, species, and self) and epistemological (such as animal, vegetable, mineral, art, science, theater, and even life). Ruskin not only pushed social reform and aesthetic innovation—changing the course of art, literature, and politics for both the Victorians and the Moderns—but also presaged postmodern and poststructuralist conceptions of a fluid subjectivity. Ruskin, once in every anthology of literary theory, has all but disappeared, while his contemporaries and students, such as Pater and Wilde, remain. *Performing the Victorian* intervenes in current criticism to demonstrate Ruskin's usefulness as a theorist today.

Part of Ruskin's reputation as an unrepentant prude surely stems from the 142-year-old story, corroborated by Ruskin himself, that he presided over the 1858 burning of Turner's drawings "of the most shameful sort— of the pudenda of women" (Harris 400) in order to protect the great artist's reputation, having concluded that Turner would only have drawn them "under a certain condition of insanity" (Warrell "Exploring" 2003, 7). But Ian Warrell, curator at the Tate Gallery in London, has recently concluded that the supposedly burnt drawings remain intact at the Tate. Far from having torched them, Ruskin had merely tucked them away in an elaborate cataloging system. The news of Ruskin's not having destroyed the drawings made major newspapers on both sides of the Atlantic in December 2004 and January 2005. Warrell speculates that Ruskin might have deceived the world in order to save the drawings and to protect those responsible for their safety, in response to the 1857 Obscene Publications

Act, which could have resulted in the curators' prosecution for holding pornography. Besides rescuing Ruskin from a reputation as an over-zealous, art-burning, Puritanical ultra-censor, Warrell's discovery puts Ruskin in the position of playing the expected role of prude in order to safeguard art and those responsible for it. From our current perspective, that means that Ruskin was already "performing the Victorian."[9]

Ruskin certainly recognized his own role-playing, warning readers in *Fors Clavigera*, "If I took off the Harlequin's mask for a moment, you would say I was simply mad" (*The Works of John Ruskin* 28. 513).[10] He also noticed both the function of theater to help establish identity and the ways in which the self forms through other kinds of performance. Because theater best illustrates Ruskin's notion of identity as performed, *Performing the Victorian* focuses on Ruskin's recurrent writing about theater as it appears throughout his enormous oeuvre. Sprinkled in books as celebrated as *Modern Painters* (1843–1860) and as obscure as *Love's Meinie* (1873–1881), Ruskin's theatrical metaphors and examples drawn from his frequent attendance at the theater illustrate his points about social justice, aesthetic practice, and epistemology. Employing opera, Shakespeare, pantomime, puppet shows, French comedies, melodrama, minstrel shows, juggling acts, and dance to tease out a variety of issues seemingly unrelated to the stage, Ruskin displays fascination with performed identities that cross gender and other boundaries. These discussions are obviously of particular relevance in Ruskin's writing on drama and spectacle, but they also reveal the primacy of performance to his understanding of science and education.[11]

A professional critic of painting and architecture rather than of the performing arts, Ruskin might seem more likely to display a static theory of ontology and of epistemology than a dynamic one. But his organic vision of architecture and his belief in painting from nature are both dynamic; ideas of movement, change, and metamorphosis drive his understanding of identity, of existence, and of knowledge. Ruskin's stressing organicism might suggest an unfolding of an innate or true nature, a stance at odds with a notion of identity constructed through performance; yet they have the crucial similarity of change. In other words, in a critic whose most celebrated and most voluminous discourse is about solid, unmoving things (such as paintings and buildings) as opposed to ephemeral time-bound things (such as theater), the use of kinesis everywhere to picture stasis reveals Ruskin's view that everything is in flux. A good example comes in his fascination with glaciers, which he sketches, paints, describes, studies, and publishes geological discourses upon throughout his life. As Kate Flint points out, it is the movement, the liquid behavior of solid ice, that entrances Ruskin and brings him to write about them in *Deucalion* (1875–1883).[12] The paradoxical allure of fluid characteristics in solids prompts Ruskin to write about crystals in *Ethics of the Dust* (1866) as well: just as glaciers flow, so do minerals before they crystallize, another example of change in stasis. Likewise Ruskin's girl students at the progressive Winnington school, whom he identifies with crystals throughout the *Ethics of the Dust,* flow randomly by his direction about the playground before coalescing in pre-arranged dances to form crystalline shapes.[13] In the same vein, theater provides the most vibrant example of how something seemingly immovable—a person's core or essence—similarly shifts and reifies with each performed iteration.

Reuben's Curse

Ruskin even describes himself as "unstable as water" (28.275). He uses the words in a pleasantly self-deprecating fashion. Having just shown a facsimile of his awkward childhood handwriting, he pokes fun at himself, calling attention to the misshapen letters as "evidence . . . of the incurably desultory character which has brought upon me the curse of Reuben, 'Unstable as water, thou shalt not excel'" (28.275). To prevent anyone from thinking that he is too harsh on his child-self, he goes on merrily: "But I reflect, hereupon, with resolute self-complacency, that water, when good, is a good thing, though it be not stable; and that it may be better sometimes to irrigate than to excel" (28.275). Certainly, Ruskin's affinity for water is of long standing: he wrote three chapters in *Modern Painters II* on how water is represented and what it represents. Ruskin's invocation of Reuben closes the notorious (and disingenuous) memory of his toyless childhood, in which he claimed he had nothing to amuse himself but examining the intricate patterns of his carpet. In this same section of both *Fors* and *Praeterita,* Ruskin vividly recalls "the most radiant Punch and Judy" puppet set, given to him for his birthday by his Croydon aunt but confiscated and disposed of by his evangelical mother, who disapproved of all kinds of theater.[14] While in these early memories Ruskin sees instability as largely positive, elsewhere he is less sanguine about suffering from what we might now call Attention Deficit Disorder. Ruskin even considered the phrase "Unstable as water, thou shalt not excel" for his epitaph, feeling mightily displeased with his difficulty in sticking to one task.[15]

But there is much more to the words Ruskin claims for his identity than he elaborates on here. The phrase "unstable as water" comes from a passage in Genesis, in which Jacob calls his sons to him as he lies dying. It is the moment the men have long awaited, knowing that their father will bless them. Jacob says to Reuben:

> Reuben, thou art my firstborn, my might, and the beginning of my strength, the excellency of dignity, and the excellency of power: Unstable as water, thou shalt not excel; because thou wentest up to thy father's bed; then defiledst thou it: he went up to my couch. (*Genesis* 49:3–4)[16]

Given that this quotation from the Bible tells of how Jacob curses his oldest son Reuben for incestuously sleeping with Jacob's wife (*Genesis* 35:22), one might expect Ruskin's describing himself as "unstable as water" to be an insult. Ruskin ignores the Oedipal transgression that causes Jacob to curse Reuben precisely when and where his son might have expected a blessing, at his father's death-bed, symbolically the very bed that Reuben defiled.[17] Yet Ruskin's characterization of his creative contributions as stemming from his being "unstable as water" seems unconscious of this aspect of the story.

Two things make Ruskin's omission worthy of note. First, Ruskin knew the Bible as well as anyone and far better than most, having, as a child, read it aloud with his mother chapter by chapter every morning after breakfast, from beginning to end and over again, leaving nothing out, not even the "hard names, numbers, or Levitical law" (28.318). Thus one must presume that, in however limited a way he uses the phrase "unstable as water" in this discussion of his own identity, he knows its full Biblical context. Second, while we can safely assume that Ruskin never went to bed with his mother, he never went to bed with anybody else either. The great transgression of Ruskin's sex life was that of inactivity, and all of his romantic relationships remained unconsummated. As a result (or as the cause), his deepest reciprocal emotional attachment to any woman was to his mother. While I do not want to wallow too deeply in Freudian analysis of a man who has been dead for over a hundred years, Ruskin's obliviousness—or sublimation—of the passage's connection to Oedipal incest seems striking. It is almost irresistible to point out that the instability of water as a shaky foundation for character (Ruskin's and everyone else's) is connected at heart with sexual transgression, which, in Ruskin's case, is sexual purity.

Tim Hilton reports that Ruskin understood the curse as negatively describing his difficulty completing projects (2000, 154). John Rosenberg goes farther and reads the quotation as representing Ruskin's increasingly unbalanced mind, culminating in his final madness (147). I would like to take the image farther still to suggest that "unstable as water" articulates the ontological and epistemological instability that Ruskin also expresses through metaphors of performance, as this book shows. Certainly Ruskin's psychology and sexuality bear not only on his personal identity but also on his views about identity formation.

Too often an effort to think seriously about Ruskin's unconsummated marriage to Effie Gray and his later love for the adolescent Rose La Touche has resulted in an overt focus on pathology. Both scholarship and popular staging have speculated on what could have caused Ruskin to reject his bride on their wedding night and every night thereafter for six years. As interesting and revealing as such studies focusing on Ruskin's nocturnal omissions are, it is his odd sex life that provokes continued interest, not because of his later mental illness, but instead because it does not fit into current paradigms that define people within a polarity of heterosexuality and homosexuality. Neither homosexuality nor bisexuality, figured as oscillating between homo- and heterosexual behavior, unsettles people as much as Ruskin's enigmatic transgression against the dominant ideology of sex and its available identities. While some consider Ruskin's intense love of Rose and his teaching at the Winnington school for girls to make him a pedophile, the truth is that we know almost nothing of what Ruskin's sexual feelings were, or even if he had any. Of his sexual actions, if they took place, we know virtually nothing either.[18] Critics, biographers, playwrights, librettists, students, teachers, and curators all seem nonplused by his aberrant inactivity as we cast about for an appropriate identity label based on sexual orientation. Ruskin's transgressive behavior of mysterious inactivity skews or queers our expectations and operates as a kind of sexual dissidence.[19] The function of Ruskin in literary criticism at the present time could be to create a current of fresh ideas about sexual identity, to irrigate—if not inseminate—through what one is tempted to call non-performance theory.

As we will see in the remainder of this book, for Ruskin everything seemingly stationary continually shifts, like water. His fascination with the natural world is largely an enchantment with evolution masked as metamorphosis. He loves glaciers for their motion in apparent fixity. Hard rocks flow before they crystallize. Ruskin's affection for theater and most particularly for pantomime is largely delight in its potential to realize fantastical transformations; indeed, the transformation scene for which Victorian pantomime is so famous is always his favorite. His devotion to girls' education is a dogged attempt to channel what he knows to be their inevitable but unpredictable patterns of development. In his characterization of himself as unstable as water, without a permanent base or solid core, Ruskin notes an ever-changing fluid self, one that always has the potential to crystallize through performance of an action, then to melt back again. As we will see in his writing on theater and his use of theatrical and performance metaphors in his other works on education and science, this mutability is the volatile foundation of all existence.

TERMS OF PERFORMANCE

In this book I use the words *identity, subjectivity,* and *self* almost interchangeably. Other critics, such as Regenia Gagnier and Donald Hall, have pointed out that the terms *identity* and *subjectivity* are not synonymous[20]; an elegant way to describe the difference is to say subjectivity is identity plus a critical self-consciousness of how identity is constructed (Hall 2004, 2–3). Ruskin's own word is *self.* For him *identity* usually suggests correctly naming a plant or mineral, while *subjectivity* means the opposite of *objectivity,* as he explains in his definition of the pathetic fallacy, where he derides the vocabulary of German philosophy (5.204). While acknowledging the usefulness of the term *subjectivity* as one that designates this linguistic foundation of the self or subject and heightens readers' awareness of identity as constructed rather than essential, I find that *identity* does the job just as well, once we establish that identities result from social factors, that the supposed core of being exists more extrinsically than intrinsically.[21]

How does Ruskin's understanding of the self fit into this postmodern insight? As the following chapters will show, he reluctantly recognizes the instability of the self, both predicated by and undermined by processes of performance. As he invokes the theater to make important points about society, education, science, art, and the theater itself, Ruskin reacts anxiously when confronting performances that blur boundaries between basic categories of existence, such as gender, species, and the difference between animate and inanimate objects. At the same time, he continually undermines those distinctions in his writing and performances. In addition, Ruskin's theatrical qualities as lecturer and even as audience underscore the importance of identity performance.

Judith Butler's ground-breaking insights have been most influential in driving contemporary discussions of gender construction as the result of performance. In Butler's philosophy, performances of gendered acts cite previously performed gendered acts, which further reinforce existing gender paradigms—while also allowing for change through altered performances for later citation.[22] While in *Gender Trouble* and *Bodies that Matter* Butler considers all kinds of gendered acts, her points apply clearly to the theater (as she discusses in "Performative Acts and Gender Constitution"), because theater supplies both stereotyped characters that reinforce existing gender distinctions and a range of others that subvert them. Theater, in which live performers may recreate a realistic portrayal of contemporary life or may just as easily produce the illusion of fantastical bodies unthought of before, is part of a system that molds and remolds genders, and if genders, then all aspects of identity and embodiment. It is one of the "regulatory schemas that produce intelligible morphological possibilities" (Butler 1993, 14) that can be revolutionary as well as repressive in its constitution of norms.

Janelle Reinelt reminds us that for Derrida, theater—like all language—is *iterable;* its iterability makes theater not only a language but also both a metaphor for and an example of how gender comes into being through repeated performance. Even more pressingly relevant to Ruskin, for whom—as we will see—process is more vital than product, gender only maintains existence if it is continually performed. As Elin Diamond explains, "It's not just that gender is culturally determined and historically contingent, but rather that 'it' doesn't exist unless it's being done" (4). This is finally the point of Judith Butler's recent book title *Undoing Gender.* It is in this sense of reiterated performance producing identity that I use *performativity* and *performance* in *Performing the Victorian;* however, *performance* encompasses acting, singing, dancing, and juggling before an audience as well as ritualized reiteration of behaviors that constitute identity. *Theatricality* I reserve for moments of discussion that suggest a heightened awareness of a performance experience's artifice and its effect on an audience.[23] Of these words, Ruskin, of course, only uses *performance,* which for him often means "accomplishing" or "doing." But as we have just seen from Diamond and Butler, performing gender and (un)doing gender are the same thing.

IDENTITY AND WORK

Ruskin's reluctant recognition that identity is performed rather than innate obviously differs from Matthew Arnold's understanding of a core or "genuine self," to quote his poem "The Buried Life." It also differs from Thomas Carlyle's and George Eliot's idea that we are what we do, that our work defines us. The difference between them and Ruskin lies in Ruskin's reliance on process rather than product. For Carlyle and for Eliot, it is work that matters; accomplishing something means being someone. For example, by the end of *Middlemarch,* Eliot's Dorothea marries Ladislaw, taking on a more traditional role than she imagined for herself when she married Casaubon to help find the Key to all Mythologies. We read that what matters finally is her incalculably diffusive influence in her new job as Ladislaw's wife. She gives up a fortune in order to take on that task, her goal being not only love but also usefulness. While Eliot recognizes society's control over the development of women's subjectivity (Hall 2004, 46–49), she nevertheless maintains that within limits we can remake ourselves through work.

For Ruskin, in contrast, what makes us who we are is not just our utility (and certainly not our money, clearly not Eliot's contention either). In *Unto this Last,* Ruskin influentially announces that "there is no wealth but life" (17.105), and, for Ruskin, life is transformation, dynamism, change, metamorphosis, performance. Norman Anderson and Margene Weiss point out that for Ruskin "being or selfhood" is "a state of becoming" (12). We exist in performing not solely through a Calvinist "work while there is day" notion of labor that Carlyle proclaims in *Sartor Resartus* (and that, at a fundamental level, binds all three of these Victorian sages together), but also through reiteration of acts that shape us for the moment and only for the moment, thus requiring continual reiteration. Thus it is the *process* of work, not the product or good result or incalculable influence or Carlyle's anti–self-consciousness deriving from work (which so impressed John Stuart Mill), that differentiates Ruskin's notion from the others' we-are-what-we-do mentality.[24] A better way of explaining it might be to say we are what we are doing.

Perhaps Ruskin's particular obsession with the teenage Rose and his appreciation of young girls in general is a profound vision of the fleeting quality of existence and a fascination with the temporality of beauty, which exists only in the moment that it is appreciated. In other words, the point for Ruskin is not a lascivious warning to virgins to get busy gathering rosebuds because life is short, but instead a rueful recognition that life consists entirely of change. Each moment even of a young girl's life so far is already over, and each new moment is also already over, and so on. For example, Ruskin wistfully remarks to the Winnington girls that Rose, with whom he has just visited, is growing and changing so rapidly, that "I shan't see her again for ever so long . . . and then she'll be somebody else—children are as bad as clouds at sunrise—golden change—but change always" (Hilton 2000, 21; Burd 1969, 312). This is different from a *carpe diem* philosophy because the point is not to seize the day for pleasure because soon we will die or at least lose our bloom, but rather to recognize that all we think of as fixed and permanent is in reality constantly changing.[25]

The insight Ruskin offers is the kind of aesthetic criticism we associate with Walter Pater and Oscar Wilde, whom Ruskin influenced. The notions of a fin-de-siècle transgressive identity may be more solidly Victorian than we are used to thinking, at least as far as Ruskin is concerned. We see this in Ruskin's writing not only about art and architecture, but also about science, education, theater, and so on, as he expresses his fascinated uneasiness over universal flux. For instance, evolution clearly unnerves him, so he explains it by way of mythic metamorphosis instead of natural selection. The example of identity transformations on stage, which stand for transformations in life, causes anxieties far different from the solace and comfort of self-knowledge that Carlyle paradoxically draws from the anti-self-consciousness of labor. Eliot seeks identity for Dorothea from purposeful intellectual effort, but Ruskin cannot find identity in work alone because the work—art, acting, writing, building, teaching, or learning—requires a viewer, an audience, a reader, a tourist, a student, a teacher. In other words, because it is the result of performance, identity for Ruskin is a fundamentally social phenomenon.[26]

Identity built through performance requires an audience to reify it as well as other performers to model it. Dinah Birch has hinted that, after his father John James Ruskin's death, Ruskin changed his career from writer to lecturer, from focusing on the written product to the performed experience (2002, 127). Although Ruskin subsequently brought out those lecture series as books, the point is that his published lectures, such as *Sesame and Lilies* and *The Eagle's Nest,* and his published open letters, such as those in *Time and Tide* and *Fors Clavigera,* are as close to performed conversation as possible in a written form. After 1864, for Ruskin all writing aspires to the condition of performance.

What Follows

In the chapters that follow, we will see that, for Ruskin, belief in a stable self falters when confronted with the theater's manifest purpose in entertainment through role-playing, with scientific evidence of change through evolution, and with education's point in fostering improvement. Finally, turn-of-the-twenty-first-century performances portray a fictive Ruskin's sexual repression in order to establish current identities as more advanced and more liberated than the Victorians'; in contrast, concurrent portrayals of Oscar Wilde create in him an example of gay existence for contemporary audiences to use in building present-day identities. However, a closer glance at Ruskin's enigmatic sexuality emphasizes the constructedness of our own dominant sexual ideology that establishes subjectivities within a narrow bipolar paradigm of homo- and heterosexuality.

Chapter 1, "'Mechanical Sheep' and 'Monstrous Powers': John Ruskin's Pantomime Reality," delineates Ruskin's ideas about the theater, which he attended voraciously, often going several times a week. For him, theater best exemplifies the pliability of the self: actors construct alternative identities on stage, highlighting the ways in which we all perform our parts in life. Ruskin sees theater serving many conflicting purposes: it offers amusement, role models to imitate, skillful artists to appreciate, and an abundance of popular culture examples that he uses in his most prominent works to make important points about social justice. Moreover, pantomimes boast fantastically beautiful transformations that Ruskin views as a truer vision of reality than the poverty, pollution, and misery he finds outside the theater in the streets of London. For Ruskin, the theater creates a heightened ontological state in which existence is more real even for the audience than in non-theatrical spaces. But paradoxically, Ruskin is unnerved by the permeability of identity boundaries he observes in theatrical performance. His descriptions of operas, plays, and pantomimes reveal a surprisingly pronounced ambivalence toward staged performance from *Modern Painters* IV (1856) to *Fors Clavigera* (1871–84). His remarks generally focus on performance moments that blur identity boundaries, including divisions between races, species, and the categories of reality and fantasy, but most particularly the gender divide. For example, in his book *Time and Tide* (1867), Ruskin criticizes several instances that both attract and disturb him: a crossed-dressed pantomime of *Ali Baba and the Forty Thieves* in which a cigar is not just a cigar, a juggling act by a Japanese family in which nationality and species categories collapse, and a serpentine dance by a teenage girl. Each of these examples flouts divisions between gender, race, nationality, and species. Ruskin fiercely yearns for adamantine boundaries; yet their portrayal on stage as fluid, along with his own alternately fascinated and horrified depictions of metamorphosis, shows how strongly if reluctantly he recognizes the instability of all orders of identity and epistemology.

Chapter 2, "'Pretty Frou-Frou' Goes Demon Dancing: Performing Species and Gender in Ruskin's Science," shows how in four scientific books, *The Eagle's Nest* (1872) on reconciling art and science, *Love's Meinie* (1873–1881) on ornithology, *Proserpina* (1875–1886) on botany, and *Deucalion* on glaciology (1875–1883), Ruskin creates a feminine science. Throughout these works, he uses theatrical examples as a vehicle to articulate the performative quality of all existence. As a by-product of his effort to devise a new kind of scientific inquiry based on principles different from his contemporaries, he undermines the gender hierarchy that partially constitutes Victorian science. A respected member of the Royal Geological Society, Ruskin attacks violent and intrusive aspects of science that have been gender-coded as masculine; he offers instead a gentle and more passive approach based on quiet observation, corresponding to stereotypically feminine characteristics, constituting the identity of "scientist" both as feminine and as a good audience, appreciating nature's performance. Ruskin also casts women as participants in scientific study, appealing to authorities they would know and using arguments designed to appeal to them. More surprisingly, Ruskin revises Darwinian evolution, which depends upon deadly competition for resources and for females, into a mythic principle of metamorphosis that he identifies as feminine. The shape-shifting of one species into another suggests to Ruskin not the species' origin, as it does for Darwin, but rather a natural language that Ruskin teaches. Ruskin also rewrites Linnaean taxonomy, based on a hierarchy of male over female parts of flowers, into a system of moral classification that privileges the female. The new system takes its nomenclature from the names of Shakespeare's heroines, suggesting that even plants perform their place in Ruskin's botany, where art and science merge. By identifying women with their object of study, Ruskin demolishes the walls between scientist and specimen. Traditional classifications evaporate: nonhuman species are named according to their behavior instead of their form; science fuses both with art and with ethics.

Chapter 3, "Playground and Playhouse: Identity Performance in Ruskin's Education for Girls," demonstrates that Ruskin's plan for the education of girls is not only far more progressive than he is generally credited with, but also a script for identity performance. In his best-seller *Sesame and Lilies* (1865), in his crystallography textbook for girls *Ethics of the Dust* (1866), and in his letters to the real-life girls whom he lectured at the liberal Winnington school, Ruskin considers how young women should be educated to take on their gendered duty. Critics justly complain that part of Ruskin's aim in improving women's education is to make them more suitable companions for future husbands; however, this expressed goal cannot explain the very rigorous improvements he proposes (and helped to implement at the Winnington School). As I have already shown in *Ruskin's Mythic Queen*, rather than nullifying Ruskin's suggestions for reform, this slippage between Ruskin's theory and practice undercuts his stated goal and hints at the instability inherent in his gender classifications. Indeed, he erases gender from student identity. He subverts divisions and hierarchies by couching all the mineralogy lessons in *Ethics of the Dust* in the form of Socratic dialogues; these playlets de-center his own authority and question the notion of identity. Ruskin questions what a "self" is and provokes the girls into wondering if crystals are alive. Likewise, by presenting education as performance, Ruskin hints that the roles the girls learn to play both in their classroom theater and in life are malleable. Ruskin undermines distinctions between animate and inanimate, teacher and student, performer and audience, lecturer and listener as radically as he subverts the distinctions between genders and species in his scientific and theatrical writings. The girls learn that, just like the crystals with which their teacher links them so strongly, their seemingly essential selves only appear to be stable, but instead flow—unstable as water—before crystallizing; they can re-crystallize differently in the future.

In chapter 4, "Ruskin and the Wilde Life: Self and Other on the Millennial Stage," we shift from considering Ruskin's ideas about theater to considering theater about Ruskin—and his friend Oscar Wilde. The chapters preceding this one argue that, for Ruskin, identity and indeed all ontological and epistemological categories are in flux. Yet the Ruskin that we know from current theatrical representations erases the multivalent Ruskin that his own contemporaries revered as a sage or reviled as a radical. These productions include David Lang and Manuela Hoelterhoff's opera *Modern Painters* (1995), Gregory Murphy's off-Broadway success *The Countess* (1999), and Tom Stoppard's critically acclaimed *The Invention of Love* (1997), which also showcases Oscar Wilde. Thousands of theater-goers, viewing Ruskin's repression as prototypically Victorian, learn only self-complacency, a point that James Kincaid has made about current uses of other Victorians, such as Charles Dickens (Epstein 129–32); other Victorianists, such as James Eli Adams, have also noted this about Victorian culture more generally (1999, 126).[27] Instead of presenting Ruskin's revolutionary art, architecture, or social criticism, contemporary enactment of John Ruskin as a stage character satisfies our most caricatured expectations of Victorian culture, giving us a foil against which to define ourselves as more progressive, more feminist, more liberated. The historical Ruskin's unreadable sexuality makes labeling him to our advantage very easy. As a stage character, Ruskin becomes our stodgy Other.

In recent depictions, Oscar Wilde, however, becomes an equally stereotyped model, but for emulation instead of rejection. In addition to *The Invention of Love* (and others), two more plays appeared during the same years as those about Ruskin: Moisés Kaufman's brilliant *Gross Indecency: The Three Trials of Oscar Wilde* (1997) and David Hare's *The Judas Kiss* (1998). Audiences identify profoundly with representations of Wilde as a gay icon, locating in him the possibility of a public homosexual existence; nevertheless, as with Ruskin, these theatrical representations flatten out the historical Wilde, largely ignoring his art, his aesthetics, his concern for social issues, and significant aspects of the biographical record in order to make room for his utility in constructing current identity categories based on sexuality. Yet each of these powerfully poetic critics describes a fluid, performed self that contrasts vividly with the fixed types now appearing on stage. Likewise, both offer social critique that could question the efficacy of these very plays. All of these plays offer examples of what happens when life writing and criticism become theater, raising important theoretical questions about performance, identity, and realism. Based on an unexamined assumption that our own modes of being must be more expansive and pliable than the nineteenth century's, fin-de-millennium theatrical representations of Ruskin and Wilde offer a set of static identity labels that constrain contemporary audiences more rigidly than does the flexible prose of either Ruskin's or Wilde's Victorian writing.

The Conclusion, "Queering Ruskin," analyzes Ruskin's sexuality in more detail, particularly regarding his scandalously unconsummated marriage and his much discussed relationship with the young girl Rose La Touche. It questions current constructions of identity based on sexuality, which the anomaly of Ruskin's desire resists; Ruskin's unusual sex life suggests a postmodern queering of the heterosexual/homosexual/bisexual triad. "Queering Ruskin" does not argue that Ruskin is gay, but rather points to the transgressive effect of Ruskin's sexuality on our rigid set of identities based on recognized sexual orientations. The verb *to queer* does not mean *to out,* but rather to ask that we look from an alternative perspective, to recognize how something not-fitting proves the inadequacy of existing paradigms.[28] Although *queer* has expanded in meaning as an identity label since its reclamation by gay activists in the 1980s from the status of slur, the primary synonym for *queer* is still *strange.* Everyone knows Ruskin's sexuality is odd; the point is that seriously confronting Ruskin's strangeness—rather than dismissing it and disposing of it as pathology—

unsettles our own polarities of gender and sexuality. Ruskin's concern over
the instability of gender, nation, race, and species distinctions in the theater and enacted in science and education broaden our own recognition of
gender identity as performed. Instances of identity performance unnerve
Ruskin; he recoils in purple prose that has echoed across time. Ruskin's sexuality unnerves us; we register our worry in derision that eclipses his significance and utility.

As a preeminent Victorian polymath, the multi-talented Ruskin exemplifies the man of many masks. Mary Ann Caws points to Ruskin's claim
in *Praeterita* (35.457) that he was "no orator, no actor, no painter," but of
course she argues correctly that he's all three (27). He slips in and out of
his myriad roles as author, artist, art critic, art historian, architecture scholar, social critic, economic prophet, collector, museum curator, professor,
school teacher, geologist, botanist, ornithologist, old lecturer, passionate
moralist, mad governess, Victorian sage, and the Master of St. George's
Guild. His variable identities illustrate the shape-shifting he writes about
in his theater writing, his scientific studies, and his educational efforts. As
he performs for the students of Winnington, he not only transforms them
from girls into rocks, snakes, and birds, he also transforms himself. Such
shifting identities do not appear in current theatrical representations of
Ruskin, which marginalize him as the ultimate sexual Other who deflects
sexuality from life onto art. In other words, Ruskin's primacy in Victorian
aesthetics makes him the perfect foil to establish postmodern identities not
only as sexually and socially more liberated, but also as somehow more genuine, because in contrast to Ruskin's sublimation into artifice, present-day
sexualities seem direct and unmediated. But this view—aside from its
overly simplified inference about both current and Victorian sexualities—
obscures Ruskin's radically metamorphic vision in which the ostensible
core identity is as mercurial as any, because it too is established through
reiterated acts.

"Engaging Children for the Christmas Pantomime at the Drury Lane Theatre."
The Illustrated London News 51 (December 7, 1867): 612.

⇥1⇤

"Mechanical Sheep" and
"Monstrous Powers"
John Ruskin's Pantomime Reality

John Ruskin avidly attended and defended the theater throughout his life, often seeing shows of all kinds several times a week when in London. We might expect the author of high brow criticism such as *Modern Painters* to write about opera. But often he rushed to the tremendous variety of popular performances available to him. Edward Burne-Jones describes Ruskin's delightedly dragging him to the front row at the Christy Minstrels, which provided the critic with "afternoons of oblivion" (29.xx); others recall him almost falling off his chair laughing and clapping at charades (Hilton 2000, 405); he confesses a horrified fascination with Punch and Judy (35.20)[1]; his works *Fors Clavigera* and *Time and Tide* both depend on detailed descriptions of fairy-tale pantomimes to make important points. Besides all this, Ruskin also writes about juggling acts and ballet. His pleasure in these theatrical events carries with it a continually suppressed and expressed anxiety—and excitement—that the reality they portray is somehow more real than the world outside, and that the shape-shifting and role playing on stage is a truer representation of identity than the core or "genuine self" (in Matthew Arnold's phrase from his poem "The Buried Life")[2] that Victorian culture more generally recognizes. Ruskin's writing on performance reveals a kind of intensified ontological experience in the theater as he asks it to achieve several contradictory goals. He wants theater to provide hours of escapist entertainment, but he also wants it to present what he calls the True Ideal (6.390), which, as I will show, is a paradoxical claim for the greater truth of theatrical illusion. He seeks a venue for actors to display their artistry and to cultivate aesthetic appreciation and sympathy in the audience. But what Ruskin wants most is for the theater to provide a link to the world outside, not, as one might think, to represent that world more accurately or realistically and also not simply to function as a didactic tool, but rather to make manifest in performance the possibility of other ways to act. In other words, for Ruskin the enactment of a fictional existence, identity, or idea on stage momentarily realizes it.[3]

Despite his fiercely negative response to certain theatrical moments, Ruskin testifies to his love of the theater repeatedly. In addition to the above mentioned operas, pantomimes, puppet shows, ballets, and minstrelsy, Ruskin frequently attended drawing room comedies, French farces, productions of Shakespeare, melodrama, and circuses. His diaries indicate that he often saw as many as two or three shows a week. As a child every trip to a pantomime "was a matter of intense rapture" (35.175), and as an old man, the theater remained one of his few unsullied pleasures (34.669, 37.478).[4] While a student at Oxford in 1838 he heartily defended the frivolous fun of theater from an attack on its ability to convey moral instruction (1.xxxiv); but throughout his life, both moral purpose and sheer entertainment supplied adequate justification for the theater. He records trying to cheer up the dyspeptic Carlyle with an invitation to some Drury Lane "fooling" (Hunt, 39), and as late as 1880 he still planned to write an essay on the importance of the theater for moral and intellectual education (34.549). His public and private writings overflow with references to theater and with often enthusiastic informal reviews of recent plays and performers.[5] Nevertheless, no criticism has yet considered what the theatrical medium itself suggests to Ruskin, especially in terms of gender performance.[6]

John Ruskin writes about theater with characteristically contradictory emotions, often revealing pronounced ambivalence toward staged performance. The tension appears throughout his career: the passages analyzed in this chapter span from *Modern Painters* IV, published in 1856, to *Fors Clavigera*, published 1871–84. Each time, he uses the theater to illustrate what is wrong and right in his society. His remarks generally focus on performance moments that blur boundaries, including divisions between races, species, and the categories of reality and fantasy, but most particularly the gender divide. For example, in his book *Time and Tide*, published in 1867, Ruskin criticizes several instances that both attract and disturb him: a crossed-dressed pantomime of *Ali Baba and the Forty Thieves*, a seemingly simian juggling act by a Japanese family, and a serpentine dance by a teenage girl. Ruskin's intense reaction to each suggests a special concern for the effect of performance on identity. Current gender theorists such as Judith Butler have argued that far from being stable or anchored in biology, gender is constructed in part through reiterated performances of gendered acts.[7] But just as performance helps to establish gender, it also inevitably helps to erase distinct gender categories. Even while Victorian performances threaten Ruskin's already unstable pretense that genders are immutable, they manifest his belief in a world burgeoning with metamorphic possibility.[8]

Theater historians and literary critics have already pointed out that the stage poses a paradox for the Victorians. On the one hand, the use of stereotypical characters, particularly in melodrama and in stock companies, reinforces accepted gender norms.[9] On the other hand, all acting undermines the humanist notion of a core identity. According to Nina Auerbach, theater for the Victorians "connotes not only lies, but a fluidity of character that decomposes the uniform integrity of the self" (1990, 4).[10] Likewise for theater historian Kerry Powell, "performance by its very nature endangered the Victorian belief in a stable identity, the true or 'buried' self that lies for Matthew Arnold at the core of being" (23). The stage makes explicit the performativity of all identity, including gender, on stage and off.

In *Bodies that Matter*, Butler argues that the categories of sex, male and female, are socially constructed though the repeated performance of gendered acts. Since, in her words, "there is no reference to a pure body which is not at the same time further formulation of that body" (10), even the most bizarre representations of bodies help to constitute or formulate them. For Butler, whatever is repeatedly represented can exist, or rather, already is. Construction of sex or gender is a "process which operates through the reiteration of norms; sex is both produced and destabilized in the course of this reiteration" (10). No discourse reiterates fantastical bodily forms more elaborately than Victorian pantomime and other extravaganzas, with their superabundance of bizarre fairy-tale transformations, teeming with fabulous formulations of what bodies can become (Auerbach 1990, 14–15). With long runs of successful shows, with annual mounting of popular Christmas pantomimes that routinely cast a woman as Principal Boy and a man as the Dame, with continual productions of cross-dressed Shakespeare, Victorian theater ritually reiterated notions of gender identity that fell outside Victorian social norms, helping to destabilize them.

In Butler's terms, theater reveals that all of our identities are the result of reiterated performance. It models in fiction what Butler calls "morphological possibilities" unthought of otherwise (1993, 14); that is, theater provides a site for citation, a staged original to be imitated in what is called real life, then to be portrayed again on stage in turn.[11] When the performance overtly suggests the mutability of gender, race, or species, it is perhaps even more disturbing for the Victorians, who worked hard to maintain these distinctions, despite mounting evidence undermining rigid demarcations. Ruskin in particular struggled between his yearning for Platonic eternal forms and his fundamental recognition that forms dissolve through evolution, as his vacillation about Darwin and the theory of natural selection demonstrates.[12] Ruskin is continually fascinated with and repelled by examples of metamorphosis and hybridity, a pattern that many Victorian stage performances fit.

Despite Ruskin's frequent attendance at the theater, his published *Works* contain no formal essays on the theater, but they do include a number of short responses to theatrical performance as part of discussions of something else. Before turning to Ruskin's mid-career *Time and Tide* (1867), where the bulk of the theatrical digressions most interesting for their gender references appear, I examine passages from two other texts, one earlier and one later, *Modern Painters* IV (1856) and *Fors Clavigera* Letter 39 (1873); in these Ruskin explores his ideas about the social significance of theater. Ruskin's affection for a good show, his concern for its promotion of an ethical world, and his anxiety over the way performances blur important boundaries continue throughout his life.

PAINTED WOMEN AND MODERN PAINTERS

Perhaps Ruskin's best known invocation of the theater—actually an opera—comes in *Modern Painters* IV (1856), in the acclaimed chapter "Mountain Gloom." In this book about beauty in art and on earth, Ruskin often conjures pitiful contrasts between the splendor that nature provides and the miserable social circumstances humans create from it.[13] This example (and the next from *Fors Clavigera*) establishes Ruskin's attitudes toward the social utility of theatrical performance. Here Ruskin also uses the performance as an illustration of the disjuncture between theater and reality. He describes an unnamed opera scene depicting Swiss peasants (probably from Donizetti's *Linda di Chamounix,* which Effie Ruskin reports having seen with her husband in Venice in 1850).[14] Ruskin first contrasts the lighthearted beauty of the theatrical representation of rural life in Switzerland with the penury and distress in the cottage life he has personally witnessed in the Swiss countryside. He goes on to say:

> [H]ardly an evening passes in London or Paris, but one of those cottages is painted for the better amusement of the fair and idle[.] . . . [G]ood and kind people, poetically-minded, delight themselves in imagining the happy life led by peasants who dwell by Alpine fountains, and kneel to crosses upon peaks of rock . . . [N]ightly we give our gold, to fashion forth simulacra of peasants, in gay ribands and white bodices, singing sweet songs, and bowing gracefully to the picturesque crosses: and all the while the veritable peasants are kneeling, songlessly to veritable crosses, in another temper than the kind and fair audiences dream of. . . . (6.390)

One anxiety expressed here (that theater, like poetry, is falsehood) does not reflect Ruskin's position in its entirety. He uses the charge as a rhetorical ploy to get his readers' attention, to get them to feel guilty for not doing anything to alleviate poverty. The pejoratively named "idle" viewers are also "good and kind people," "kind and fair," who surely want to work for social justice, but are distracted rather than inspired by the "False Ideal" (6.390), as he calls it, of happy peasantry depicted on stage. Disdaining the Puritan who regards "theatrical amusement as wrong or harmful," Ruskin describes himself as yearning not for more Realism on stage, but for a way to make real the theatrical representations of happiness, to realize them in the world beyond the opera house. Predating Bertolt Brecht's indictment of the numbing entrancement of bourgeois theater, Ruskin believes the theatrical experience palliates the audience's cathartic impulse to do good by purging their emotions of sympathy too soon, before they themselves have a chance to act.

But Ruskin's goal is not only to point out the irony of this contrast between real and play poverty, but also to urge action:

> If all the gold that has gone to paint the simulacra of the cottages, and to put new songs in the mouths of the simulacra of the peasants, had gone to brighten the existent cottages, and to put new songs in the mouths of the existent peasants, it might in the end, perhaps, have turned out better so, not only for the peasant, but for even the audience. For that form of

the False Ideal has also its correspondent True Ideal. . . . Night after night, the desire of such an ideal springs up in every idle human heart; and night after night, as far as idleness can, we work out this desire in costly lies. We paint the faded actress, build the lath landscape, feed our benevolence with fallacies of felicity, and satisfy our righteousness with poetry of justice. (6.390–91)

Ruskin the theater critic preaches the same message as Ruskin the art critic: good painting and acting depend upon creating a better world to depict.[15] He would prefer his companions were "painting cheeks with health, rather than rouge" (6.393). He goes so far as to detail the prices for mounting an elaborate production and calculates what good could be done with that specific sum in charitable effort, feeding whole Alpine valleys (6.391).[16] Sounding remarkably like more recent drama critics (and consistent with his position on fine art), Ruskin continues by urging less spectacle and more acting, smaller productions and better voices, less money and more quality (6.392).

Though not a Puritan denouncing ungodly theater, Ruskin rejects opiate entertainment that dulls and misdirects sensitivity to social problems.[17] Again, the theatrical experience seems so real that it allows the audience to feel as though they have acted benevolently, without actually helping anyone outside the theater, once the show ends. But even more, his worry over theatricality as artifice stands out. The "faded actress" symbolizes most palpably his concern, because she is the only human—indeed the only animate—example of falsity; Ruskin's list of "lath landscape," "fallacies of felicity," and "poetry of justice" in parallel with her makes the actress as fake and fallacious as they are. The problem has suddenly shifted from money misspent to fear of feminine duplicity; in painting the faded actress, we might pass her off as blooming. Her appearance, or rather her performance, as a younger or healthier woman troubles Ruskin: she embodies "costly lies." As Auerbach explains, this is a typical Victorian concern with actresses, who epitomize the age's terror of deceptive women. Acting equals lying, just as painting equals prostitution.[18]

Ruskin makes the connection to lack of philanthropic action explicit a moment later:

[A]s the heavy-folded curtain falls upon our own stage of life, we shall begin to comprehend that the justice we loved was intended to have been done in fact, and not in poetry. . . . We talk much of money's worth, yet . . . what the wise and charitable European public gave to one night's rehearsal of hypocrisy,—to one hour's pleasant warbling of Linda or Lucia,—would have filled a whole Alpine valley with happiness, and poured the waves of harvest over the famine of many a Lammermoor. (6.391)

The moral force of his message that real justice is better than "poetry of justice" stands, but his choice of metaphor implies that, ultimately, the distinction between the real and the sham is illusory: embracing the theater that he has just attacked, Ruskin concludes with an image of Judgment Day as the final curtain call.[19]

Pantomime Truth in *Fors Clavigera*

Nevertheless, Ruskin's indictment of opera's erroneous depiction of happy peasants does not jibe with his own lifelong devotion to all forms of theatrical entertainment. The point of this attack and similar ones elsewhere in his writing is not that the theater depicts society unrealistically, but that the audience fails to make the proper use of the theater they see performed. His vision for how theater should function comes in a much later example in which he explicitly contrasts and co-mingles the two worlds of stage and street: in Letter 39 (1874) of *Fors Clavigera* (1871–84), his series of open letters to workers.

Written almost twenty years after *Modern Painters* IV, long after Ruskin's famous unconversion in 1858, *Fors Clavigera* abandons the religious orthodoxy of the earlier text, although its moral certainty remains.[20] Also changed is Ruskin's audience: not the expensive book-buying and opera-going readers of *Modern Painters,* but the working class. Here Ruskin does not charge dramatic production with siphoning funds from charity, nor does he revile it for falsely representing joy instead of sorrow. Indeed, it is specifically the fantasy Ruskin admires in his teasing admission that he cannot tell the difference between pantomime and reality. He means his playfulness to emphasize the surreal quality of ugliness in London, where life should be as pretty as the theatrical representations of fairy tales that he describes. Here Ruskin tells of having just bought tickets for his fifth visit to see the current production of *Cinderella:*

> [D]uring the last three weeks, the greater part of my available leisure has been spent between Cinderella and Jack in the Box; with this curious result upon my mind, that the intermediate scenes of Archer Street and

Prince's Street, Soho, have become to me merely as one part of the drama,
or pantomime, which I happen to have seen last; . . . I begin to ask myself,
Which is the reality, and which the pantomime? Nay, it appears to me not
of much moment which we choose to call Reality. Both are equally real;
and the only question is whether the cheerful state of things which the
spectators, especially the youngest and wisest, entirely applaud and
approve at Hengler's and Drury Lane, must necessarily be interrupted
always by the woeful interlude of the outside world. (28.50–51)

By declaring the difference between Reality and Pantomime insignifi-
cant, Ruskin erases his indictment of "fallacies of felicity" and poetry justice. Moreover, by making London life merely "part of the drama," Ruskin
turns theater into the encompassing truth, while our so-called real lives are
relegated to woeful interludes within the show. While the idea that we are
all just acting our parts in life may sound familiar, this is not quite the same
as saying "all the world's a stage." The kind of show Ruskin elevates to the
greater reality is not Shakespeare, not Jaques's cynical sequence of roles
that life requires. Instead, Ruskin champions pantomime, an extravagant
transformation spectacle in which everything is possible.[21] Recalling both
Auerbach's point about the fabulous metamorphoses abounding in
Victorian pantomimes and Butler's point about the way repeated performances develop new "morphological possibilities," we see the liberating
advantage of a fairy-tale reality in which we can become anything.

Ruskin's longing for the make-believe world of the theater transforms it
from the False to the True Ideal he had pleaded for in *Modern Painters*. Far
from failing in mimesis, theater provides the ideal that the real should imitate. Ruskin describes the actors in *Cinderella* "all doing the most splendid
feats of strength, and patience, and skill. . . . [T]he pretty children [are]
beautifully dressed, taught thoroughly how to behave, and how to dance,
and how to sit still, and giving everybody delight that looks at them"
(28.51). In contrast, Ruskin complains that "the instant I come outside the
door, I find all the children about the streets ill-dressed, and ill-taught, and
ill-behaved, and nobody cares to look at them" (28.51–2). The stage children are still as unlike the children in the streets as the simulacra of peasants were unlike real peasants in *Modern Painters;* the message for the
audience that they neglect their duty to the poor stands, but the ire against
the falsehood of dramatic presentation is gone. Abandoning dreams of
repainting the faded cheek of the actress with health, Ruskin views the cast
as the acme of strength, skill, and exuberant youth.[22]

The contrast serves Ruskin's usual purpose: he rouses his readership to recognize injustice by underscoring what seems best about the child actors. He does so without reference to the fact that their good behavior is part of an act, their nice clothes merely costumes, and the delight they offer an aspect both of their art and their need to earn money. While ignoring that the young actors are themselves child laborers, Ruskin focuses on the dreary circumstances of London's impoverished children. Here he invokes scenes both of the London poor and the London entertainment that he knows his working-class readership will recognize in order to place before them a contrast between what ought to be and what is.[23]

He goes on to decry the audience's reactions to pantomime special effects. At Drury Lane, these include a meadow or

> Green, with its flock of mechanical sheep, which the whole audience claps because they are of pasteboard, as they do the sheep in Little Red Riding Hood because they are alive; but in either case, must have them on the stage in order to be pleased with them, and never clap when they see the creatures in a field outside. (28.52)

Ruskin simultaneously highlights and collapses the distinction between theater and not-theater in pointing out what would be the absurdity of clapping for sheep performing themselves off stage; furthermore, he implies that our values are skewed by theater-going conventions that allow us to view the world inside the theater as less true than of that outside. Conversely, to Ruskin we are wrong to imagine that the world outside is less valuable, less intense, and less ideal than the world inside. The contiguity Ruskin sees between stage sheep, either animal or cardboard, and field sheep is the same that he hints at in his contrast between stage children and street children. His goal in collapsing the difference between stage and street or field is to inspire his readers to strive for social change. Yet the sharp irony of Ruskin's frustration stresses the audience's unwillingness to use the performance in the theater as a link to the outer world. The audience

> can't have enough . . . of the loving duet between Tom Tucker and little Bo Peep: they would make the dark fairy dance all night long in her amber light if they could; and yet contentedly return to what they call a necessary state of things outside, where their corn is reaped by machinery, and the only duets are between steam whistles. . . . They still seem to have human ears and eyes, in the Theater; to know *there*, for an hour or two, that golden light, and song, and human skill and grace, are better than

smoke-blackness, and shrieks of iron and fire, and monstrous powers of
constrained elements. (28.52)

His rhetorical purpose is to stress the importance of the staged world
not only as one depicting fairy-tale happiness but also as a venue for the
display of the performers' art and skill as compared to the despair, poverty, and ill-will beyond the theater walls, which he contrasts vividly to the
loveliness of the panto. The contrast resembles his method in *Modern
Painters,* yet here his playful insistence that the two worlds are equally real
suggests more than a rhetorician's ploy contrasting the idealized harmony
on stage with the gritty reality of the street; in this 1873 text as in 1856,
there is no need to claim the fictive to be real in order to make the point
that he loathes neglect of the poor. Something more is going on—as we
shall see. Ruskin echoes both Carlyle's rejection of Victorian machinery
and Dickens's exaltation of Sleary's Circus over Bounderby's Coketown in
Hard Times.[24] As Ruskin idealizes Hengler's circus and Drury Lane pantomimes, he suggests that only within the golden light of the theater, performing the role of spectator, does the audience become fully human.
Outside they merely tend machines, or become machines, or worse.
Although Ruskin begins by saying that he doesn't know the difference
between performance and reality, of course he does, and he prefers the performance.

What all this adds up to is a remarkably complicated attitude toward
the theater, which operates simultaneously as opposites: on the one hand,
as described in *Modern Painters* IV regarding opera, theater functions as a
parasite entertainment blunting the potential philanthropy of its satiated
bourgeois audience; on the other hand, as shown in *Fors Clavigera* regarding pantomime, theater offers an idealized world of art, beauty, and skill
that contrasts with a blighted reality as well as models an alternative to it.
Although the first example comes from an earlier book and the second
from a later one, Ruskin does not grow from one position to the other;
instead, he exhibits both attitudes—contradictory though they are—
throughout his career.[25] However, there is at least one way in which the two
texts are very similar: in both Ruskin subverts the distinction between life
and performance. Ruskin's rejection of the faded actress's fallacious beauty and his embrace of pantomime reality are two sides of the same coin:
anxious attraction to the hazy border between truth and illusion.

This is what we might expect from a time famous both for its anti-theatrical prejudice and for its corollary worshiping of stage celebrity, when
actresses in particular were simultaneously reviled for fakery and desired as

sexually appealing (attitudes that Ruskin also participates in at various times). And this is where the instability of identity enters in. As we shall see shortly in our discussion of *Time and Tide,* Ruskin's notions of gender, nation, and species are all fluid despite his efforts to keep them separate; that fluidity manifests itself in staged performances of transformation across sexual, national, and animal boundaries that are occasions for his most vivid writing on the theater. The relationship between stage and street works the same way, simultaneously distinct and identical. He wants to keep the stage existence purely ideal, so that it can be even more real than the street. In other words, he goes further than rejecting the notion of theater as mimetic, further than proposing theater as a didactic model for others to imitate; for Ruskin, theater seems almost the repository of something like Platonic ideals, realer than the real.[26] If all the world really were a stage, then all its men and women and sheep could live as players, protected by the frame of the stage from the poverty, pollution, and monstrous powers of a mechanized, capitalist, industrial society.[27]

FORTY CIGARS IN *Time and Tide*

These two examples discussed above, with their focus on the social impact of theater, help to put into perspective the vehemence of Ruskin's reaction to the boundary-blurring performances in *Time and Tide.* Appearing in 1867, it comes in the decade sandwiched between *Modern Painters* IV in 1856 and *Fors Clavigera* Letter 39 in 1874. *Time and Tide* consists of Ruskin's published letters to his friend Thomas Dixon, a cork cutter. Like the better-known letters to workmen in *Fors,* Ruskin chooses events from his everyday life as occasions for thoughtful social criticism. In creating a sequel to *Unto this Last* (1860), Ruskin outlines responsibilities for workers in an ideal society, finding ample opportunity to inveigh against the real society surrounding him. In the three letters focusing on theatrical performance I discuss next, Ruskin argues for the importance of healthy amusement; he wants a kinder world in which working men will have the leisure time after a reasonable work day to enjoy noble recreation, rather than suffering such long hours that they are too exhausted to take any pleasure in art or culture. But the crux of the matter for Ruskin is that people do not always want to be amused in a wholesome way. The choice of entertainment available cheaply enough for most laborers worries him.

Although *Time and Tide* belongs to Ruskin's economic works, he wrote it smack in the middle of his most active period writing on women, which not coincidently was when he was most involved in his doomed courtship of Rose La Touche. He brought out "Of Queens' Gardens," his famous essay enlarging women's domestic role, in 1865; *Ethics of the Dust,* his crystallography textbook for girls, in 1866[28]; *Time and Tide* in 1867; and *The Queen of the Air,* his mythographic study of the goddess Athena as his ideal of womanhood, in 1869. While in *Time and Tide* Ruskin is, as always, concerned with economics and social justice, here at the height of his literary power we find a text that develops the conjunction of Ruskin's interests in the stage, in the idea of theater as a false or true ideal, and in women's proper contribution to society, resulting in a forceful expression of ambivalence about gender identity.

In *Time and Tide* Letter V, Ruskin sardonically describes the pantomime *Ali Baba and the Forty Thieves* he has just seen at Covent Garden Theater. Because Victorian pantomimes were wildly popular and appealed to all classes, they provide Ruskin with a perfect example for analyzing a likely amusement for workers.[29] In this first passage, he wryly reports the famed proliferation of cross-dressing supernumeraries or extras:

> The forty thieves were girls. The forty thieves had forty companions, who were girls. The forty thieves and their forty companions were in some way mixed up with about four hundred and forty fairies, who were girls. There was an Oxford and Cambridge boat-race, in which the Oxford and Cambridge men were girls. There was a transformation scene, with a forest, in which the flowers were girls, and a chandelier, in which the lamps were girls, and a great rainbow which was all of girls. (17.336–37)[30]

It is characteristic of Ruskin to enjoy the spectacle of young women as flowers; he often identifies girls with flowers and is, after all, the author of *Proserpina,* which develops a floral taxonomy based entirely on girls' names, as we shall see in the next chapter. Also typical of Ruskin is how clearly he revels in the whimsy of a show that casts a girlish multitude as fairies and lamps and colors of the rainbow. More surprisingly for Ruskin, whose strong ideas about appropriately separate spheres for men and women make up his famous essay "Of Queens' Gardens," he even appears to relish describing the gender-bending performance of actresses as Ali Baba's thieves and as College men, which was in fact conventional in Victorian pantomime. He registers neither surprise nor concern at the Orientalism inherent in portraying Ali Baba and his men as feminine, also typical of Victorian culture. But there is one part of the show that Ruskin enjoys unabashedly, without irony. He admires the little girl playing Ali

Baba's daughter, eight or nine years old, who dances gracefully with a pantomime donkey made up of two fellow actors:

> She did it beautifully and simply, as a child ought to dance. . . .—she looked and behaved innocently,—and she danced her joyful dance with perfect grace, spirit, sweetness, and self-forgetfulness. And through all the vast theater, full of English fathers and mothers and children, there was not one hand lifted to give her sign of praise but mine. (17.337–38)

As much as the lack of enthusiasm for the little girl's simple dance distresses Ruskin, something much worse occurs:

> Presently after this, came on the forty thieves, who, as I told you, were girls; and, there being no thieving to be presently done, and time hanging heavy on their hands, arms, and legs, the forty thief-girls proceeded to light forty cigars. Whereupon the British public gave them a round of applause. Whereupon I fell a thinking; and saw little more of the piece, except as an ugly and disturbing dream. (17.338)

The previous good humor with which Ruskin describes the fantastical abundance of thief-girls is disingenuous, a preparation to decry what follows. The innocent and decent girl-child who dances beautifully and naturally (even with a stage donkey) far outshines the hundreds of young women who not only cross-dress and portray thieves, but also who do not bother dancing and who, finally and most damnably, smoke.

So why does Ruskin loathe the cigar-smoking so much? First, he hated tobacco; he considered it a terrible evil, corrupting the young men of Europe.[31] Second, with Ruskin's idealization of women as moral guides of men, the idea that young girls would smoke publicly, encouraging rather than discouraging such debilitating behavior, would seem a moral perversion of their queenly responsibilities.[32] Third, applause for a shocking visual joke that had been withheld from an artistic and skillful dance appalls the aesthetic critic. The contrast is especially distressing for Ruskin because dancing represents for him part of the duty of girls; he explains in the *Ethics of the Dust* that "dancing is the first of girls' virtues" (18.293), meaning not that they should entertain an audience, but that it is their parents' responsibility that they should be made "intensely happy;—so that they don't know what to do with themselves for happiness,—and dance, instead of walking" (18.296). Finally, the episode highlights what was wrong with the forty thieves and their forty companions all along: the girls are un-girling themselves both by smoking and by playing outlaw men. Not only are they engaging in masculine behavior by smoking at all, but also they are smoking cigars: the phallic symbolism of the cigar needs no Freud to declare itself.

The Victorian public accepted women in pants roles, comic and serious. Theater historians record more than half a dozen famous female Hamlets; Charlotte Cushman successfully played even Romeo (Booth 130; Davis [1991] 112–14); as is still customary, pantomimes routinely employed a woman to play Principal Boy, parodied in Barrie's *Peter Pan* (Auerbach 1990, 46–51).[33] However, Victorian critical uneasiness surfaces when the cross-dressing exceeds particular limits. For example, Powell points out that while most Victorian critics do not seem to mind women playing beardless adolescents, they find preposterous women playing mature men, specifically men with beards (29–30). Likewise, Ruskin does not object to women playing men in the pantomime until they whip out their cigars. So the problem for Ruskin as for his contemporaries seems to be that the beard, like the cigar, symbolizes masculinity too forcefully for critical comfort. A conventionally feminine pantomime boy poses less of a sexual threat, especially since tights show off shapely female legs, often specifically admired by Victorian theater critics.[34] But women with beards or cigars symbolically suggest morphological possibilities too unsettling and compromise gender boundaries too bluntly to pass unremarked.[35]

In *Time and Tide* Letter VI, Ruskin continues his exposition on disturbing theater, here focusing not on gender but on how performance blurs boundaries between races and between species. He mentions having seen, just the night before the Covent Garden pantomime of *Ali Baba,* a performance by jugglers from Japan. He begins the new letter by explaining that he must carry his reader "back to the evil light and uncalm, of the places I was taking you to," a description that sounds more like a tour to the castle of the un-dead than a trip to a circus.[36] But his vexation over the show seems based on the unbalancing effect of witnessing an exhibition of skill that strikes him as impossible because inhuman. The racism in this account is obvious and unfortunately commonplace among Victorians, but what is surprising is the discomfort Ruskin experiences in viewing the acrobatics. He describes the Japanese juggler's "exercises on a suspended pole": the performance's

> special character was a close approximation to the action and power of the
> monkey; even to the prehensile power in the foot; so that I asked a sculp-

tor friend who sat in front of me, whether he thought such a grasp could be acquired by practice, or indicated difference in race. He said he thought it might be got by practice. . . . [T]he father perform[ed] in the presence of his two children, who encouraged him continually with short, sharp cries, like those of animals[,] . . . ending with a dance by the juggler, first as an animal, and then as a goblin . . .

The impression . . . was that of being in the presence of human creatures of a partially inferior race, but not without great human gentleness, domestic affection, and ingenious intellect; who were, nevertheless, as a nation, afflicted by an evil spirit, and driven by it to recreate themselves in achieving, or beholding in achievement, through years of patience, of a certain correspondence with the nature of lower animals. (17.341–2)

Ruskin is disconcerted by the analogy he draws between the juggler's and monkey's ability to climb; he views it not as a skill to laud but as an unpleasant "correspondence with the nature of lower animals." Indeed Ruskin likens the jugglers to beasts four times in this passage. He does not want any "human creature" to seem too much like an animal, even though throughout his prose his imagery is full of such metamorphoses. The bestial resemblance makes the jugglers into demons as well. If the demoniacal quality could remain with the Japanese, Ruskin would probably not have too much trouble with it, but his final sentence in this passage exposes the real problem: he denounces the evil spirit driving the Japanese to enjoy or "recreate" themselves through practicing or appreciating this monkey-like skill. However, the exhibition Ruskin watches is in London, and the audience beholding the achievement is British, not Japanese. In other words, Ruskin worries about the possibly debasing effect on the British worker of watching the distinction between human and animal evaporate. Laborers need recreation, but not this kind. The pun on "recreation" as "re-creation" functions here; if the Japanese can re-create themselves as beasts by juggling or by watching jugglers, so can the English. In Judith Butler's terms, the repeated demonstration of a skill that weakens the perceived difference between man and beast suggests a morphology that is not so imaginary after all: people are monkeys, men are goblins, and women have cigars.

Even more disturbing to Ruskin than the animalistic Japanese jugglers or the cross-dressing, cigar-smoking girls is a performance depicted later in *Time and Tide* Letter VII,[37] where Ruskin describes a dance that imaginatively carries the young performer across lines of both species and gender:

It was also a dance by a little girl—though older than Ali Baba's daughter,
(I suppose a girl of twelve or fourteen). A dance, so called, which consist-
ed only in a series of short, sharp contractions and jerks of the body and
limbs, resulting in attitudes of distorted and quaint ugliness, such as
might be produced in a puppet by sharp twitching of strings at its joints:
these movements being made to the sound of two instruments, which
between them accomplished only a quick vibratory beating and strum-
ming, . . . only in the monotony and aimless construction of it, reminding one of various other insect and reptile cries or warnings: partly of the
cicala's hiss; . . . and partly of the deadened quivering and intense contin-
uousness of the alarm of the rattlesnake. (17.343)

Ruskin's contrast between the graceful, innocent dance from *Ali Baba* and
this pubescent girl's reptilian performance brings together the most distressing qualities from the previous two examples: worse than a monkey,
she resembles an insect or serpent.[38] The mechanical, bestial imagery dehu-
manizes the young dancer, but mentioning the phallic rattlesnake in particular also masculinizes her. Her serpent association, which becomes so
important in *The Queen of the Air*, disturbs Ruskin even more than the
simian effect of the Japanese jugglers because she blurs double boundaries,
merging genders as well as mingling species.[39]

In *The Darkening Glass*, John Rosenberg comments on precisely these
three passages from *Time and Tide*. He points out that although "Ruskin's
digression on the cigar-smoking girls is an indictment of the perversity of
British taste . . . , its underlying energy springs from his self-disgust at his
own perversity, his horrified fascination at child-like innocence . . . becoming suddenly and loathsomely adult" (168).[40] While Rosenberg is unequiv-
ocally right to identify Ruskin's psychological state as an explanation of his
vehemence, I ask why Ruskin digresses on the theater at all, in this book
about laws for an ideal commonwealth.[41] The practical answer is that these
theatrical entertainments are popular culture, and he knows his readers will
be familiar with them. But another answer is that Victorian pantomimes
and spectacles offer repeated enactment of boundary-blurring transformations otherwise available only in the imagination or in fairy-tale or in
myth, but which appear realized on stage in extravagant splendor. As long
as the transformations seem to reinforce gender dichotomy by playing up
sexual difference, Ruskin enjoys himself: Dames are obviously men and the
fun comes from their ludicrousness in drag; Principal Boys are obviously
women and their costumes highlight rather than hide that fact. But somehow in these three performances described in *Time and Tide* the transfor-

mation goes sour, revealing how stage performance not only models but also muddies distinction in categories of identity such as gender or race or species. Once any performance underscores the instability of gender, race, or species as categories, all performances are suspect, and so are all categories, ultimately collapsing even the difference between pantomime and reality. No wonder that Ruskin reacts so strongly to those cigars that the rest of the performance passes "as an ugly and disturbing dream."

HALF LIKE A MONKEY

In his diaries Ruskin often chronicles his dreams about the theater; several recorded dreams correlate precisely with shows he has attended.[42] The most telling example of Ruskin's reactions to gender performance comes not from *Time and Tide,* but from a dream he details in his diary entry on August 9, 1867, about six months after seeing *Ali Baba* and the Japanese juggling exhibition. With its concern with race, species, gender, sexuality, and performance, it ties together all three theatrical experiences from *Time and Tide:*

> A most singular dream last night. I was laying out a garden somewhere and a little child, half like a monkey, brought me a bunch of keys to sell. I looked at them and saw they were ivory and silver, and of exquisite old pattern, but I could not make out on what terms they were to be sold. Then I was in a theater, and a girl of some far-away nation—half like Japanese, but prettier—was dancing, and she had never been used to show her face or neck, and was ashamed; and behind there was a small gallery full of children of the same foreign type, singing, and the one who brought me the keys was one of them, and my father was there with me. And then it came back—the dream—to the keys, and I was talking about them with some one who said they were the keys of a grand old Arabian fortress; and suddenly we were at the gate of it, and we could not agree about the key; and at last the person who held them said: "Would it not be better no one should have them?" and I said, "Yes"; and he took a stone, and crushed them to pieces, and I thought no one could now ever get into the fortress for its treasures, and it would all moulder into ruin; and I was sorry, and woke. (*Diaries* 2.628)

As he had with the Japanese jugglers, Ruskin describes the performer in simian terms, replacing racial difference with one of species.[43] Again he locates his anxiousness about dual identity in the theater. He emphasizes the child's odd morphology in almost evolutionary terms: she is "half like a monkey" and "half like Japanese," a racist hierarchy of physical beauty placing the Japanese below something "prettier."

Keys often represent women's domestic power, as seen in the bunch of household keys proudly carried by Dickens's Agnes Whitfield and Esther Summerson. But like the cigars in the first example from *Time and Tide,* here the keys become phallic symbols.[44] They make the dreamed dancer not only half-human and half-Japanese, but also partly invest her with a masculine attribute. Surely being half-monkey, half-racially other, and half-male contributes to her sense of shame in Ruskin's dream as much as having to exhibit too much of her body to public view: Ruskin here maps hybridity in gender, race, and species as sexual anxiety. Unlike the cigars, however, the keys potentially lead to a treasure trove of beautiful Eastern artifacts. While the sexual symbolism of a key whose purpose is to penetrate a lock and enter a fortress of delight is so blatant that it needs no special explanation, it is worth noting that the fortress is Arabian, not only conflating the East with the feminine in typically Orientalist fashion, but also recalling the five hundred girls in *Ali Baba and the Forty Thieves.* While Ruskin unreservedly abhors the corrupting cigars in *Ali Baba,* he vacillates about the Arabian keys. The dream's strange solution to the problem of who should have the phallus is that no one should; better castration for all than that the young girl be shamed. Ruskin finally regrets the destruction of phallic power when it could lead to art and knowledge and Eastern treasures. Most of all Ruskin regrets that locked away, the treasures will "all moulder into ruin," suggesting that without appreciation, they decay. Both the literal interpretation of deteriorating artifacts for the art critic and the metaphorical interpretation of wasting sexuality for the frustrated lover are obvious,[45] but also this idea applies to the avid theatergoer: just as performing requires an audience, so later in *Fors,* the spectators only become fully human while watching the performance. The dream suggests that protecting young girls from the shame of public display or from the dangers of phallic power comes at too high a price.

While the dreamed performance of the girl dancing and the children singing in the background is short, far briefer than either the whole dream or than the descriptions of performances in *Modern Painters, Time and Tide,* or *Fors Clavigera,* Ruskin's uneasy reactions to real stage performances have already done their work. The imaginary young dancer reiterates the "morphological possibilities" modeled by performances that prompted Ruskin's dream in the first place. What Ruskin experiences in the heightened reality of reiterated performances and their repetition in his dreams is the notion that bodies can be simultaneously male and female, human and animal, British and Japanese, painted and real, effectively making bitter nonsense of distinctions he holds dear, while holding him in fascinated attraction to their transformative magic.

We have seen in this chapter that Ruskin wants theater to provide several different and conflicting functions, a situation that testifies to its importance for him. First, he wants theater to entertain, to succor and sustain, to provide oblivion. Second, he wants it to showcase human talent, skill, and artistry, and to promote sympathetic appreciation in its audience for these qualities. Third, he also wants it to be an aesthetic experience, one that can be valued highly as art. Interestingly, he finds this high-brow characteristic in even the lowliest forms of pantomime and minstrelsy. But fourth, most importantly and quite at odds with the purposes of entertaining escapist oblivion and almost irrelevant to its value as art for art's sake, Ruskin recognizes in the theater a heightened reality that is more real than the "real" world outside. For him, the performed reality is in some sense truer both for the performers *and* for the audience, than the less intensely and less beautifully lived reality outside.

Ruskin's aestheticism here does not stop with the intensely and beautifully lived life Oscar Wilde describes (whom it influenced, of course). Ruskin fiercely insists that the result of performance or aesthetic experience be a more ethical world that manifests improved social justice.[46] For him truth is beauty only if beauty is just: "truth," "justice," and "beauty" become synonymous. As post-Wildeans and postmodernists we understand didacticism to be at odds with aestheticism; Ruskin has already seen that impending split and attempts to reconcile the two.

"Pantomimes at the London Theatres." *The Illustrated London News* 60 (January 13, 1872): 49. Top: *Pygmalion* at the Haymarket; middle: *Tom Thumb* at Drury Lane; bottom: *Ali Baba* at the Crystal Palace.

❧2❧

"Pretty Frou-Frou"
Goes Demon Dancing

Performing Species and Gender in Ruskin's Science

Athletic dancers at the Gaiety Theatre and the French play *Frou-Frou* (1867) might seem odd vehicles for the reconciliation of art and science, but Ruskin describes both for his Oxford students in *The Eagle's Nest: Ten Lectures on the Relation of Natural Science to Art* (1872). He uses these theatrical performances and their audience's reactions to illustrate the importance of gender-coded qualities such as appreciation and sympathy, which he sees as vital for audiences, artists, and scientists alike. *The Eagle's Nest* and Ruskin's other books on science—*Love's Meinie* (1873–1881), *Proserpina* (1875–1886), and *Deucalion* (1875–1883)—raise basic questions for the Victorians and for us, such as, What is science? How does scientific knowledge relate to aesthetic knowledge? To identity performance and to ethics? To ontology and epistemology?

Ruskin's contemporaries John Stuart Mill, John Henry Newman, and Matthew Arnold each urge universities to teach science, ethics and aesthetics, or the True, the Good, and the Beautiful, concerns that go back as far at least as Plato's *Republic*.[1] For Ruskin, these three categories overlap, and with their merger comes a concurrent blending of seemingly separate epistemological and ontological classifications. Ruskin's great skill at minute observation and his genius for vivid particularity in describing what he sees serve

39

him just as well in botany and geology as in art and theater. Famously he declared as a young man that art should follow nature, a position he held throughout his life (3.624); similarly, he wants science to operate as a kind of reverence for nature both in choosing it as its topic of study and in proceeding without harm. If pursued in such reverential fashion, both science and art will respond ethically.

When Ruskin tells his Oxford students in *The Eagle's Nest,* "you will never love art well until you love what it mirrors better" (22.153), he builds upon his belief that aesthetics depends on accurate, empirical scientific knowledge imbued with a kind of mythic animation of the natural world, and that the methods of both art and science require that we submit ourselves to the topic we study (22.150).[2] This approach is not typical either for artists or for scientists. Critics have rightly noted that Ruskin's natural history is old-fashioned even among Victorians. He disputes some of the greatest scientific innovators of his time, such as Charles Darwin and John Tyndall.[3] However, his mythological approach to knowledge has some surprisingly radical side-effects: he creates an alternative science that is both feminized and performative. As a by-product of Ruskin's effort to devise a different kind of science from his contemporaries, he undermines the gender hierarchy that partially constitutes Victorian science and he emphasizes the fluidity of epistemological categories through performed identity. He also calls upon theatrical examples to prove his point.

It has been well documented that within Victorian culture, science stands in gendered opposition to the Nature it studies.[4] In contrast, Ruskin feminizes science. Most simply, in his "grammars" of botany and ornithology, as he called *Proserpina* and *Love's Meinie* (25.xxx), as well as in his books on geology and mineralogy, *Deucalion* and *Ethics of the Dust* (1866), Ruskin includes women as active participants in scientific inquiry, appealing to authorities they would know and using arguments designed (rather condescendingly) to appeal to them. He also attacks violent and intrusive aspects of traditional science that have been gender-coded as masculine; he offers instead a gentle and frankly more passive science based on quiet, sympathetic observation, a science which corresponds to stereotypically feminine characteristics. In a sense, this perspective suggests not only that Ruskin encourages women to become scientists, but also that he encourages scientists to become (or at least to act like) women. Even more surprisingly he revises Darwinian evolution, which depends upon deadly competition for resources and for females, into a mythic principle of metamorphosis that Ruskin identifies as feminine. Ruskin expresses the transmution of species in language suggesting that one species performs another. Ruskin also rewrites

Linnaean taxonomy, based on a hierarchy of male over female parts of flowers, into a system of moral classification that privileges the female. He renames botanical orders according to the names of women in Shakespeare's plays, classifying plants according to characteristics that reflect on what Ruskin sees as their moral bearing. Even flowers perform their species identity in Ruskin's view, establishing their ethos through action-read-as-language rather than, as in more acceptable botanical classifications that rely on form, through origin or heredity.

The most subtle and most pervasive feminization of science comes from Ruskin's placing all animals under the syncretic and formative power of the Greek goddess Athena as part of a system of natural hieroglyphs, in which every living and non-living object represents something else. I have argued extensively in the final two chapters of *Ruskin's Mythic Queen* that Ruskin feminizes both metaphor and language through his use of mythology in the *Ethics of the Dust* and *The Queen of the Air;* my chapter here builds on my work in that book.[5] An aspect of learning to decipher this language of nature is to study what in *The Queen of the Air* Ruskin calls "living hieroglyphs" or "Words of God" (the snakes, birds, crystals, and flowers Ruskin analyzes in his scientific texts). Empirically and appreciatively observing how the living signifiers move or grow or die leads to an understanding of what they mean. For Ruskin, "it is not the arrangement of new systems, not the discovery of new facts, which constitutes the man of science, but the submission to an eternal system" (22.150). Because he feminizes language in *The Queen of the Air* by (among other things) making it the province of Athena, and because scientific study is a mode of reading Athena's natural hieroglyphics, science is feminized, too. Since Ruskin rejects the search for origin and focuses instead always on things as they change and what they represent at that moment, it is as though the world performs itself for him. The scientist is like the sympathetic, receptive audience or spectator at a play that the universe puts on. Under Athena's rule, everything personifies something else; in nature's play of signifiers, we can just sit back and watch the show of eternal signification.

WOMEN IN RUSKIN'S SCIENCE

Technologies that ravage the landscape have long been figured as male: the common image of "raping the earth" expresses this tradition. Even pure science—exclusive of technological application—has generally pictured its object of study as feminine. Certainly Darwin follows this convention in *The Origin of Species,* where he personifies Nature as female, and other instances abound. This construction of science and scientists as male and the subject they study as female implies not only bipolar opposition but also a power dynamic. Critics particularly point to Francis Bacon, founder of empiricism, who spoke of science as binding Nature and all her children to service and making her a slave (Mellor 305).[6] Ludmilla Jordanova cites an iconographic example: the late-nineteenth-century statue in the Paris medical faculty of a robed woman with exposed breasts removing her veil, called *Nature Unveiling Herself before Science,* implies an erotics of gender hierarchy in scientific culture (87). There is also a theatrical aspect to Victorian medical science, most literally manifested in the operating theater, in which a doctor performs an operation before an audience of eager students; the oldest surviving operating theater (in use from 1822 to 1847) is St. Thomas's, where all the patients for these public surgeries were women and all the doctors and medical students were men.[7] Even when scientific inquiry involves no cruelty to organic creatures and no plunder of the earth, the controlling metaphor of the Rational conquering the Mysterious, of the quest to penetrate the unknown and unseen, contributes to the stereotype of male scientist mastering female nature.

Substantial research suggests that nineteenth-century science regarded women as not only more closely tied to nature than men, but also so inferior to men as to be almost a different species, less evolved, not fully human.[8] Londa Schiebinger points out that most European visual depictions of apes were of females, and that debates about whether apes could be educated paralleled those about women and Negroes, suggesting the liminal position all three groups held in Victorian scientific imagination (186). Darwin would not be so sloppy as to hint that women belong to a different species; Charles Darwin and Herbert Spencer usually present women's supposedly lower development in terms of their being child-like rather than animalistic. Woman is "intermediate between the child and the man" (Charles Darwin 717). In other words, because women generally do not grow as big or as hairy as men, they have appeared to these thinkers to remain less fully developed: the male appearance is considered the appropriate adult human state, while the smaller, less hirsute female appearance seems immature. The need for women's arrested development was explained in reproductive terms: the energy required to come to full maturity was necessarily spent producing and nurturing young (Charles Darwin 295–96). But, like Freud, other Victorians managed to suggest that "ontogeny recapitulates phylogeny," so that a less developed human is a less evolved and a less human one, after all.[9] In each of these examples, women are understood by Victorian scientists to be closer than man to nature.[10]

Ruskin's writing undermines the general Victorian hierarchy of masculine science over feminine nature. He redefines science as an exercise in wonder at nature rather than control over nature. Ruskin rejected those aspects of Victorian science and technology that were tied to aggression, to imperialism, to control, to mastery over nature, to greed that would result in bad stewardship of the earth, or to harsh use of colonial women and children (Sawyer 1985, 272). Whereas the early-nineteenth-century scientist Humphrey Davy applauded chemistry for inventing gunpowder (Mellor 292), Ruskin cites the power to blow up people as an example of precisely how modern science and industry have failed (34. 314). Ruskin loathed dissection to learn anatomy for either "a young boy, or girl" (22.233) and hated vivisection for any scientific purpose. He named the university's decision to allow vivisection in Oxford laboratories as his reason for resigning the Slade professorship (Rosenberg 211).[11] He disdained materialist science or "nescience" (22.130) that kills birds or insects in order to study them, and reviled technology that pollutes as it harnesses nature's power. A spiritual or mythic science, science grounded in love of beauty rather than in its denial, would conserve rather than exploit (Sawyer 1985, 272). In short, he proposes a scientific approach in which the scientist, as nature's non-intrusive, respectful observer, correlates to the audience's proper role in watching a theatrical performance: appreciative, supportive, and sympathetic.

An example of this relationship between theater and science comes in *The Eagle's Nest*. Ruskin describes having just gone to see the French play *Frou-Frou* (1869) by Henri Meilhac and Ludovic Halévy, which he saw in a French-language London production at the Gaiety Theater on January 26, 1872.[12] Nicknamed "Frou-Frou" for the sound her silk dress makes when it rustles, the vivacious main character Gilberte and her virtuous sister strike Ruskin with painful sympathy:

> The most complete rest and refreshment I can get, when I am overworked, in London . . . is in seeing a French play. But the French act so perfectly that I am obliged to make sure beforehand that all is to end well, or it is as bad as being helplessly present at some real misery.
>
> I was beguiled the other day, by seeing announced as a "Comédie," into going to see "Frou-Frou." Most of you probably know that the three first of its five acts are comedy, or at least playful drama, and that it plunges down, in the two last, to the sorrowfullest catastrophe of all conceivable— though too frequent in daily life—in which irretrievable grief is brought about by the passion of a moment, and the ruin of all that she loves, caused by the heroic error of an entirely good and unselfish person. The sight of

it made me thoroughly ill, and I was not myself again for a week.
(22.173–74)

Ruskin goes on to wonder how it is that people can "endure such an action
before them of a sorrow so poignant" without being pierced with feeling
(22.174). He finds his answer in one young French woman's response that
the play is sad, yes, but "how pretty Frou-Frou looks in her silk dress" (22.174).
Ruskin's worry that audiences focus on fashion rather than the tragedy is
well founded, since all we remember of this play he found so moving, 135
years later, is the English adjective "frou-frou," meaning excessively frilly.[13]
But Ruskin's point in describing this emotionless audience reaction in *The
Eagle's Nest* is that it parallels what is wrong in science. Such "apathy checks
us in our highest spheres of thought, and chills our most solemn purposes"
(22.174). The problem is that scientists do not feel sympathy with and admiration for what they study, but feel only curiosity and ambition. "The insa-
tiableness and immodesty of Science" is "perilous" because it "tempts us through
our very virtues" (22.175). He wants scientists to avoid vanity, but fears that
as "every day [we] are more passionate in discovering,—more violent in competition," are we not also "every day more cold in admiration, and more
dull in reverence?" (22.176). By imagining a reverential science that values
life and champions meticulous but passive observation of nature, rather than
dominates or destroys it, Ruskin subverts the masculine/feminine hierarchy that partly constitutes Victorian scientific culture.[14]

In *The Stones of Venice* (1851–53), written long before Ruskin's angriest
diatribes against contemporary scientists in the 1870s and 1880s, Ruskin
describes two kinds of knowledge-seekers, the scientist and the artist; Robert
Hewison identifies the artistic perceiving man as Ruskin the naturalist (176).

> The thoughtful man is gone far away to seek; but the perceiving man
> must sit still, and open his heart to receive. The thoughtful man is knit-
> ting and sharpening himself into a two-edged sword, wherewith to pierce.
> The perceiving man is stretching himself into a four cornered sheet,
> wherewith to catch. (11.52)

Ruskin presents both men positively, but he represents their opposition through
sexual imagery. Given the gender polarity conventionally assigned the pairs
of terms that Ruskin includes (active/passive, seeking/sitting, sword/sheet,
pierce/catch) and given Ruskin's choice of other words associated with the
feminine that he gives to the perceiving man (open, heart, receive), the artist
or perceiving naturalist becomes feminized within this dyad. This feminine

type is Ruskin's model for scientists who perceive without piercing; who need no phallic swords or dissection tools or engines of war; and who open their hearts to receive the knowledge nature provides. And again, the parallel between a good scientist and a good audience is already at play: sitting still, opening one's heart, receiving the message, and catching (the jokes).

Ruskin also feminizes science by removing scientific education from an exclusively masculine province; by constructing a female audience within his scientific prose; by teaching science to girls at the forward-looking Winnington School; and by often lecturing to women on scientific topics. He repeatedly comments that his books on botany and ornithology are for young people, explicitly including girls (25.35, 413, 45, 483, 504). He writes a mineralogy textbook for "little housewives" (*Ethics of the Dust,* discussed in chapter 3), despite the fact that mineralogy was not typically seen as a subject of study for the female sex. An additional way in which Ruskin endeavors to include women in scientific study is to quote profusely from botanical authorities that women readers would know and find non-threatening. The source of this kind that he most frequently alludes to (albeit condescendingly) is Lindley's *Ladies' Botany,* and on more than one occasion he refers to "Aunt Judy" (naturalist and children's author Juliana Gatty), whose 1859 *Aunt Judy's Tales* were well known. By giving authorities like these almost equal footing with Linnaeus, Ruskin undermines the privilege that the "master" texts (aimed at and written by men) normally have, especially since in this case the standard authorities are by far the more respected, for good reason. He also implicitly gives an aura of feminine authority to scientific inquiry by subordinating empirical knowledge to mythical, so that he invokes Proserpina, Demeter, Athena, Iris, and the Egyptian Neith as authorizing his scientific texts.[15]

Despite the patronizing tone Ruskin often uses when directly addressing his female readers and listeners in his scientific treatises, the mere fact that he includes them at all is significant. An example is a lecture in *Deucalion* on gems called "The Iris of the Earth," where he urges women to be tabernacles, to adorn themselves wisely with jewels. Here women establish their identity as holy temples through appropriate costume and performance of the scientific principles he has outlined: reverence for and conservation of the earth that produced such gemstones and wearing the gems out of an appreciation for both their beauty and their significance rather than through a superficial desire for status. As Paul Sawyer points out, Ruskin uses his "characteristic tone of saccharine condescension" when speaking to young women (1985, 27n). Yet by constructing the readers of *Deucalion* as women, Ruskin alters the notion that geology—or any science—is the exclusive province of men.

The effort is compromised by his patronizing attitude and by the sudden address of this particular lecture, on jewelry, to women, when the lectures in *Deucalion* on glacial movement are addressed to a universal (and thus silently understood as male) reader. However, even in *The Eagle's Nest*, his Oxford lectures of 1872 reconciling science and art, where the audience is specifically identified as male, Ruskin conjures the image of women as successfully engaging in scientific investigations. He requires his male undergraduate listeners to imagine two young women resolute in pursuit of astronomy, and he applauds the one who braves catching a cold in the observatory to view the night sky (22.141–43). Despite his grating sweetness in referring to the starry-eyed girls, he puts them in the masculine preserve of the observatory, where serious astronomical observation takes place; that the Victorians saw this as a men's sanctuary is clear also from *The Mill on the Floss,* in which George Eliot depicts Maggie's assumption that all astronomers hate women and refuse to allow them into their "high towers" because "if the women came there they might talk and hinder them from looking at the stars" (162). Moreover, Ruskin speaks of his girl astronomers in the all-male classrooms of Oxford, where he indoctrinates the young college men toward acceptance of female scientists.

Ruskin defines scientific activity as suitable for women; nevertheless, he retains the traditional sense that the material studied is feminine, complicating his diffusion of the rigid gender hierarchy he writes against. For example, he names his book on botany *Proserpina* and then claims that every young woman *is* Proserpina (25.435), indicating every girl's right to study science and simultaneously every girl's identity with the topic itself: young women are both subject and object of botanical inquiry.[16] He thus intensifies the convention that positions women closer than men to nature. He repeatedly identifies women as women with birds, flowers, and gems. These are entirely traditional identifications; for example, according to the *Oxford English Dictionary,* calling a young woman a "bird" goes back to the fourteenth century. Naming a girl a "jewel" or a "flower" is just as trite. But Ruskin makes unusual use of the convention, because these traditionally feminine objects are exactly those he examines in his natural histories and encourages women to examine, too. Science as the empirical study of these objects becomes for women a kind of ontology, as they study the nature of their own being. The clearest example of how he redoubles women's connection to the material studied is his description of the swallow from *Love's Meinie,* an ornithological incarnation of the ideal housewife in "Of Queens' Gardens."

When describing the swallow's virtues, Ruskin echoes that essay from

Sesame and Lilies (1865), Ruskin's best seller and a volume often presented to young women as a gift (18.5; Helsinger 1983, 96). First, here is the passage from "Of Queens' Gardens":

> This is the true nature of home—it is the place of Peace; the shelter, not only from all injury, but from all terror, doubt, and division. In so far as . . . the hostile society of the outer world is allowed . . . to cross the threshold, it ceases to be home. . . . But so far as it is a sacred place, a vestal temple, a temple of the hearth, . . . so far it vindicates the name, and fulfils the praise, of Home.
>
> And wherever a true wife comes, this home is always round her. The stars only may be over her head; the glowworm in the night-cold grass may be the only fire at her foot; but home is yet wherever she is. (18.122)

Kate Millett's attack on Ruskin in *Sexual Politics* has prompted decades of debate between critics who, agreeing with Millett, consider Ruskin's mythic vision to limit women's role and those who consider the essay to widen women's sphere of action by redefining domestic power more broadly.[17] Complicating either conclusion about "Of Queens' Gardens" are the parallels between the wife and the swallow in *Love's Meinie*. The bird seems always to be female:

> Understand the beauty of the bird which lives with you in your own houses, and which purifies for you, from its insect pestilence, the air that you breathe. Thus the sweet domestic thing has done, for men, at least these four thousand years. She has been their companion, not of the home merely, but of the hearth, and the threshold; . . . showing better her loving-kindness by her faithful return. . . . [I]n her feeble presence, the cowardice, or the wrath, of sacrilege has changed into the fidelities of sanctuary. (25.71)

Like the "true wife," the "sweet domestic" swallow guards the home, the hearth, the threshold. Both keep their homes for men, and have done so for as long as there have been women and birds. The swallow purifies the home from pestilence, cowardice, wrath, and sacrilege; likewise, the woman protects from injury, terror, doubt and division. The woman is at home in the wilderness, the wild creature is at home in a house. Like any "true wife," the bird is a faithful companion, loving and kind. In making the swallow so startlingly like the celebrated woman from "Of Queens' Gardens,"

Ruskin does more than emphasize attractively domestic qualities in the feral bird: he mythologizes both real women and real birds, investing each with far more power than a practical Victorian audience might willingly admit. He also exalts the notion of identity between observer and observed, between the female naturalist and the objects of nature she studies, foreshadowing such twentieth-century notions of feminist science as expressed by Nobel Prize-winning geneticist Barbara McClintock in becoming one with what she studied.[18] In another sense, as the woman becomes the swallow, so the bird becomes the housewife, playing her domestic role, just as later we will see Ruskin portraying flowers in the roles of Shakespeare's Juliet and Viola. Women's special connection to birds or flowers does not disable their understanding. For Ruskin, disconnection and objective distance from the material studied are more debilitating to genuine knowledge than a sympathetic bond.

Evolution and Metamorphosis

Refusing to recognize Darwinian evolution that occurs meaninglessly through cut-throat competition, Ruskin seeks instead an alternative paradigm that allows for transformations between species to occur without competition and with transcendent significance. Ruskin accomplishes his revision of Darwin by advocating a science based on traditionally feminine principles that substitute metamorphosis for evolution.

Natural selection depends on excess population and on rabid competition to produce conditions in which only the "fittest" survive; Ruskin exiles such a scenario to a nightmare landscape exemplified in the barren, choking brambles he describes at Brantwood (25.293). Unlike Darwin or Malthus, for Ruskin there can be no excess population when, aphoristically, "there is no wealth but life" (17.105). He disapproves of competition in any form, even among students (22.243).[19] He offers instead—as I shall show in a moment—a rich world of chaotic flux, traditionally characterized as feminine. The identification of competition as masculine is clear from "Of Queens' Gardens," where women guide men away from the fatal competition of political economy. Because women "enter no contest," they remain morally untainted by the "inevitable error" that corrupts men, who must enter the rough world of the free marketplace (18.122).

Critics often talk about Ruskin's disagreement with Darwin's ideas. He repeatedly makes fun of Darwin's theory of evolution, much to his friends' and editors' embarrassment (25.xlvi). In the overtly scientific books, *Love's*

Meinie and *Proserpina,* Ruskin's speculations on the descent of various plants contain numerous low jokes and irritated outbursts about the theory of evolution that support the critical commonplace that Ruskin opposed Darwin (25.263, 268, 291, 301). But despite Ruskin's often deserved reputation as anti-Darwinist, his position is not so simple, and occasionally he admits that Darwin is right.[20] For example, in *The Queen of the Air,* Ruskin claims that his own theories "are in nowise antagonistic to the theories which Mr. Darwin's unwearied and unerring investigations are every day rendering more probable" (19.358n). Even in *Proserpina* Ruskin uses Darwin to uphold his point when it is convenient; for example, he twice respectfully refers to Darwin's work with carnivorous orchids as an authoritative source for his own analysis (25.224, 25.546). In fact, Darwin epitomizes what Ruskin demands from scientists: a meticulous observer who loves the profusion of nature without exploiting it, who records resemblances in richly metaphorical language (Beer 62). But after claiming no antagonism to Darwin's "unerring investigations," Ruskin continues: "The aesthetic relations of species are independent of their origin" (19.358n). He shifts the significance of species from their origin through natural selection to their mythic or aesthetic or moral meaning, which for Ruskin is the same thing.

Why does Ruskin display such ambivalence toward Darwin's ideas? For two reasons: aesthetics and spirituality. Darwin's discussion of the peacock provokes two of Ruskin's most blatant attacks in both *Love's Meinie* and *Proserpina* (25.36, 25.262–63). To Ruskin, explaining those fabulous feathers as the result of generations of sexual selection misses the point by distracting the observer's attention away from what is really important about the peacock, its beauty.[21] Far different from the creationist arguments brought against Darwin by Samuel Wilberforce and others, Ruskin's objections to natural selection stem from his sense of aesthetics as moral: natural selection seems ugly and meaningless, while for Ruskin the world's beauty manifests intensely felt spiritual truths. Although Ruskin lost his evangelical certitude as he matured, his belief in a direct correspondence between material and spiritual beauty remained, infusing empirical study with a kind of religious meaning. Darwinian correlations among species depend on mere descent, on accidents of time, and on deathly competition, not on mythic significance.

Ruskin cannot deny evolution through natural selection on empirical grounds. Like Darwin he knows that organic forms shift continually. But he is hostile to a science that degrades the interpretation of these variations into a mere quest for beginnings. He alters the explanation of continual change in natural forms from linear evolution to free-flowing metamorphosis. Gillian Beer has pointed out that Darwin draws on the notion of metamorphosis to establish the idea of evolution through natural selection (104–45), so in a sense Ruskin reverses Darwin's revision. In providing a mythic alternative to evolution, Ruskin unwittingly feminizes it; mysterious shape-shifting has long had feminine associations in Western culture.

The wifely swallow from *Love's Meinie* serves as an example of Ruskinian flux as opposed to Darwinian evolution. Ruskin describes the swallow metamorphosing from one creature to another:

> You can only rightly describe the bird by the resemblances, and images of what it seems to have changed from,—then adding the fantastic and beautiful contrast of the unimaginable change. It is an owl that has been trained by the Graces. It is a bat that loves the morning light. It is the aerial reflection of a dolphin. It is the tender domestication of a trout.[22] (25.57)

The metamorphic quality of Ruskin's description self-consciously invokes evolutionary change, only to debunk it a moment later: "the transformations believed in by the anatomist are as yet proved true in no single instance, and in no substance, spiritual or material"; Ruskin opts instead for a mythological understanding of animal significance: "the transformations believed in by the mythologist are at least spiritually true; you cannot too carefully trace or too accurately consider them" (25.57). The parallel structure of the prose here gives the two kinds of transformation equal weight, even though Ruskin knows perfectly well that, though not yet proven, Darwin's theory of evolution is very likely (19.358n). His point is not to promote curmudgeonly disapproval of new-fangled science, but to enjoin his reader to love and appreciate the natural beauty around him or her: "I cannot too often, or too earnestly, urge you not to waste your time in guessing what animals may once have been, while you remain in nearly total ignorance of what they are" (25.57). Seeing the swallow as potentially owl, bat, dolphin, and trout helps us understand not only the spiritual truths about the swallow, but also that everything can be similarly seen as incipiently something else. Each creature plays at being another, blurring our sense of distinct species as we recognize the startling similitude across previously sturdy boundaries. Since both nature and the principle of change are typically figured as feminine, to picture nature in constant chaotic flux (as opposed to linear evolutionary progress) is to intensify the feminine quality of what is already seen as feminine in Western civilization.[23] This metamorphic understanding of species identity is in a sense another kind of performance: each aspect of the swallow depends upon how she acts, upon what other creatures she can impersonate rather than on an inherited or inherent essence. The swallow's seeming metamorphoses are part of being the bird version of the housewife-queen of the earlier essay. There Ruskin praises women for their capacity for change.

This notion of the performed fluidity of form as feminine shows up appropriately enough in Ruskin's discussion of water plants in *Proserpina.* The leaves that remind Ruskin of Persephone's field of flowers he calls "Arethusan" for the Sicilian fountain near the site of her abduction. The chief characteristic of the Arethusan leaves are their capacity for infinite change in form, which is a traditionally feminine feature, based on the female body's changing shape in pregnancy.[24] Flowers are in rapid, continual flux: "they grow as you draw them, and will not stay quite the same creatures for a half-an-hour" (25.252–23), reminding us of what Ruskin says about his maturing young friend Rose: "children are as bad as clouds at sunrise—golden change—but change always" (Hilton 2000, 21; *Winnington Letters* 312). This sense that the universe shifts as Ruskin attempts to record it, even in half an hour, pervades the whole of *Proserpina,* reflected in the book's wild attempts at codification and cavalier admissions of the impossibility of the task.

For Ruskin, as for Darwin, no species remains fixed. Physical forms shift. The difference is that while for Darwin the shifting morphology signifies the species' origin through natural selection, for Ruskin the shifting morphology signifies the current moment's performance of continual metamorphosis.[25] Beauty resides in the momentary form, for Ruskin every bit as much as for his younger colleague Walter Pater, whose *The Renaissance* (1873) famously urges readers to refine their aesthetic sense to apprehend each fleeting moment of beauty. As Ruskin puts it, the aim of the fruit is the flower, not the other way around (25.250). "How far flowers invite or require, flies to interfere in their family affairs—which of them are carnivorous and what forms of pestilence or infection are most favorable to some vegetable and animal growths," these questions, typical of Victorian botany, seem obscenely wrong-headed to Ruskin. He complains, "They will next hear that the rose was made for the canker and the body of man for the worm" (25.414). He objects not to recognizing the fact of insects, cankers, and worms, or to empirical evidence of their roles in plant reproduction and decomposition, but to a science that subordinates beauty to biological process, and whose greatest metaphor for change relies on chance and violence. Ruskin prefers the feminine paradigm of free-flowing multiple metamorphoses instantiating species through a moment's performance that is replete with eternal, mythic significance; he rejects the masculine paradigm of one-way linear movement of species, focused on a point of origin, dependent upon fatal combat, disregard for life, and spiritless sexuality.

SHAKESPEAREAN TAXONOMY

While Ruskin's studies of plants and animals react to Darwin and to the Victorian acceptance of evolution, in *Proserpina* Ruskin also responds to the eighteenth-century botanist Carl Linnaeus, abandoning Linnaean method and the great taxonomist's gender-based hierarchy in plant classification. As with his revision of Darwin, Ruskin's impetus in rewriting Linnaeus is squeamishness about a taxonomy that focuses on reproductive organs instead of floral beauty. Ruskin turns to myth and to dramatic literature for help in reorganizing botany. By developing a nomenclature that reverses Linnaeus and generally privileges women's names, Ruskin again unconsciously feminizes science and emphasizes species performance.

Most people who set out to create a new and better terminology expect its success to depend upon its fixity, its reliability, its authoritativeness. Not Ruskin. He pokes fun at Linnaeus (whom Ruskin clearly also respected and borrowed from heavily), by basing his orders and classes and species of flowers on Greek goddesses and Shakespearean heroines, replacing the father of botany with myth, theater, and fictional females. Linnaeus organizes his Orders and Classes on plant morphology; physical similarities demonstrate relatedness. Ruskin, on the other hand, defines his Orders of plants with a play on words: plant orders are like religious orders or orders of knighthood, based on the plants' symbolic spiritual, ethical, or chivalric qualities, such as grace (26.348). As in *Ethics of the Dust,* in *Proserpina* Ruskin elides scientific education and ethical prescription. He delineates a hierarchy of ideal women very similar to his discussion of literary role models for girls in "Of Queens' Gardens." He ranks "levels of loving tempers in Shakespearean wives and maids," from the most nobly spiritual and greatest to the still completely positive but simplest and most earthly. Isabel, a novice, rises to the top; Viola and Juliet stand at the bottom (25.416–17). The stage heroines give their names to families of flowers in the Order that Ruskin calls Cytherides: Cytherea is a name for Venus; all the flowers in this category are associated with love. The floral families of Viola and Giulietta each share a name with one of Shakespeare's characters; these two families, made up of violets and pansies, are placed in Cytherides to emphasize their connection to "those who love simply, and to the death" (25.416).[26] Ruskin finds the source for his revised categories in the theater, suggesting that more important than the plants' biological processes are the meaningful roles that pansies and violets play. What matters is what they signify.

In addition to creating mythic and Shakespearean nomenclature that Victorian women would find more accessible than Linnaeus, Ruskin makes his botany into an opportunity to preach about ideal characters and behavior for women; he can more successfully control the botanical Viola and Juliet in his prose than his lost almost-fiancée Rose or even his little cousin Lily in real life. The parallel listing again links flowers to females in Ruskin's world, and shows Ruskin at his most conventionally Victorian in ranking sexless over carnal love. The linkage works both ways, though. While he aims both to include women in scientific study and to preach his ideas of ethical behavior, he suggests that plants (like the birds we discussed in *Love's Meinie*) also in some sense "behave" or act. Each entity manifests a sort of ethos that exists, in his view, because it performs in certain ways. [27] This idea is a radical departure from the notion that organisms merely receive a label constituted solely by their appearance or morphology or—worst of all for Ruskin—their origin. Personifying flowers, Ruskin implies that the botanical orders based on girls' names describe the plants' significance because of the plants' own actions. He further implies that such significance or identity could change—indeed must change—if their behavior changes, as over time it will. Such a modification in behavior would require another revision in nomenclature and thus in species designation. The interchangeability of action and language moves us into the realm of a performative science, as I will discuss later in this chapter.

This is very different from Linnaeus, who not only uses plants' reproductive characteristics as the primary method of classification, but also—in contrast to Ruskin—describes plants' sexual relations with great gusto, although always through metaphors that replicated his society's gender relations. For example, for Linnaeus plants are not just male or female, but husbands and wives, who wear wedding gowns; more suggestively "flower petals spread as 'bridal beds,'" . . . while the curtain of the *corolla*" lends "privacy to the amorous newlyweds" (Schiebinger 23); and the marriages are either "public or clandestine" (Schiebinger 25). Likewise, Erasmus Darwin viewed the plant world through the lens of human sexuality, as in his steamy botanical poem *The Loves of the Plants* (1789), where flowers indulge in wanton passion, incest, and suicide.

In response, Ruskin embarks on his project of creating new terms because the old ones are "apt to be founded on some unclean or debasing association, so that to interpret them is to defile the reader's mind." He continues, "I will give no instance; too many will at once occur to any learned reader, and the unlearned I need not vex with so much as one" (25.201). He even scruples against pointing out when he has changed the authoritative term, so as not to call attention to the old corrupting name, even making up new ones in cases where he considered the old ones acceptable, to prevent arousing curiosity and pointing out the offending terms (25.202). Botany's emphasis on sexuality disturbs Ruskin, and his new system silently "corrects" it.[28] Although his motivation stems from personal and cultural sexual repression, Ruskin more urgently sees the change in names as a progressive one that will enable him to teach botany to girls. In a letter to Daniel Oliver (herbarian and librarian at Kew Gardens) Ruskin complained that existing botanical nomenclature "is in many ways disgusting and cannot be translated to girls" (Birch 1981, 152). Ruskin's fanciful rejection of Linnaeas's botanical sexuality allows him to educate boys and girls identically in their scientific studies, as I discuss in chapter 3.

Ruskin revises an even more significant structural aspect of Linnaeun taxonomy. Linnaeus defines Orders of plants by characteristics of the flowers' pistils or female parts, and defines Classes (above Orders in Linnaeus's taxonomy) on the characteristics of flowers' stamens, or male parts, resulting in a botanical reflection of eighteenth-century European gender hierarchy (Schiebinger 17). Because Ruskin avoids classifying kinds of plants along sexual lines, he resists inscribing in his botanical system the same hierarchy that Linnaeus has. Ruskin uses linguistic gender in assigning flowers Latin names to create a syrupy compliment to women: masculine endings only indicate a flower's strength and endurance; feminine endings may also be used of strong flowers, but they must also be good and/or pretty to achieve a feminine name. Existing flower names that are also already established names for women "always signify flowers of great beauty, and noble historic association" (25.345). In his effort to avoid reproductive discussion, Ruskin also reverses Linnaeun hierarchy by ranking the female higher than the male.

Proserpina is amazingly fragmented, with chapters that start sometimes twenty years before they finish, often recording their own evolution—including dates—as much as any subject matter.[29] Just as the natural world that Ruskin tries to define is always in flux, so his "grammar of botany" is a process rather than a product (25.216).[30] The instability of Ruskin's system coupled with the fragmentation of the text undercuts not just his own classifications, but all scientific classifications; as he says in *Deucalion,* "no existing scientific classification can possibly be permanent" (26.418).[31] To expose flaws in existing scientific systems, Ruskin performs what Kirchhoff calls "systematic desystematizing" (1977, 257).[32] This scientific deconstruction produces a text that remains always unfinished; the nomenclature never gels. Ironically, like Darwin's tangled bank, Ruskin's depiction of botany produces more ideas and images than can possibly survive in a single text. The result is a dizzying picture of nature that is as untamable and unstable and prolific as Ruskin himself. But in that superabundant chaos lies the opportunity both to revise science as feminine and to recognize that the natural world defies notions of fixed species, permanent categories, or stable identities. Instead, Ruskin creates a performative science in which plants' and animals' identities depend upon what roles they play.

ATHENA'S NATURAL HIEROGLYPHS
AND THE PLAY OF SIGNIFICATION

Ruskin subverts the Victorian sense of science as masculine more subtly by reading the objects of Naturalist study mythically, as living, acting hieroglyphs within the Greek goddess Athena's "natural language." Finding that Athena ultimately controls science through language should not surprise us since, in *The Eagle's Nest*, Ruskin specifically identifies Sophia—the Christian abstraction of Athena—as controlling both science and art (22.132–34).

The Athena that Ruskin creates in *The Queen of the Air* governs language in several ways: she is goddess of the air, personifying and controlling the medium through which sound waves and thus spoken discourse travels; she wields "formative" or syncretic power, bringing together like and unlike elements to build crystals, to give life, to make metaphors, to bind signifier to signified; and she controls a system of "natural hieroglyphs." In Ruskin's thinking, each corporeal animal is a hieroglyph: real living, breathing, flying, crawling creatures are signs; the "grammars of zoology" that followed *The Queen of the Air* during the next fifteen years interpret Athena's hieroglyphics. Every item in Ruskin's hieroglyphic code, in which serpents and birds are "living Words," is "wholly under the rule of Athena" (19.345). His most vivid example is the snake, which Ruskin describes as "that running brook of horror on the ground"; the serpent evokes "horror . . . of the myth, not of the creature" (19.362). It is "a divine hieroglyph of the demoniac power of the earth. . . . As the bird is the clothed power of the air, so this is the clothed power of the dust; as the bird is the symbol of the spirit of life, so this of the grasp and sting of death" (19.362–63).

Ruskin thus feminizes signification itself, not only by giving Athena governance over the "living hieroglyph," but also and more importantly by having Athena's formative power forge the linguistic link between each hieroglyphic signifier and its inevitable signified.[33] Because for Ruskin all living things and natural objects are signs in Athena's grand system of hieroglyphics, and because scientific investigation is in part an effort to decipher their meaning, Ruskin's sciences on any topic are already positioned under Athena's control. But even more to the point, two of his science books are about animals specifically identified as Athena's hieroglyphs in *The Queen of the Air: Love's Meinie* on birds and *Deucalion's* chapter "The Living Wave" on snakes. Furthermore, the crystals in the *Ethics of the Dust* (and the jewels from "The Iris in the Earth" in *Deucalion*) are the province of Neith, whom Ruskin identifies as the Egyptian Athena.

Flowers ruled by Proserpina also fit into Athena's hieroglyphic code. One way Ruskin manages this is to turn flowers into birds and snakes, and vice-versa.[34] For example, he compares blossoms to birds by explaining an etymology for "petalos" in Greek meaning "to fly" "so that you may think of a bird as spreading its petals to the wind" (25.231). He recognizes the fundamentally metamorphic method of his hieroglyphic thinking by quoting Charles Bonnet, the eighteenth-century discoverer of parthenogenesis, to say "sometimes it was difficult to distinguish a cat from a rosebush" (25.220). Ruskin is joking, but he also means it. Athena's living hieroglyphs shape-shift not only across species, but also from animal to vegetable to mineral and back again.[35] Even in the order of Cytherides (home to all of Shakespeare's heroines), a serpent influence appears: the Viola Cornuta's stalk is "thickest in the middle, like a viper." Its calyx has a "fanged or forked effect; feebly ophidian." Ruskin sums up this flower by complaining, "On the whole, a plant entirely mismanaging itself,—reprehensible and awkward, with taints of worse than awkwardness; and clearly, no true 'species,' but only a link" (25.40–42). The corruption of this flower is not just in its being half violet (or Viola), half pansy (or Juliet), but it in its inability to decide if it is a runner or not. Again he identifies the plants by their behavior or performance, not by their hereditary stock or any other traditional Linnaean method of classification. Paradoxically, Ruskin expects his hieroglyphs to incarnate eternal types, so that pansies and violets, as similar as they are, remain distinct; runners should stay runners and not individual stems. He envisions a universe where living signifiers transmute themselves metaphorically rather than physically, where, even while dissolving and reforming, the ideal forms and what they represent are still identifiable. Yet he knows, with his flimsy Darwinian joke about "species" and "link," that there are no fixed species and that there are myriad links. Ruskin here abominates all things hybrid and mutated and half-evolved, but he evokes them in fascination. His powerful descriptions revel in their existence and in the process of metamorphosis, because finally mutations are hieroglyphs, too.

The serpent ranks as a hieroglyph for Ruskin not only because of its mythic and cultural associations, but also because of its ability to perform symbolic serpent feats. Ultimately, a serpent represents a serpent because it acts like a serpent: were a serpent to look exactly the same—having inherited precisely the same physique and claiming exactly the same descent—but were to behave in some other fashion, for Ruskin it would not represent "serpent." It is the snake's observed action that earns it Ruskin's horror and admiration, not its origin in the primordial slime—or as he calls it, the "calcareous earth" (19.359). Nor is he interested in its originary source of energy, as other scientists would be, which as he acknowledges in *The Eagle's Nest* is the heat and light of the sun. What interests Ruskin, as he describes a "small steel-grey serpent" by the Lake of Brientz (22.196), is the snake's "exquisite grace, strength, and precision of the action" that the animal displays as "[w]ith an almost imperceptible motion, it began to withdraw itself beneath a cluster of leaves" (22.197):

> Without in the least hastening its action, it gradually concealed the whole of its body. . . . I saw what I thought was the glance of another serpent, . . . but it was the same one, which . . . used its utmost agility to spring into the wood; and with so instantaneous a flash of motion, that I never saw it leave the covert, and only caught the gleam of light as it glided away into the copse. (22.197)

Ruskin's fascination with the serpent, as with the Japanese jugglers and the little dancer with the donkey I discussed in chapter 1, is with its skill. Even though the snake is not on any stage, not acting with an audience in mind, still Ruskin reacts to its precision, strength, and grace in action with the same tribute he gave to performers who demonstrate similarly astonishing talents. Just as the swallow establishes its ethos of wholesome domesticity though its behavior, so the snake establishes its ethos of mystery and unnaturalness though the execution of its seemingly unaccountable motion. Living hieroglyphs gain their mythic meaning through performance.

As with the codification of flower names and their mythic significances in *Proserpina*, the correlation of gemstones with moral qualities in *Deucalion* builds a readable language of "natural hieroglyphs," like that described in *The Queen of the Air*.[36] When women dress themselves in the right jewels (which are not so much the gold, crystal, and onyx of the subtitle as moral characteristics, such as charity or grace, as in *Proserpina*), they take on an important role. The tabernacle they should decorate turns out to be both their own bodies, equally with those of their "poor sisters" (26.196).[37] As Sawyer explains,

> In the logic of the lecture, jewels are the primary signifier that renders three

other systems interchangeable—women, the nation (Tabernacles), the natural order. In all these 'grammars,' and in so much of Ruskin's thought, the
unacknowledged wish appears to be to control the world through signs,
which are made ontologically primary to the things they signify. (275n)

Again women perform both the subject and object of study. Like the
crystals personified as little girls and the little girls themselves as readers of
crystal-signs both within and without the *Ethics of the Dust*,[38] like the women-
as-flowers and readers of flower-signs in *Proserpina*, like the wives and swallows in *Sesame and Lilies* and *Love's Meinie*, in *Deucalion* the reader,
constructed here specifically as female, cannot stand outside the system to
read from a meta-position, but is already implicated in it as another sign.
Sawyer suggests that the psychological motivation for creating these signs
is a wish to control (or at least to organize) the outer world through them.
This is certainly true for Ruskin, as it is to some extent for all of us. It is
the fiction that language offers us; we structure disorder and pretend to control it by naming what we experience and manipulating the names. Since
for Ruskin a species achieves its species identity through action and the nomenclature must adapt, action and language become identical, bringing us ver-
tiginously into the realm of a performative science.

Ruskin's rhapsody on the swallow and his glorification of the wife in such
similar terms sometimes backfire and belittle women rather than elevate them.
But his syntheses emphasize not only that Ruskin sees everything hieroglyphically,
but also that for him these likened terms are again interchangeable, reminding us of Fischer-Lichte's insight into the semiotics of the theater, in which
actors are signs of signs, and so on. For Ruskin, a swallow is a woman; we
have seen that a woman is a tabernacle (26.195–96); clearly a tabernacle is a
church (26.196); a church is a crystal (18.320–24); a crystal is a girl (18.271,
221); a girl is a flower (25.388); a flower is a snake (25.221, 283); a snake is
a bird (26.308–309). The circle of slipping signifiers works in any other direction, and the distinction between girl and woman is not significant here: for
example, a woman is also a flower (18.142), a bird is a flower (25.242), a flower
is a crystal (25.250), and so on in dizzyingly metamorphic vision of the world
as each unit acts like, performs, or becomes the next. Since all these objects,
including women, are interchangeable signs, not only can everything be seen
as performing something else, but also everything, including girls and
women and swallows, is a hieroglyph in Athena's language. To pursue botany,
mineralogy, geology, ornithology, or astronomy rightly, in Ruskin's view, brings
the scientist to a better understanding of each hieroglyph studied and to a
better chance of learning to read its (interchangeable) meaning.[39]

CONCLUSION

Ruskin's view of nature as revealing spiritual truth sounds at times like Natural Theology, which reads nature as God's other scripture. This movement was vanquished by mainstream Victorian science. Ruskin, like Tennyson and so many others, had already lost his childhood belief to the clink of geologists' "dreadful Hammers" (36.115) even before *The Origin of Species* (1859) was published and rocked the Christian world's religious confidence. Nevertheless, in rejecting so much that he felt was wrong about his century's science and technology, Ruskin did not simply return to the position of Natural Theology. Despite his interpreting the living hieroglyphs as "Words of God" and despite the often reactionary tone Ruskin takes regarding Darwin and others, his late scientific studies do not evince an orthodox Christianity; his luminous hieroglyphs have too much independent life and are too pagan to be satisfying evidence for the argument from design.[40] Instead of religion, Ruskin uses notions of myth and performance to interpret transcendent truths that he feels materialist science necessarily overlooks.

I have argued that for Ruskin the feminized scientist plays the role of the appreciative audience at nature's play, but he uses a theatrical analogy to put the scientist on stage, too. The opening chapter of *The Eagle's Nest* describes a dance performance Ruskin attended at the Gaiety Theatre about two years earlier, and the purpose of his story is to point out that the great skill, artistry, imagination, and good can be subverted, used for what he sees as ultimately an evil purpose:

> The supposed scene of the dance was Hell, which was painted in the background with its flames. The dancers were supposed to be demons, and wore black masks, with red tinsel for fiery eyes; the same red light was represented as coming out of their ears also. They began their dance by ascending through the stage on spring trap-doors, which threw them at once ten feet into the air; and its performance consisted in the expression of every kind of evil passion, in frantic excess. (22.133)

Having previously told his sports-prone undergraduates that the opposite of good rowing is not bad rowing, but ignorance of how to row, Ruskin here distinguishes between the wisdom and folly in rowing versus the wisdom and folly in dancing. Unlike rowing, "the folly . . . of dancing does not consist in not being able to dance, but in dancing well with an evil purpose; and the better the dancing, the worse the result" (22.133). He explains his point:

These demon dancers . . . were earning their bread by severe and honest
labor. The skill they possessed could not have been acquired but by great
patience and resolute self-denial; and the very power with which they
were able to express, with precision, states of evil passion, indicated that
they have been brought up in a society which, in some measure, knew evil
from good, and which had, therefore, some measure of good in the midst
of it. Nay, the farther probability is, that if you inquired into the life of
these men, you would find that this demon dance had been invented by
some of them with a great imaginative power, and was performed by them
not at all in preference of evil, but to meet the demand of a public whose
admiration was capable of being excited only by violence of gesture, and
vice of emotion. (22.134–35)

The moral point Ruskin makes is obvious: great artistry can be employed
for ethically suspect purposes. Although norms change over time (and whatever disturbed Ruskin about this dance might appear very tame in the age
of MTV and late-night digital cable), the point that art and ethics messily
intertwine remains with us. What Ruskin asks his students and readers is
that as scientists, artists, and stage performers, we refuse to devote our best
work to evil ends.

In employing mythical and theatrical examples to remake scientific study
into a way to read and to appreciate the natural world, to understand and
to love it better, to serve it and to preserve it, Ruskin feminizes science. Indeed,
Ruskin's nineteenth-century vision of science presages twentieth-century eco-
feminism, which also bases its philosophy on valorizing ancient claims of
innate connections between women and the earth. Ruskin's life-long effort
to reconcile science and art culminates in his late "grammars" of ornithology, botany, and mineralogy. That he should try to capture science as his
ally is not surprising in a time when science had just become the "new mythology" (Levine 1987, 8). In effect, Ruskin tries to redefine science so that he
can pursue it in good conscience. This is what makes it finally feminine,
since in his view women are men's moral guides. In *The Laws of Fésole* Ruskin
declared "all great Art is Praise" (15.351). He picks up the aphorism again
and applies it to history in *The Bible of Amiens:* "all great Art is Praise. So
is all faithful History and High Philosophy" (33.29). But what of all great
science, of what Victorians still called Natural History and Natural
Philosophy? The science Ruskin proposes in these books is a science of praise.
As he tells his undergraduates in *The Eagle's Nest,* he wishes to teach "to all
persons entering life—the power of unselfish admiration" (22.286); here
he goes so far as to say that the highest form of charity is justly "giving praise"

(22.268). Appreciative applause in a theater, too, is a necessary "sign of praise" (17.337). This great task of praise that comprises the work of artists, historians, philosophers, philanthropists, audiences, and scientists, happens also to be that of women. In "Of Queens' Gardens" Ruskin charges women that their "great function is Praise" (18.122). A science that nurtures and preserves the natural world, that sees beauty without destroying it, that builds upon a sense of identity with rather than antagonism toward nature, that studies nature to understand it and to appreciate it better rather than to enslave it, that praises rather than dissects, this is—in Victorian terms and in the terms Ruskin himself uses—a feminine science.

Throughout Ruskin's scientific texts, his scrupulously careful empirical appreciation of nature becomes indistinguishable from his technique for remarking with equal meticulousness on art, architecture, or theater. While recognizing the conservatism of Ruskin's science as he reacts against some of the most significant innovations and discoveries of his time, we must also recognize the progressive and even revolutionary qualities of Ruskin's scientific thinking: there is first his promotion of women in science through the many avenues discussed here, but also there is the way in which his thinking undermines fixed epistemological and ontological categories, and finally there is the way in which he insists that all modes of intellectual endeavor connect. For Ruskin, actions constitute identity even for non-human species, concern for the environment and for social justice converge, aesthetics cannot retreat from science or vice versa. Nature acts upon scientists who respond as an analytical but reverent audience. Ruskin draws on mythic symbolism to anthropomorphize stones, flowers, and birds; as they perform their roles in a universe burgeoning with metamorphosis, so we learn to perform ours, he hopes, in a better, more compassionate way. But we also learn the fragility of all categories of knowledge and thus of our own ever-shifting identities.

"Pantomimes at the London Theatres." *The Illustrated London News* 66 (January 2, 1875): 12.

Top: *Beauty and the Beast* at the Princess; middle: *Cinderella* at the Crystal Palace; bottom: *Harlequin, the Children in the Woods, the Old Father Aesop, Cock Robin,* and *Jenny Wren* at the Adelphi.

⊰3⊱

Playground and Playhouse
Identity Performance in Ruskin's Education for Girls

As late as 1888, Ruskin insisted on theater's usefulness for teaching: "I have always held the stage quite among the best and most necessary means of education" (34.549). He even refers to actors as "stage tutors" (34.550). Certainly in mid-century and mid-life, he was putting his long-held belief into practice. Ruskin wrote explicitly and practically about improving women's education in "Of Queens' Gardens," an essay from his best-selling *Sesame and Lilies* (1865),[1] a popular high school graduation gift for girls in the late nineteenth and early twentieth centuries. He put his theories into practice with the girls at Margaret Bell's liberal Winnington School, where he lectured regularly. That practical experience found literary expression in the series of ten Socratic dialogues called *Ethics of the Dust: Ten Lectures to Little Housewives, or the Elements of Crystallisation* (1866), in which an unnamed Old Lecturer[2] discusses the science of crystallography with a group of schoolgirls. Letters between Ruskin and those real-life Winnington students (whom he depicted arguing with and laughing at their teacher in *Ethics of the Dust*), have been collected in *The Winnington Letters*, revealing more about his theatrically inflected educational theory and practice. Throughout both the historical and the fictionalized Winnginton experiences, Ruskin draws examples from the theater, he uses theatrical metaphors in illustration of major points, he performs for the girls, and he directs the girls' performances for others and himself.

Not only does Ruskin perform when lecturing, but he also gets the girls to act, dance, sing, and otherwise perform, too, as a means to learning. Cathy Shuman points out in *Pedagogical Economies* that learning "only happens through an identification that transforms students as well as objects of study" (206).[3] The transformation, the impersonation, the getting out of oneself is what teaches, or rather causes understanding, so that in such a method a good teacher resembles a director who manipulates others into acting, pretending, breaking down the barriers of subjectivity. An aspect of Ruskin's feminized science, Ruskin uses this technique of identification between the girls and what they study throughout *Ethics of the Dust*. Ruskin advocates a similar process of identification in assuming a permeable self as the mode of reading in "Of Kings' Treasures," the first essay in *Sesame and Lilies* (Helsinger 2002, 116).[4]

Although in "Of Queens' Gardens" and the *Ethics of the Dust* Ruskin never uses the now popular word "subjectivity" in the sense of "conscious identity" and rarely even uses "identity" in this manner, he often talks of the girls' establishing and maintaining a "self."[5] In doing so, he resists the Victorian notion of an innate or core identity, seeing instead a self developed through various kinds of performance and play in the educational process. These texts are a particularly fruitful source of information on how Ruskin understands selfhood as he discusses selfishness, self-sacrifice, self-culture, and finally interrogates what a "self" is, resulting in a view of identity as constructed through reiterated performances (*Winnington Letters* 129).

In "Of Queens' Gardens," the *Ethics of the Dust*, and the *Winnington Letters*, Ruskin relies on a role-playing pedagogy that depends upon the malleability of the self. The playfulness of Ruskin's educational method stresses performance in the games he invents for his students in *Ethics of the Dust* and records in the Winnington letters. He stresses a process of change through education that goes beyond the notion of linear development to a dislocation of identities, prefiguring his later books on science, as discussed in chapter 2. His play-acting tutorials disrupt epistemological categories as they cut across multiple boundaries, including the dichotomies of performer/audience, teacher/student, lecturer/class, collector/collectible, scientist/nature, subject/object, human/beast, and animate/inanimate. As we have seen with Ruskin's writing about theater and science, all epistemological and ontological categories dissolve in Ruskin's multifaceted vision of learning as performing. Elin Diamond points out that performance is "a contested space, where meanings and desires are generated, occluded, and of course multiply interpreted" (1996, 4). Ruskin's Socratic dialogues in the *Ethics* offer such a contested space: both as a record of past performance and a script for imagined future performances, the iterated enactments embody new meanings.

But before moving on to subtler issues, I will first demonstrate that Ruskin did in fact argue in "Of Queens' Gardens" for vastly improved schools for girls, removing most discrepancies between men's and women's education. These innovations often involved performance in one sense or another, stripping away typical Victorian differences between boys' and girls' education, empowering girls in the near eradication of gender from student identity.

Seven More Lamps of Architecture, or How to Build a Better Girl

As we have seen of Ruskin's writing on theater and on science, his progressive plan for girls' education reveals an anxious recognition of identity performance. Critics justly complain that part of Ruskin's objective in vigorously improving instruction for girls in both "Of Queens' Gardens" and *Ethics of the Dust* is to make them suitable companions for future husbands.[6] However, this expressed goal is counteracted by the many practical improvements he urges that erase differences between education for men and women. Further, his depictions of girls constructing their identities through gender-bending performances challenge traditional gender roles.

Recent scholarship has brought attention to Ruskin's real-world, practical efforts to improve women's education. Jan Marsh and Pamela Garish Nunn uncover Ruskin's work mentoring and even underwriting women artists; Dinah Birch details Ruskin's direct contributions not only to institutions where he had an acknowledged position, such as the Winnington School and Oxford, but also to the other women's colleges at Cambridge (Girton and Newnham), at Whitelands College, and Cheltenham Ladies College (2002).[7] Today, even after so much research has demonstrated Ruskin's exertion on behalf of women's education, even though Linda Peterson has detailed the philosophical debt of "Of Queens' Gardens" to Anna Jameson and Bessie Parkes (Peterson 88–97), and even though Seth Koven has proven that "Of Queens' Gardens" helped Victorian feminists to justify their demands for independence, education, and jobs, and suffrage (Koven 190), "Of Queens' Gardens" persists in common critical opinion as the text best epitomizing oppressive Victorian patriarchy (Phegley 2). Kate Millett's famous attack in *Sexual Politics* on Ruskin's woman-worshiping chauvinism still pervades most Victorianists' understanding of his gender politics. To clarify precisely what is so progressive about Ruskin's curriculum, I enumerate his seven specific suggestions in "Of Queens' Gardens" for improving education for girls: 1) physical education, 2) happiness, 3) uncensored reading, 4) nature, 5) better treatment for girls' teachers, equal to boys', 6) avoiding theology, 7) science. Some of these suggestions correlate to performance more obviously than others (as I will show), but all eliminate differences between men's and women's education, encouraging the construction of an identity based on study and action rather than gender.

Like Plato (for boys, that is), the very first thing Ruskin requires for a girl's education is physical training.[8] Few Victorian girls' schools taught physical education. Ruskin gives it priority: "The first of our duties to her—no thoughtful persons now doubt this,—is to secure for her such physical training as may confirm her health, and perfect her beauty; the highest refinement of that beauty being unattainable without splendour of activity and of delicate strength" (18.123). Although Ruskin tells the middle-class Manchester audience that first came to hear this lecture in December 1864 that no thoughtful person doubts that girls need exercise, he knew that Winnington, where he taught, was rare in including team sports for its students.[9] In this essay famous for its rich prose describing the "true wife," Ruskin redefines feminine refinement performatively as a "splendour of activity." Exercise makes for "the highest refinement of that beauty"; one might otherwise think physical exercise produces brute strength, not delicacy. Throughout the passage he yokes the terms that will gain the approval and consent of his gender-conscious, socially aspiring audience ("beauty," "delicate," "refinement") with terms that make his real point ("health," "physical training," "activity," "strength"). He posits a new aesthetic of vigorous womanly beauty that incorporates health, strength, and action. Through the reiterated act of exercise, we physically remake ourselves.

Ruskin next insists that girls be made happy: "Do not think you can make a girl lovely, if you do not make her happy" (18.124)[10] He comes back to this discussion later in *Ethics of the Dust*, where he claims that girls should be made so happy that they must dance for sheer bliss. I will discuss dancing and happiness in relation to performance in *Ethics of the Dust* below, but for the moment, Ruskin redefines feminine beauty in performative terms: one manifests loveliness by dancing for joy.

The most significant injunction Ruskin makes to parents concerns what their daughters should read: "The chance and scattered evil that may here and there haunt, or hide itself in, a powerful book, never does any harm to a noble girl; but the emptiness of an author oppresses her, and his amiable folly degrades her" (18.130). Recommending uncensored reading, he insists that "if she can have access to a good library of old and classical books, there need be no choosing at all. . . . turn her loose in the old library every wet day, and let her alone. She will find what is good for her; you cannot. . . . Let her loose in the library, I say" (18.130–31). Peterson points out that this is the same free access to a library that Victorian feminist Bessie Parkes urges (Peterson 97).[11] To a Victorian audience, the advice to let a girl read uncensored books from an old library without direction or pre-selection could mean her poring over the ribald novels, plays, and politically radical essays of the eighteenth century, rather than the approved moral fiction and the religious sentiment of the nineteenth. She would plunge into the uncut Shakespeare, not Bowdler or other "family" versions. Consider the difference between Ruskin's injunction here and Lewis Carroll's advice in the preface to *Sylvie and Bruno* that someone should write a "'Shakespeare' for girls" since no currently available editions are suitable for girls between 10 and 17 years of age because "they are not sufficiently 'expurgated'" (497).[12] In contrast, Ruskin would have girls read Greek and Latin classics, which he encourages them to study in their original languages, and which include sexual, military, political, and philosophical material normally deemed inappropriate for young women of the period. Ruskin makes no distinction between boys and girls in this issue.[13] The solitary acts of exploring a library and reading books are the defining rituals for a scholar; Ruskin's insistence that girls perform them fully is his most stringent blow at gender difference within student identity, despite the syrupy and gendered justification he offers to support it.[14]

Another force Ruskin considers significant in girls' education is nature, not surprising when we remember how in his writing on science—as is true of Victorian culture more generally—he sees women and nature as closely allied.[15] In "Of Queens' Gardens," Ruskin makes two points in using nature to educate girls. First, regarding the importance of happiness just mentioned above, he wants girls to enjoy less restricted childhoods that involve unfettered access to wild and beautiful spaces. Second, he wants nature itself to be protected, as discussed in chapter 2. In "Of Queens' Gardens" he reasons that because nature teaches children, we must protect nature. It is a pedagogical argument for cleaning and conserving the planet:

> [D]o not think your daughters can be trained to the truth of their own
> human beauty, while the pleasant places, which God made at once for their
> schoolroom and their playground, lie desolate and defiled. You cannot
> baptize them rightly in those inch-deep fonts of yours, unless you baptize
> them also in the sweet waters which the great Lawgiver strikes forth for
> ever from the rocks of your native land—waters which a Pagan would
> have worshipped in their purity, and you worship only with pollution.
> (18.135–36)

Performing the public religious ritual of baptism becomes a metaphor
of the most basic stewardship of the earth and a mode of participating in
the reverent and supportive attitude he promotes in his overtly scientific
works. Once again he correlates women with nature as both worshiper and
worshiped, as previously we saw them as both subject and object of scientific inquiry. In keeping with Ruskin's pattern of taking ancient Greek religion seriously (as in *The Queen of the Air*),[16] this passage upends the typical
British Victorian hierarchy of Christianity over every other religion by
capitalizing "Pagan" and by reversing expectation in linking pagan practice with purity and Christian practice with pollution. This reversal stresses Ruskin's point that self-conscious action (or, to put it in theological
terms, works)—not salvation—ultimately determines who we are. For
Ruskin, the identity "Christian" depends neither on church baptism nor
on purity nor on belief, but on repairing the human destruction of the natural world.

Ruskin next urges respect for girls' teachers with a logic and persuasive
impact that must have won him the admiration and gratitude of many people who, like Emily Davies, were working hard to improve the conditions
of governesses and teachers:[17]

> But what teachers do you give your girls, and what reverence do you show
> to the teachers you have chosen? Is a girl likely to think her own conduct,
> or her own intellect, of much importance, when you trust the entire for-
> mation of her character, moral and intellectual, to a person whom you let
> your servants treat with less respect than they do your housekeeper (as if
> the soul of your child were a less charge than jams and groceries), and
> whom you yourself think you confer an honour upon by letting her some-
> times sit in the drawing-room in the evening? (18.132–33)

Such a plea for the improvement of the status of governesses and teachers,
which earlier in the passage he contrasts specifically and bitterly with the

much superior status of boys' tutors and teachers, speaks directly to the center of Victorian feminist activity.[18] Again Ruskin presses the boundaries of gender difference by insisting on equal conditions and equal status for male and female teachers.

The sixth suggestion Ruskin makes is that girls be discouraged from over-involvement in studying theology. In "Of Queens' Gardens," Ruskin redirects middle-class women's energy away from embroidering altar cloths toward more useful philanthropic action, making a material difference for social justice in the wider world. That such action should be substantial and influential is evident in the identity he invents for his audience as "queens" in "Of Queens' Gardens"; even the point of the title is to open up women's domestic sphere to include England and all the world as a venue for practical activity. In comparison with the claustrophobically house-bound role of Patmore's heroine in *Angel in the House,* Ruskin's politically engaged queen is a far more powerful figure.[19] Ruskin sees women's abilities squandered on church-related triviality when they could be channeled into significant productive use.

The question of Ruskin's distrust of theology has already been fully discussed by other critics, who note his frustration with the religious fanaticism of Rose La Touche.[20] Her adolescence involved a major mental (and ultimately physical) health crisis brought on by her decision, against her mother's wishes, to join her father in taking communion before having been confirmed in the Anglican church. Despite the conflict between her parents, both of them joined Rose in disapproving of Ruskin's heathenish notions.[21] In other words, at the bottom Ruskin's negative reaction to girls' study of theology is a personal distress over Rose's beliefs. The issue dividing Rose and Ruskin seems not to have been their thirty-year age difference, but Ruskin's devastating loss of faith. The years during which he met, became friends with, corresponded with, fell in love with, and proposed to Rose coincided with the Winnington years, which we will discuss below. This period also, after the death of his father on March 2, 1864, saw Ruskin's biggest changes in identity, both from believer to unbeliever and from professional writer to professional lecturer or performer (Birch 1989, 148; Shuman 174).

The Winnington Letters—particularly those to headmistress Margaret Alexis Bell—are full of Ruskin's unconversion angst, which he discusses more obliquely in *Ethics of the Dust.* In *Ethics,* after recounting to the children a dream of how the Egyptian goddess Neith and god Pthah visit him, Ruskin says to the girl he dubs Egypt, "you could not think, Egypt, what a strange feeling of utter loneliness came over me when the presences of the two gods passed away. It seemed to me as if I had never known what it was to be alone before." (18.229). Ruskin's description of the Old Lecturer's loneliness sounds very much like Ruskin's despair at losing his belief in God about this time. He never refers to it directly in the *Ethics*, but he refers to it often in letters to the free-thinking Miss Bell. His Sunday lectures on the Bible were unorthodox enough to raise the complaints of at least one parent, but he wrote nothing about his loss of faith publicly because of a promise he had made to Rose La Touche's mother not to publish anything about his religious doubts for at least ten years (Burd 1969, 82).

Ruskin couches his loneliness in walking without his god in mythological terms, bringing home the religious sincerity of ancient Egyptian beliefs (so often thought of as merely stories), promoting respect for ancient religions as he did in discussion of the Pagan above. Also, as I demonstrate momentarily, he emphasizes the character Egypt's participation in the play-within-a-play: Egypt, one of the twelve school girls, consistently refers to herself as having lived in a time "when I was queen" (18.229). Called Egypt "for her dark eyes," her primary role is a student-character at the fictional school. But she generally also maintains her character-within-a-character as the queen of Egypt or as a personification of Egypt itself. While casting Egypt as a little girl participates in a typically Victorian patronizing feminization of the North African country, Ruskin nevertheless introduces to an audience of British school girls and other readers the notion that non-Christian religions, both ancient and modern, deserve respect. Furthermore, as Queen of Egypt, she can model how to provide better stewardship of the earth.

Girls' study of at least one science is the seventh and last in Ruskin's list of innovations. We have already seen that Ruskin feminizes science in *Proserpina, Love's Meinie, Deucalion,* and *The Eagle's Nest,* so it should not come as a surprise that in "Of Queens' Gardens" he advocates women's scientific education: "she should be trained in the habits of accurate thought; . . . she should understand the meaning, the inevitableness, and the loveliness of natural laws; and follow at least some one path of scientific attainment" (18.125–26). Here again Ruskin eliminates any difference between boys' and girls' curriculum; he uses precisely this formula for boys at Oxford, where he feels that to procure a "very good first-class" degree a student should achieve a high level of proficiency in either "chemistry *or* botany *or* physiology" (16.453; emphasis is Ruskin's). A more troubling question of degree of attainment arises a moment later regarding girls' scientific study: "as far as to the threshold of that bitter Valley of Humiliation, into which only the wisest and bravest of men can descend, owning themselves for ever children, gathering pebbles on a boundless shore" (18.125–26). Interestingly, although he uses the gendered word "men" here, these scientists become gender-neutral in their journey toward admitting ultimate ignorance. I noted in chapter 2 that for Ruskin women can become scientists and that male scientists are feminized. Here, as men transform into children, we see that the humbling and even infantilizing act of scientific inquiry ultimately eradicates gender altogether.

In a passage reminiscent of Jane Eyre's feminist exclamation from the leaden roof of Thornfield Hall, Ruskin makes a final plea to his audience in "Of Queens' Gardens" to provide their daughters with an education equal to their sons:

> And not only in the material and in the course, but yet more earnestly in the spirit of it, let a girl's education be as serious as a boy's. You bring up your girls as if they were meant for sideboard ornaments, and then complain of their frivolity. Give them the same advantages that you give their brothers—appeal to the same grand instincts of virtue in them; teach *them*, also, that courage and truth are the pillars of their being:—do you think that they would not answer that appeal, brave and true as they are even now, when you know that there is hardly a girls' school in the Christian kingdom where the children's courage or sincerity would be thought of half so much importance as their way of coming in at a door. (18.132)

Victorian culture's emphasis on a girl's deportment or her "way of coming in at a door" dismays Ruskin. Here in 1865 he prefigures an image from the play *Frou-Frou*, which we have already seen will cause Ruskin so much distress in 1872. In *Frou-Frou*, the eponymous heroine's admirer effusively describes her mode of entry: "a door opens,—and hark! . . . A rustling flutter of silken skirts sweeping along like a whirlwind—Frou-Frou! Into the room with a twirl, . . . always Frou-Frou!" (4). Reacting against such a superficial model of womanhood, Ruskin sees the foundation of a girl's (or boy's) identity—"the pillars of her being"—as sincerity and courage. Just as good deportment must be practiced, abstract qualities that constitute identity also need to be established through rehearsal and performance. Rather than merely making a good entrance, girls need to train for a much more traditionally masculine role in which they learn to be "brave and true" rather than to be pouting and kittenish like the protagonist of *Frou-Frou*. Just as Ruskin redefines feminine beauty as strength

and activity, here he redefines feminine virtue (with the Latin root meaning "manliness") as courage and sincerity.

As a final example of how startlingly radical Ruskin's gender-neutral
pedagogical ideas become, Ruskin proposes the establishment of frank and
honest sex education. He does not do so in a public lecture. In a letter to
a friend who wants to teach continence to the youth of England, he says
this:

> But I shall at least ask of modern science so much help as shall enable me
> to begin to teach them at that age [fifteen] the physical laws relating to
> their own bodies, openly, thoroughly, and with awe. . . . But really, the
> essential thing is the founding of real schools of instruction for both boys
> and girls—first, in domestic medicine and all that it means; and second-
> ly, in the plain moral law of all humanity: "Thou shalt not commit adul-
> tery," with all that *it* means. (34.529)

Ruskin, who never had sex with his own wife, who consistently fell in
love with the innocence of young girls, who felt uncomfortable discussing
the reproductive capacity of plants in *Proserpina,* who conceived of feminine perfection as the virgin Athena, encourages the straightforward explanation of their bodies and how they function and perform to young people
of both sexes. One would not have thought that the quintessential idealiz-
er of chaste Victorian womanhood would have urged detailed sex education for both boys and girls, but we have here another instance of how
Ruskin's practical suggestions for education subvert gender differentiation.
While Ruskin never escapes a notion of complementary spheres for men
and women, the process he designs and puts into practice to fit women for
their gendered role involves a curriculum that asks students to perform as
students, eliminating gender as an aspect of student identity.

Like theater, education lays bare the paradox or inconsistency informing
a core identity that is true and eternal. We change. We grow. We learn, for
good or ill. And among other categories of identity, we learn gender. Ruskin
believes that what he suggests is a change in curriculum only; boys and girls
study virtually the same thing[22] because women must act as men's ethical
guides and they need an equal education to do it effectively. However,
changing the curriculum results in learning gender differently from before;
Ruskin's plan in "Of Queens' Gardens" produces girls' growing away from
the gender dichotomy he also famously upholds in the same text.

In the Playhouse

In *Ethics of the Dust*, Ruskin (as the Old Lecturer) addresses young female students themselves, instead of their mothers and fathers as in *Sesame and Lilies*.[23] Published shortly after *Sesame and Lilies*, the *Ethics of the Dust* derives from Ruskin's experiences from 1859 to 1868 at the Winnington school, where he lectured and which he helped support (Burd 1969, 19). Ruskin admired the school's progressive plan enough to help the school's director, Margaret Bell, financially; Ruskin's father suspected Miss Bell of cultivating Ruskin's friendship as much for his ability to help her monetarily as for his talent in teaching the girls. Ruskin's experiences at the school have a theatrical hue; his sweetest memories from that time are of watching the girls dance. Observers besides Ruskin note a theatrical undercurrent to the Winnington School and students; Georgiana Burnes-Jones describes the pretty spectacle of many girls dancing in unison in the gallery (Burd 1969, 37) and even of Ruskin's tall, thin figure as a black line moving in a quadrille among the white-clad girls (Hilton 2000, 59). Ruskin sprinkles references to plays throughout the dialogues of *Ethics of the Dust* (Molière's *Le Bourgeois Gentilhomme*, Burnand's *Villikins and his Dinah*, and Shakespeare's *Twelfth Night* all appear); he likely included such allusions in his real life lectures to the Winnington girls as well. Ruskin puns on the school's Thespian ambiance in a telling letter to his father John James Ruskin dated August 8, 1863; Ruskin writes that all the girls do at the Winnington schoolhouse is play, "except that if Miss Bell called it a 'playhouse' it might be mistaken for a theatre" (*Winnington Letters* 412).[24]

I have shown that in "Of Queens' Gardens," Ruskin establishes seven aspects of an ideal education for girls. In that essay, he also offers as girls' role models the great female characters of Shakespeare, who, he says, "has no heroes—. . . only heroines" (18.112). In that lecture aimed at the girls' parents, the goal for young women is to acquire the intellect of Portia, the bravery of Juliet, "the patience of Hero," "the passion of Beatrice," and so on, as they take on the role of ruling queens.[25] In *Ethics of the Dust*, so long as each character acts the part of Mary, Lily, Florrie, Sybil, or Egypt, and so on, as named in the dialogues, all she need do is become a good scholar, studying French, arithmetic, and music (18.266). Curiously, the subjects the lecturer mentions are the most traditional possible to imagine for Victorian girls. There is no self-referential mention of this text-book on ethics and mineralogy. Nor is there mention of the entirely unconventional subjects that the *dramatis personae* are actually engaged in studying, both within the fictional frame of the book, and without it in the mirror relationship between writer and reader. Nor is there mention of the progressive curriculum covered by the historical Winnington students. The list of stereotypical subjects lulls the reading audience into imagining for a moment that the world depicting Socratic dialogues between an internationally famous scholar and a dozen average schoolgirls, where children discourse on philosophy and fairy tales, where myth and magic hold their own with crystallography and architecture, is entirely normal, after all, and would provide any typical Victorian girl a place to study and flourish, if only she can learn the part.

Ethics of the Dust takes the form of ten dialogues between the lecturer and a group of twelve female students, ranging in age from nine to twenty. Most readers have not found the book compelling as literature— Ruskin wryly mentions his publisher's request that he "write no more in dialogue!"; nevertheless, Ruskin declared the *Ethics of the Dust* his own favorite among all his works (18.203). Carlyle praised it highly as "radiant with talent, ingenuity, and lambent fire" (Cate 1982, 113). Compounding critical reaction against the work on aesthetic grounds is the book's indisputably patriarchal tone. Throughout *Ethics of the Dust,* more than with *Sesame and Lilies,* we hear avuncular joking and heavy-handed playfulness, which Raymond Fitch characterizes as "jocular chauvinism" (525). It brings Dinah Birch to say that the book is "especially irritating for a woman to read" (1989, 150), and may be part of John Rosenberg's remark that the book is "charming if trivial" (160). It is certainly a factor in Paul Sawyer's opinion that Ruskin's

> sugared phrases . . . rationalize submission and reduce the range of moral action to a dollhouse scale, the only scale on which perfect behavior is attainable. . . . Ruskin's Winnington, in short, stands for a never-never land of harmony, before there ever broke out a contradiction between government and liberty, duty and desire, or the wishes of the parent and the child. (1985, 248)

Nevertheless, the *Ethics of the Dust* fits a pattern of encouraging scientific education for girls, of taking their ethical capacity seriously, of demonstrating that identity is fluid and is constituted through performance, and of undermining fixed epistemological and ontological categories. In terms of identity performance, *Ethics of the Dust* turns out to be a much more interesting document than the critics' dismissals would suggest.

Generically, the book is a conundrum. In a sense, Ruskin has devoted his only published drama to the issue of girls' education; both Emma

Sdegno and Cathy Shuman refer to it as a play in their criticism. Carlyle also praises the work for being properly dramatic with stage directions and a "very pretty stage and *dramatis personae*"; indeed he refers to the whole work as "a most shining Performance" (Cate 1982, 113–14). It is also fictionalized autobiography, in which Ruskin has cast the girls of Winnington as students and himself as their teacher, basing much of the book firmly on real events. As an amalgam of theater and autobiography, *Ethics of the Dust* is odd in that the girls are not only fellow performers in the dialogues, but also are the audience for Ruskin's lessons at Winnington (2002); among many other lectures, Ruskin read his own essay "Of Queens' Gardens" aloud to the Winnington girls (*Winnington Letters* 530–31). Ruskin's public lectures were famous as theatrical events; Hilton points out that "like Gladstone and Dickens, neither of whom he resembled in other ways, Ruskin was a master of the public occasion. Ruskin's lectures are all triumphs of the Victorian art of dramatic speech-making" (Birch 2000, 75). Fusing the self-reflexivity of Ruskin's and the girls' performances at Winnington and in *Ethics of the Dust*, Ruskin describes the Winnington girls as "a pleasant sight to see and a pleasant audience to read to" (*Winnington Letters* 422–23).

Ethics of the Dust is also and perhaps most obviously an example of a philosophical genre, most familiar to us from Plato's dialogues. The form is a curious choice for Ruskin, considering that Plato's dialogues are notoriously seen as anti-theatrical, presenting his low opinion of mimetic art in general and of rhapsodes, actors, and the theater in particular. Most critics do not consider Plato's dialogues to be plays,[26] but Ruskin's Socratic dialogues differ from Plato's in several ways. Plato rarely includes stage directions (*Protagoras* being an exception), let alone elaborate movement like the lecturer's choreography, in which he directs the girls to run around the playground as though they were liquid molecules and then to coalesce in crystalline shapes. Also, Plato's dialogues function as dialogue-essays, in which the interlocutors exist primarily for Socrates to refute them and so carry his argument forward (although there's plenty of humor along the way), whereas Ruskin's dialogues include moments in which the children deflect or even completely redirect the course of the lesson. While Birch correctly observes that Ruskin includes dissenting voices in order to contain them, I would counter that the girls' points do not always evaporate under the Old Lecturer's arguments; certainly the historical dissenting girls' rebuttals didn't just evaporate either, as can be seen from the letters they wrote him from Winnington and through the long years of their friendships with him afterwards. In contrast, Socrates' interlocutors are always vanquished. Also,

Plato's dialogues do not appear to be intended to instruct the fictional interlocutor or anyone he represents, but instead to instruct a later reader who
will agree with Socrates at the interlocutor's expense. Ruskin's book constructs a readership of girls similar to those in the dialogues; he hopes these
readers will identify with the Winnington students and be persuaded along
with them (at least, as he has generally depicted the interaction). Moreover,
Ruskin himself, as I have discussed in chapter 1, was more theaterphiliac
than theaterphobic. Certainly, Ruskin's former student—and occasional
theater companion—playwright Oscar Wilde could not be accused of anti-
theatricality; Wilde's Socratic dialogues "The Critic as Artist" (1890) and
"The Decay of Lying" (1891) follow Ruskin's in rejecting Plato's antithe-
atrical stance. Finally, Ruskin names his *Ethics of the Dust* for Aristotle's
Ethics, nearly half of which Ruskin had committed to memory as a young
man, selecting it as the only Greek book he took away with him from
Oxford in 1840 (Burd 1985, 64–65). Aristotle opposed Plato's antitheatricality, lauding mimetic art in general and theater in particular.

In the *Poetics,* Aristotle justifies drama (and poetry) partly on what he
calls the human instinct for imitation. Ruskin repeatedly identifies imitation as fundamental to learning, perhaps most famously in "Of Kings'
Treasuries," the companion essay to "Of Queens' Gardens." So finally theater and education have the same basis, as suggested by Ruskin's comment
that the stage is a necessary means of education (34.549). Yet the issue of
imitation is a complex one for Ruskin. Rebecca Stern points out that learning by imitation hints at a contradiction in Victorian notions of identity:
one must imitate to learn, yet for a Victorian inheriting Rousseauian
notions of education through nature, learning should be a transcendental
blossoming or unfolding of innate ability: "the repetitive, imitative aspects
of identity are disturbing in that they suggest ways in which even human
'nature' is ultimately assembled" (Stern 438). There should be no need for
imitation in the development of an authentic, natural self; nevertheless, the
Victorians—Ruskin among them—knew that one must mimic to learn.

For Ruskin, one must also play to learn. Ruskin's play on the word
"playhouse" in his quip to his father highlights an important issue regarding the relationship between imitative play and identity performance
recurring throughout the dialogues. We are all familiar with the idea that
children learn through play and that adults also can learn through role-
playing. There are also many obvious differences and similarities between
pretending in play and performing in a play. But what is the relationship
between one kind of playing and another? To what extent is pretending the
same as performing? How does playing a part on stage relate to perform-

ing an identity in life? Or rather to constituting a self through reiterated performances? These questions, which current theater and performance theorists tease out for us,[27] are already at work in *Ethics of the Dust,* as the following pages demonstrate. As discussed in chapter 1, in *Fors Clavigera* Ruskin asserts that pantomime reality is realer than the reality he finds in the streets outside the theater because theater manifests the True Ideal (defined long before in *Modern Painters*). So too in *Ethics of the Dust,* Ruskin breaks down the barriers between being and performing, between adult and child, between "real" and "play."

Ruskin prepares his readers at first to understand "playing" as "exercising imagination" in the preface to the first edition of *Ethics of the Dust* (18.202). He dramatizes this idea in a passage in which the Old Lecturer, designated by the letter "L," has just described a fanciful valley in which diamonds are strewn about like dew and must be swept away in glittering heaps if people want to walk on the grass. In this exchange between the Old Lecturer and Florrie, the youngest student at age nine, Ruskin "plays" both on the notion of play and on the correlation of size, age, and maturity:

> Florrie. Now you're just playing, you know.
>
> L. So are you, you know.
>
> Florrie. Yes, but you mustn't play.
>
> L. That's very hard, Florrie; why mustn't I, if you may?
>
> Florrie. Oh, I may, because I'm little, but you mustn't, because you're— (*hesitates for a delicate expression of magnitude*).
>
> L. (*rudely taking the first that comes*). Because I'm big? No; that's not the way of it at all, Florrie. Because you're little, you should have very little play, and because I'm big, I should have a great deal. (18.211)

Ruskin teases always with a purpose.[28] The Lecturer next demands to know why he must be more truthful than the author of fantasy, such as *The Arabian Nights,* a work familiar to the girls in both print and pantomime forms. Isabel (age 11) readily answers that she likes to know about "real things" (18.211). Predictably and maddeningly, Ruskin asks in response, "What do you call real things?" (18.211). As with his comment in *Fors* that the world inside the pantomime is more real than the world outside the theater, Ruskin complicates basic ontology (what is? and what is real?), just as elsewhere in the *Ethics of the Dust* he asks what lives and what does "alive" mean (18.238).[29] Along with these questions, what "play" is and who can play are just as serious questions, when both playing as pretending and playing as playacting add up to a fantasy realer than reality.

Human adults and children are not the only things that play. Ruskin also uses the word "play" to describe what crystals do. In one of the most memorable scenes from *Ethics of the Dust,* the Old Lecturer directs the girls to run around the playground in confluence and then stop in a prearranged pattern to crystallize themselves. In what Sawyer calls "inspired bizarreness reminiscent of the Alice books" (1985, 246), they make themselves into diamonds, rubies, emeralds, Derbyshire spar, Iceland spar, gold, and silver (18.248). Ruskin used this hands-on method to teach the historical Winnington girls; Lily Armstrong and Isabel Marshall (on whom the characters Lily and Isabel are based) close an 1865 letter to Ruskin by saying they must go because "they have to turn into particles" (*Winnington Letters* 571–72). This letter expresses their reaction to having read *Ethics of the Dust;* in another round of self-reflexivity, by making particles of themselves, they play the part that Ruskin has written for them. In the book, the Old Lecturer tells the girls that when they crystallize themselves on the playground into the shapes he has prescribed, even "when you construct the most difficult single figures, you have only learned half the game—nothing so much as the half, indeed, as the crystals themselves play it" (18.277). For crystals, playing the game correctly is absolutely a matter of identity: missteps in crystal choreography cause them to lose "all shape and honour; and even their own likeness, in the contest" (18.278). Anthropomorphizing the crystals does more than provide a combined scientific and moral lesson, it breaks down the barriers between animate and inanimate; this is no surprise coming from Ruskin, who in *The Queen of the Air* declares that "the links between dead matter and animation drift everywhere unseen" (19.362).

Ruskin's wordplay in *Ethics of the Dust* with "play," "real," and "alive" come to a head with his discussion of identity or "self." He presses the notion that crystals and girls constitute themselves into "selves" by establishing boundaries with others. A girl, a rock, or a tree exists as an entity only in its rigorous differentiation from the rest of the universe.

PLAYING ONE'S SELF

Over and over again within *Ethics of the Dust* Ruskin emphasizes how important it is that girls be educated in the fields for which they have individual—that is, not gender-based—talent. According to Cook and

Wedderburn, the manuscript version of *Ethics of the Dust* states this even more explicitly: "this, children, is what you have all to do, . . . namely, to ascertain your powers, tastes, special gifts and graces; and to cultivate these. . . . You are not to think that Titian would have helped the world by not painting, or Casella by not singing" (18.287n). By honing their art, the girls define themselves and refuse to be defined by rigid social strictures, crossing gender lines to find appropriate role models. Ruskin further argues passionately that, contrary to Victorian expectations, young women should not sacrifice themselves or their talents to others. He loathes the common Victorian notion that a woman should behave as Virginia Woolf in "Professions for Women" describes Patmore's infamous Angel in the House behaving, giving up all her own opinions and sense of separate identity, submerging herself in husband, father, or religion (Woolf 237–38). Ruskin calls such self-sacrifice suicide; again he redefines feminine behavior to disallow debilitating actions typically seen as definitively feminine. He clarifies this in dialogue with Violet (age 16):

Violet. But self-sacrifice is not suicide!

L. What is it then?

Violet. Giving up one's self for another.

L. Well, and what do you mean by "giving up one's self"?

Violet. Giving up one's tastes, one's feelings, one's time, one's happiness, and so on, to make others happy.

L. I hope you will never marry anybody, Violet, who expects you to make him happy in that way. (18.283–84)

The permeable self that Ruskin recognizes in Violet's eagerness for self-sacrifice strikes him as fearfully dangerous, even fatal. Only by rigorously exercising one's tastes, consciously pursuing one's interests, persistently performing one's art can one maintain a separate existence and prevent obliteration. Establishing boundaries to define the self, which are always in danger of breaking down, requires continual and time-consuming effort and action to protect. Ruskin's position here, that one creates and maintains a separate identity through the repeated reassertion of defining characteristics in a conscious display before others, is a position that identity is constituted through performance. The paradox is that once one has established a self through performance, Ruskin holds it in primacy over other possible selves, giving the illusion of a core or intrinsic identity to that which requires continual performative upkeep to preserve.

When in his works on political economy Ruskin tries to imagine a

society structured on a kind of familial cooperation instead of the competition that marks free enterprise, he invokes the same ideas. In *Ethics of
the Dust* he uses precisely this imagery for social reform, stressing a "political economy of cooperation" over a "political economy of competition"
(18.360). In an excerpt plucked from *Modern Painters V,* soot, dirt, and
water compete futilely for mastery of a path, and in their struggle produce only undifferentiated mud. If the elements could cooperate instead,
each crystallizing itself separately, in place of the muddy mess, the path
would be strewn with diamonds, sapphires, and snowflakes. This image
constitutes the final lesson in *Ethics of the Dust,* as the old lecturer asks
the eldest and wisest schoolgirl Mary to perform the passage for the others, mimicking Ruskin by reading aloud from Ruskin's earlier text. So
important is this message that *Ethics of the Dust* quotes *Modern Painters*
verbatim to relay it; the fictional girls and the real readers know that it
comes from a much more famous book that exists outside the make-
believe world of the Old Lecturer and his students. This lends a peculiar
reality to the fictive realm of the dialogues while emphasizing their fictionality by calling attention to the literary frame. Ruskin does this to
highlight a point about political economy, which the girls need to understand in training as social critics and moral guides to men. Ruskin oppos-
es the market competition that pits laborers against one another in a fight
for jobs, or any kind of competition, such as school examinations,[30] that
squanders effort instead of harnessing it, just as we saw him dismiss
Darwinian competition as part of Natural Selection and deride competition among ambitious scientists. Paradoxically, the process of teaching
the girls to be true to themselves by cultivating their own talents,
indulging neither in self-sacrifice nor in competition, promotes both the
idea of a core self with intrinsic qualities (each girl perhaps preparing to
crystallize into a separate gem) and the idea of a performed constitution
of self (such crystallization can only occur after lessons, after reiterated
rehearsal, and in the act of differentiation from others).

Earlier, when the girls struggle with the old lecturer's question of what
it means to be alive, of whether crystals—which we have seen him anthropomorphize throughout the *Ethics of the Dust*—are alive, the Old Lecturer
poses the question differently: "the difficulty is not so much saying what
makes a thing alive, as what makes it a Self" (18.238). Here he raises self-
hood or identity above life as the most significant issue for the children.
He goes on: "As soon as you are shut off from the rest of the universe into
a Self, you begin to be alive" (18.238), suggesting again that one constitutes identity by establishing the boundaries between oneself and others,

in other words, between the performing self and the audience. When Mary (age 20) complains that Ruskin's definition of "alive" doesn't distinguish between a rock and a tree, he finishes up as ambiguously as he began: "if you choose to think of the crystals as alive, do, and welcome. Rocks have always been called "living" in their native place" (18.239). Ruskin playfully denies basic distinctions between animal and mineral, bringing us to a dynamic universe in which rocks live, crystals play, and they all dance.

IDENTITY DANCING

In the dialogue entitled "Home Virtues," the Old Lecturer employs a strategy that Ruskin uses everywhere in his writing: first introducing his topic with a startling assertion that shocks his audience into attention; then proceeding to reinterpret the assertion until it is no longer shocking and in fact begins to seem entirely reasonable. The bombshell in this chapter is that "dancing is the first of girls' virtues" (18.293). Not surprisingly, twentieth-century critics have found this remark offensive. Bauer, for example, says Ruskin here represents women as "intellectually inferior and morally childlike" (79). We see similar reactions to Ruskin's corollary shockers in which he offers dressing and cooking as girls' other great virtues; nevertheless, the importance of these three duties, as the Old Lecturer reinterprets them for his indignant students, is that each action is a performance that constitutes identity.

The statement that dancing is the first of girls' virtues would have been as ludicrous to the Victorian audience as to ours (at least, judging from the schoolgirls' reactions in *Ethics of the Dust*). Here he plays with the notion of deportment as a virtue that he had debunked a few months earlier in *Sesame and Lilies*. He explains his point that girls should be "always wanting to dance" as this:

> Their first virtue is to be intensely happy;—so happy that they don't know what to do with themselves for happiness,—and dance, instead of walking. . . . The last and worst thing that can be said of a nation is, that it has made its young girls sad, and weary." (18.296)

Thus we find at the most basic level another instance of the progressive Ruskin's primary lesson for educators, that any program's purpose should be to produce happy, healthy people. "Dressing" turns out to mean dressing others; women's duties include seeing that the world's poor have adequate clothing, which women should provide through philanthropy or though social action. Likewise, "cooking" turns out to mean that women should procure for everyone an adequate food supply. But dancing meant much more to Ruskin than the animal expression of joy described here, although he attaches importance to that as well. For him, girls' dancing symbolizes the idyllic Winningington experience.

Ruskin was never able to write the chapter he planned on Winnington for his autobiography *Praeterita,* but among the memories he described in 1885 as "becoming the most important" to him were "the Dances at Winnington" (Burd 1969, 21). The girls' dancing and singing held such a special meaning for him that he intended the chapter heading for *Praeterita* to be "he heard music and dancing" (1969, 20).

The Winnington Letters also records Ruskin's interest in the relationship between performance and identity as expressed in dance. We have already seen that he choreographs playground dances for them to demonstrate how crystals form, identifying them closely with the minerals they study. He also writes of the beautiful effect created by the children's singing to each other's dancing, but he focuses on how the dancing reveals aspects of identity:

> How strange the effect of climate is!—the two most graceful [dancers] of all have both been softened by warm climates, the one I chose for the Sun in my Zodiac dance having passed all her childhood at the foot of the Andes—and—don't be shocked—the other is the Bishop of Natal's youngest daughter—who moves as lightly and quietly as a leopard, having an infinite sweetness of temper joined with the African wild training. (*Winnington Letters* 425)

There are a number of startling things about these comments by Ruskin on dance, education, and identity at Winnington. They are even more apparent in his comment that "I think that education and race *are* the great means of forming character. I can not yet form even an opinion how far national scenery helps." (*Winnington Letters* 237). The most surprising point that arises out of Ruskin's statement about dancing here is that race is a means to form character.

Ruskin's word usage does not suggest that race predetermines character, an opinion we might expect given the prevailing Victorian understanding of race as hereditary, very different from our current academic definition of race as socially constructed. Instead, Ruskin's phrasing states that race is a means to form or to constitute character. Analogous to education, race becomes a process for Ruskin rather than an intrinsic trait. Contrary to what one might anticipate, Ruskin almost implies that just as one can change educational approaches to affect character in different ways, so too can one change races. This is an intriguing take on race, neither inherent nor static, but suggesting that race, like education, is manipulable and dynamic. Even given that for the Victorians, the word "race" meant species or nationality as often as it referred to attributes associated with human skin color, the malleable effect of race in this statement is astonishing.

Ruskin's final query about national scenery regarding the two girls he mentions, one of whom is the daughter of the deposed Bishop of Natal, John William Colenso, seems partially to answer his question about how education and race form character. For Ruskin, the girls living in warmer climates are made graceful by their environment, growing to resemble the leopards and so forth. Yet if race is performed (as I have already shown that it is for Ruskin in chapters 1 and 2) and if it is a means to form character (as he says it is here), than the zodiac song and dance that Ruskin devises for the girls is a method using the performance of race alongside more traditional educational means to establish their identities as he wishes.

In a letter to American poet James Lowell, Ruskin refers to play-acting and stage-movement at Winnington while reading poetry with the girls. They have been performing Lowell's poems, including the 275-line dramatic monologue "Columbus." Here Ruskin quotes (or slightly misquotes) Lowell's "The Origin of Didactic Poetry," a clunky but humorous jab at overly moralistic verse, in which most of the Roman pantheon speaks. In this poem, the goddess of wisdom, Minerva, invents and then regrets inventing didactic poetry. Lowell makes his point pithily: "The muse is unforgiving;/Put all your beauty in your rhymes,/ Your morals in your living." Didactic verse is boring; morality has no place in art. The question immediately arises as to how this Wildean perspective fits into Ruskin's fame as the passionate moralist, asking us once again to consider that Ruskin demands both (in his own mind, without contradiction) that art exist for art's sake at the same time that art be ethical.

He tells Lowell:

We had Columbus and Cromwell—and nearly all the prettiest minor poems on successive evenings—the last evening I got a nice blue-eyed girl to be Minerva, and recited the "when wise Minerva yet was young." You should have heard the silver laughing (n. b.—I had studied curtseying all the afternoon before—in order to get myself nicely out as Venus—). (36.327)

While teaching contemporary American poetry to the girls at
Winnington, Ruskin also teaches them the fun of being Columbus,
Cromwell, Minerva, Venus, and so on, building an imaginative set of identities to stretch their own. In another inspired moment of bizarreness, the
tall, angular Ruskin acts the part of not just any woman, but of the volup-
tuous Goddess of Love. No one really needs to practice curtseying; Ruskin
reiterates a gendered act that identifies him with the girls.

CONCLUSION

In Ruskin's writing on education, the notion of identity performance goes
beyond the formation of character to a disruption of a belief in a core or
essential self. According to Shuman, Ruskin prefers "pedagogical rituals
that transform the relations between the subject and object of knowledge
and blur the lines between observer and spectacle, teacher and student"
(171). "Of Queens' Gardens" erases gender from student identity by creating a curriculum for girls that is virtually identical to that of boys and
initiates girls into the fundamental rituals of the scholar. In *Ethics of the
Dust*, Ruskin subverts traditional pedagogical hierarchy by couching all the
mineralogy lessons in the form of dialogues, decentering his own authority, and questioning the very notion of self-hood. Likewise, by presenting
education as performance, Ruskin hints that the roles the girls learn to play
both in their classroom theater and in life are malleable. Acting as teacher
and casting the students as audience and then reversing their positions
demonstrates the interchangeability of identities between performer and
spectator. When Ruskin insists that the girls do not merely play-act crystals but *are* crystals, he undermines distinctions between animate and
inanimate, subject and object, animal and mineral, as radically as he subverts the distinctions between genders and species in his other scientific and
theatrical writings. Finally, Ruskin figures the Winnington experience
most nostalgically as a dance, a ritual performance that registers how identities dissolve and coalesce with each step, turn, and curtsey.

SCENE FROM "ALADDIN AND HIS WONDERFUL LAMP," AT DRURY LANE THEATRE.

"Scene from 'Aladdin and His Wonderful Lamp' at the Drury Lane Theatre" and "Scene from 'The Babes in the Wood' at Covent Garden." *The Illustrated London News* 66 (January 9, 1875): 28.

⚜4⚜

Ruskin and the Wilde Life

Self and Other on the Millennial Stage

Contemporary theater exhibits a fascination with Victorian culture as a vehicle to explore current concerns. The 1990s and early 2000s have brought us several blockbuster musicals based on Victorian materials, such as an opulent revival of *The King and I* (1996), the pop phenomenon *Jekyll and Hyde* (1997), followed less successfully by *Jane Eyre: The Musical* (2000), *Dracula* (2004), and Andrew Lloyd Webber's mediocre but well-received *The Woman in White* (2004). Both *The King and I* and *Jane Eyre* reach back to their nineteenth-century sources for examples of spirited feminism, appealing strongly to turn-of-the-twenty-first-century audiences. Plays showcasing the wit and tragedy of Oscar Wilde, such as off-Broadway's *Gross Indecency: The Three Trials of Oscar Wilde* (1997) and *The Judas Kiss* (1998), have found an avid audience. These plays highlight Wilde's iconic function in contemporary culture as the definitive victim of homophobia and the founding father of gay identity.[1] More surprisingly, the life story of Ruskin has inspired two major American stage adaptations that offer a feminist reading of the Victorian era, indicting a patriarchal Ruskin for his marriage's failure. While playing to more limited audiences than either the hugely popular musicals based on nineteenth-century stories or the widely performed plays about Wilde,[2] both the 1995 opera *Modern Painters* and the 1999 hit off-Broadway play *The Countess* succeeded, one at the packed open-air opera venue in Santa Fe, the other with enthusiastic New York audiences. These two pairs of shows about Wilde and Ruskin that premiered between 1995 and 1999 highlight the cultural work of contemporary theater to help mold our understanding of ourselves. Tom Stoppard's acclaimed *The Invention of Love* (1997) also brings both Ruskin and Wilde—as well as its protagonist A. E. Housman—to the stage.

As mentioned in the Introduction, Ruskin's importance in his own time can hardly be overestimated. His ideas influenced Victorian artists, architects, writers, and social theorists, promoting economic and educational reforms, defending Turner, advancing the Gothic revival, inspiring and championing the Pre-Raphaelites, and indirectly starting the Arts and Crafts movement. Among his most famous acolytes were William Morris, Charlotte Brontë, Leo Tolstoy, Marcel Proust, Frank Lloyd Wright, and Mahatma Gandhi, who translated into Gujarati *Unto this Last,* the book Gandhi credited with changing his life. In 1906 the founding group of twenty-nine Labour MPs identified *Unto this Last* as the book that most influenced them, more so even than Marx ((Rosenberg 131). But despite the fact that three towns in the United States are named for Ruskin,[3] hardly anyone in America outside of the academy now knows who he was. His relevance, according to current staged versions of his life, is as a sexually repressed and patriarchal madman. Even Ruskin's renowned eloquence, even his recognized status within these dramas as someone important to the history of ideas, serves only to emphasize his prudish chauvinism. In both cases, Ruskin's purpose is to allow contemporary audiences to feel good about how far we have come since 1854. As John Kucich and Dianne Sadoff explain in *Victorian Afterlife* about other texts and authors, at work here is "postmodernism's privileging of the Victorians as its historical 'other'" (xi). Theater's glance back at Victorian sexuality allows ours to stand out in greater relief; indeed, these revisions construct a teleology in which present-day sexual relations and sex roles are quite simply more advanced than the Victorians'. Thousands of audience members viewing Ruskin's repression as quintessentially Victorian find it easy to feel self-righteously complacent about today's more relaxed sexual attitudes. We construct an identity of liberation antithetical to a fictional Victorian identity, creating an illusion of progressiveness based on a false sense of how far we have come.[4]

In contrast to plays about Ruskin, the recent plays about Wilde that I discuss here offer a model for contemporary audiences to emulate in crafting identities that make room for the possibility of gay existence.[5] Whereas Ruskin on stage acts the pathologically repressed prude allotting us a position of superiority, Wilde on stage acts the archly urbane defender of same-sex love whose apotheosis establishes the viability of gay identity validated by his self-sacrifice. Unlike general audiences at plays about Ruskin, most theater-goers know something of Wilde's own work. They typically have read or at least have encountered a reworking of *The Picture of Dorian Gray* or have seen a production of *The Importance of Being Earnest,* perhaps even in high school. Movie and television adaptations abound, as do theatrical re-imaginings.[6] While Wilde's famous epigrams and familiar aesthetic philosophy enter the dialogue of the plays I discuss here, it is not his writing, any more than Ruskin's, that makes him important in depictions on the turn of the millennium stage, but representations of his sexuality. As valuable a service as such cultural work is in depicting what Martha Ertman calls the "poster child" for gay identity (153), these plays diminish the complexity of their subject. The historical Wilde's sexuality defies easy categorization and his understanding of his own tragedy has as much to do with losing his art and his children as with suffering martyrdom for love of men.[7] As with Ruskin, Wilde's usefulness now as stage character depends on pinning him down, flattening him out, taming the wildness—so to speak—of his self-consciously performed persona.

All five shows depend upon a sense of historical accuracy for their appeal, even the Brechtian *Gross Indecency* and even *The Invention of Love,* which takes place in a dream state. All derive their illusory aura of authenticity from the use of life-writing; in addition, both *Gross Indecency* and more briefly the opera *Modern Painters* rely on trial records, highlighting the devastating effect of legal intervention in these men's lives. Unlike the fantastical *The Invention of Love, Modern Painters* and the play *The Countess* draw from Ruskin's and his wife Effie Gray's letters and diaries as well as from Ruskin's autobiography and criticism to depict the Ruskins' miserable wedded life; likewise, *Gross Indecency* and, to a much lesser extent, *The Judas Kiss* pluck dialogue and incidents from Wilde's letters, criticism, and historical documents. Appropriately for both Wilde and Ruskin, all of these shows blur to one degree or another the boundary between criticism and art. Yet, in adapting texts that are about ideas into staged representations of a life, all five plays result finally in plots concerning domestic interaction rather than the questions of art and social justice that animate Ruskin's and Wilde's own work. All reify current notions of sexual identity as a basic category of existence at the expense of recognizing either nineteenth-century ontological categories or the slipperiness of such categories over time. None of these performances quite fits either Ruskin's or Wilde's conception of performative identity.

REALISM AND FEMINISM OFF BROADWAY

Gregory Murphy's *The Countess* received excellent reviews from *The New York Times, The New York Post,* the *New Yorker,* and *Time Out: New York.*

Production of *The Countess* by Gregory Murphy, at the Samuel Beckett Theater, off Broadway, New York, 1999. Joshua Millais, photographer. Pictured are James Riordan as John Ruskin, Jy Murphy as John Everett Millais, and Jennifer Woodward as Effie Ruskin.

Directed and produced by Ludovica Villar-Hauser, this small costume drama ran for over six hundred performances.[8] *The Countess* depicts the disintegration of Ruskin and Effie Gray's marriage and the mounting attraction between Effie and their friend, the young Pre-Raphaelite painter whom Ruskin mentored, John Everett Millais, deserving the *New York Times*'s comment that the play is "erotically charged" (E1). A straightforward, accessible, realistic drama, *The Countess* focuses tightly on a very short period of Ruskin's life, from June 1853 to April 1854. While Ruskin omitted his six-year marriage from his autobiography *Praeterita* altogether, the play uses other kinds of life writing with meticulous care.

Of course, the play takes poetic license for dramatic effect, dropping characters, imagining witty conversation and unrecorded sexual advances, but it follows recorded facts we have about these private lives surprisingly closely. *The Countess* includes myriad details from published letters and sketches, most notably those found in Mary Lutyens's book *Millais and the Ruskins*.[9] Any scholar familiar with these materials will find their continual echoes throughout the script almost eerie, but the temptation to judge these plays based on their factual correctness is a mistake. They do not aspire to the condition of scholarship: they contain no footnotes; they are not published by university presses. Like the opera *Modern Painters, The Countess* encourages the audience to take Effie's side against Ruskin; he comes across in this play as cruel and manipulative. Members of the audience audibly gasp and even hiss when Ruskin berates Effie and disdains her physical person.[10] Those knowledgeable about the importance of the historical Ruskin's cultural contributions often watch with an increasingly heavy heart while the play's Ruskin behaves in such an abominably controlling way; some want to defend or excuse the historical Ruskin, futilely taking sides in a case that was decided 150 years ago. *The Countess* even sparked a hot exchange of letters to the Editor in the *New York Times*.[11] The power of these productions to incite such a reaction is the very reason to remind ourselves of something obvious: the Ruskin and Effie and Millais in New York or Santa Fe are literary personae, interpreted on stage. Such a play or opera asks us to consider what happens when historical personages become characters, when their own written words become dialogue, when their self-representations become dramas.

Part of the fun of any show based on a true story is that it is supposed to be true. But as representations of history, such plays are at least as false as the letters, diaries, and autobiographies that they come from. While this point may be apparent to literary critics, to many in the audience, the fictionality of life writing is an unfamiliar notion. When giving post-performance remarks after productions of *The Countess* to audiences eager to know more about Ruskin's life, I have found it necessary to explain that no one claims that Effie, Millais, and Ruskin lied in narrating these events so crucial to their reputations and their happiness, just that their written experiences come to us as artificial constructs, recalled after the fact and related in artfully crafted words, prepared with rhetorical appeal to persuade readers to understand and agree that each was right in what he or she did. Even diaries involve an effort to make sense of one's own actions, to clarify motivation, if only to oneself. As James Olney and others have shown, life-writing of all kinds brims with self-justification, failed memories, and misrepresentations.[12] So the first thing to say about all these plays based on autobiography is that their attractive sense of authoritativeness is illusory. This must be true even of the renditions most faithful to their source texts.

In addition, there remains a problem that historians are very familiar with, but that play-going audiences may not realize: any particular collection of manuscripts is pre-selected for the researcher by the collectors. In this case, the group of documents now at the Pierpont Morgan Library in New York known as the Bowerswell papers, on which Gregory Murphy based *The Countess,*

The Criterion, London production of *The Countess*, West End, 2005. Andrew Muir, photographer. Pictured are Nick Moran as John Ruskin, Damian O'Hare as John Everett Millais, and Alison Pargeter as Effie Ruskin.

include many manuscripts by Effie, Millais, Ruskin, and their families and friends. But they came from the home of Effie's parents in Bowerswell, Scotland. The choice of documents Effie's family collected reflects their concern with vindicating the Grays' and Millaises' actions regarding the Ruskins' annulment and the Millaises' marriage. While in Britain or America today a wife's decision to sue for annulment of an unconsummated marriage to one famous man and subsequent marriage to another would not require much justification, the Millaises and Grays certainly felt strongly the need to safeguard their relatives' reputations. They conscientiously gathered whatever materials they could in that cause.

Beyond the illusion of authenticity provided by basing a play on life-writing, the realistic genre in drama presents additional complexities. A realistic play's nonexistent fourth wall heightens the effect of verisimilitude because the audience observes seemingly unmediated action. Paradoxically, realistic drama feels more objective than the first-person account of a letter or diary or autobiography. When we pick up documents written by husband and wife in the middle of their marriage's collapse, we would be naive to imagine they write objectively. But when we watch a play unfold, though based on the same letters, the action comes to us as though unbiased by which hand recorded which incident. But added to the biases inherent in the source material are the playwright's selections and omissions for dramatic effect, satisfying our expectations for a realistic plot with tidy cause and effect, clear motivations, and psychological verity. Yet such neatness does not exist in life and certainly does not exist in the cacophony of voices percolating in the self-representations of Ruskin, Effie, and Millais. What adds to the audience's sense of realism and objectivity in the portrayal of history is another layer of mediation created by the writer between the historical figures and the performers' action.

Along with the false sense of objectivity that comes with dramatizing autobiography, there is a strange immediacy in the theater that makes an actress playing a real historical person, such as Effie Gray Ruskin, seem more real than the long-dead Effie we meet in her own letters, now obscured by the thick interference of a century and a half gone by. This impression of reality in the theater operates very strongly. The director creates a vision of truth. A living woman a few feet away speaks and schemes and kisses and argues and cries. The audience, transported into an imagined past by the actors' talent or the playwright's skill, willingly forgets how much the most painstaking historical portrayal is still an illusion. For example, Tara Millais, a descendant of Effie's and John Everett Millais's and thus a living embodiment of Effie's DNA, spoke of how wonderful it was in watching this play to see her great-great-grandmother brought to life.[13] The unrelated actress's craft creates a palpable illusion of reality.

Evidence that the play uses its realism to reject Victorian patriarchy abounds. The play shows Ruskin and his parents unsympathetically as they try to dominate Effie, dramatizing how powerless she is legally as a married woman in early 1850s England.[14] Likewise it demonstrates the problems that arise when people receive too little education in sexual matters, as no doubt happened much more frequently in nineteenth-century Britain than now; there is a certain irony to this, considering that later in his life, Ruskin writes advocating sex education for girls and boys, as we discussed in chapter 3 (34.529). The play reveals, through Ruskin's disillusioned reaction to Effie, that a cultural idealization of women hampers real relationships; conversely, it makes the modern feminist point that when women internalize the dominant culture's expectations for their bodies and find they can not measure up, they believe they are physically defective, inadequate, deformed. In addition, the play provides a strong woman character, Lady Eastlake, who recognizes that there is nothing wrong with Effie, encouraging her to leave Ruskin. Finally, the play's plot provides Effie with the strength to achieve her freedom.

Nevertheless, the play finally does reinforce the Victorian social arrangements and even the Victorian ideology it portrays, more in its characterization of Effie than of Ruskin. Indeed, the realism and the cachet of authenticity achieved by adapting autobiographical materials perhaps mark the play as patriarchal,[15] despite the playwright Greg Murphy's stated effort to the contrary. The clearest example is that the play ends by having Effie leave her husband so that she can marry Millais, reinforcing the marriage plot. More pervasively, Effie remains extremely decorous and domestic throughout, acting uneasy in situations that could be construed as compromising; her discomfort protects her position as a gentlewoman in the eyes of the audience because it proves she is not wanton.[16] She spends her time on needlework and sketching, thoroughly suitable nineteenth-century feminine behavior. Effie is visibly agitated in trying to discuss sex even with her champion Lady Eastlake. Her likableness for the audience depends not on her bucking Victorian convention, but on her being a victim of it. The play does not include the historical Effie's flirtatiousness, her love of parties and gallery openings, the duel challenged over her stolen jewels, the young Austrian officer who squired Effie about Venice while Ruskin was busy writing or sketching, not only because of theatrical time constraints, not only because of focus on the love story between Millais and Effie, but also because these incidents would not show Effie in the light of the oppressed Victorian angel in the house. Outside of that role, as depicted in this play, she would lose even the turn of the twenty-first-century audience's intense sympathy.

The contemporary audience loves Effie because she satisfies all their expectations for a Victorian heroine. Even the protagonists of Victorian novels take more gambles sexually than this late twentieth-century play gives Effie: virtually any novel by George Eliot or Thomas Hardy will provide examples. *The Countess* does not risk the possibility of ambiguity for her, as though anyone other than a spotless paragon might not work within the Victorian context for a present-day audience. Other than a passionate and guilt-ridden kiss, the play goes to considerable lengths to resist anything that could sully her within imagined Victorian judgment. In other words, the play commits the same "sin" that it claims Ruskin does, idealizing Effie. So even though Murphy's stated intent is to defend Effie not only from her Victorian detractors, but also from her twentieth-century biographers, to help us understand how isolated and frustrated she must have felt (in which he succeeds admirably), the play exculpates Effie and condemns Ruskin exclusively within current understanding of Victorian terms. [17]

While the play's defense of Effie as a vindication of her right to a fulfilling sex life seems tremendously modern and feminist and certainly correct, it is in fact no more than what Victorian society had already granted: Effie got her annulment, and Ruskin got ridiculed. So while Murphy successfully shows Effie's untenable position with Ruskin and highlights Victorian women's vulnerability within marriage, it breaks no new ground; indeed, it recuperates Effie in the most old-fashioned way imaginable. For many years Queen Victoria refused to allow the quasi-divorced Mrs. Millais to be presented at court, relenting only when Millais lay dying; the play signals Effie's vindication by having the Queen finally receive her. The play is as patriarchal as the Victorian world it recreates, not only on stage but also in the approving mind of the audience. Perhaps more troubling to admit is that the erotic charge for present-day audiences observed by *The New York Times* surely depends in part upon the patriarchal Victorian setting: the triangle involving an abusive and powerful husband, a legally vulnerable and neglected wife, and a devoted and impetuous young lover needs the perceived power dynamics of Victorian gender relations to maintain the same erotic appeal. In twenty-first-century Britain or America, Effie Gray would not be legally bound to obey her husband, and John Ruskin would not be trapped without possibility of divorce. In chapter 1 I discussed the historical Ruskin's concern that the surrogate outrage we experience at theatrical presentations can dull our intention to make material improvements for social justice outside the theater; that point might well serve as a critique of the compromised feminist outcome of *The Countess.*

Aspiring to the Condition of Music

Even people familiar with the tragic soap opera of Ruskin's love life probably never imagined that it would become the topic of a real opera, but with 1995's world premiere at the prestigious Santa Fe Opera, it did. *Modern Painters* not only tells the story of Ruskin's marriage and its notorious dissolution, but also chronicles his doomed love for the very young Rose La Touche, whom it depicts as only thirteen (rather than eighteen) when he proposes marriage[18]; in addition it recounts the disastrous Whistler trial, in which the young American Impressionist painter James Whistler sued the influential art critic over a bad review, exacerbating the aging writer's increasingly severe bouts of mental illness. The Santa Fe Opera commissioned composer David Lang, best known for co-founding the "Bang on a Can Music Festival" in New York, and librettist Manuella Hoelterhoff, the Pulitzer-Prize winning culture critic for the *Wall Street Journal.* Francesca Zambella directed, having just won the Laurence Olivier Award for a production at the English National Opera. It received positive reviews from *Vogue* and the *Village Voice,* but has not been produced since.[19] The opera is a musically minimalist yet philosophically expansive look at all of Ruskin's adulthood, less factually accurate than *The Countess* but more committed to communicating the beauty of Ruskin's language, organized more thematically than chronologically. Although it is very odd to think of an opera as an adaptation of critical texts, this one largely is. Besides some quotations from the autobiography *Praeterita*, characters often sing lush passages directly from Ruskin's criticism, including *Modern Painters* (1843–1860), *The Stones of Venice* (1851–53), *The Seven Lamps of Architecture* (1848), *The Crown of Wild Olive* (1866), *Unto this Last* (1860), *Sesame and Lilies* (1865), and *Storm-Cloud of the Nineteenth Century* (1884). But perhaps it should not surprise us, since Wilde already tells us that "criticism . . . is the only civilized form of autobiography" (1027).

Very different issues arise in adapting autobiography to a Masterpiece Theater-like costume drama than to an opera, rarely a realistic form. As a genre it revels in artificiality, often highlighting virtuosity over content, always subordinating words to music. Of course, a realistic play is also a study in artifice and convention; William Demastes, Brian Richardson, and others point out that what defines a play as realistic or not changes over time and across cultures.[20] Nevertheless, as a genre today, realistic drama depends upon the audience's acceptance of these established conventions (linear time, reasonable cause and effect, plausible plot, likely dialogue, ignoring the audience), as marking it somehow true to life. In contrast, opera traditionally depends upon the audience's expectation of grandeur and excess. Although some of the same issues of authenticity arise in watching an opera based on life-writing as in a play, the historical accuracy of an opera does not increase its appeal to the same degree. Opera promises extravagant emotion and mythic circumstances, no matter how prosaic the narrative it presents. Far from creating an illusion of greater objectivity than its autobiographical sources, *Modern Painters*—with its stylized sets, lengthy arias, and richly metaphorical language—seems outside discussions of subjective and objective portrayal of real events. Neither does opera offer the same sense of immediacy that a realistic play does; the medium acts as a buffer between the audience and the character, no matter how good the acting and singing, because the conventions of realism do not include song as a likely mode of conversation. Far from following the record as rigorously as *The Countess, Modern Painters* radically rearranges chronology, changes facts, and combines circumstances.[21] Highlighting some of Ruskin's most purple prose as lyrics, its creators concentrate more on transmitting the poetry of Ruskin's language than in telling his story.

Modern Painters, Santa Fe Opera, July 1995.Hans Fahrmeyer, photographer. Ann Panagulias as Effie, François Le Roux as John Ruskin.

The opera takes its title from Ruskin's magisterial five-volume analysis of J. M. W. Turner and many other artists, which he wrote over seventeen years, from 1843 to 1860, documenting his own intellectual development as well as offering a fount of social, mythological, and (as I have shown in chapter 1) opera criticism. However, the opera's seven scenes are organized around the chapter titles of another of Ruskin's famous books, *The Seven Lamps of Architecture,* published in 1849, soon after Ruskin's marriage began. The seven lamps are Sacrifice, Truth, Power, Beauty, Life, Memory, and Obedience. The opera provides little direct relationship between its action and the seven elements Ruskin describes as necessary for a nation's healthy architecture, but as abstract terms they resonate thematically with the subject matter of each of the roughly chronological episodes from Ruskin's life. The result of naming and structuring the creative work after the critical suggests that Matthew Arnold was in this respect right: criticism provides the stream of ideas for artists, quite literally. The opera also dramatizes art as criticism and criticism as art, almost as though the subject matter were Wilde's "The Critic as Artist," insinuating that the boundary between the two is meaningless.[22] In addition the show implies that opera is structured like architecture[23]: it is meant to last, to be worthy of sacrifice, to be a monument and a living, inhabitable cathedral of music, meant as much for future generations as for us. In organizing their opera along the *Seven Lamps,* Lang and Hoelterhoff make a very grand claim.

Nevertheless, although beguiled by the beauty of Ruskin's writing and the significance of his ideas, the creators are faced with the fact that what is opera-worthy about Ruskin is the story of his scandalous marriage and the other personal tragedies of his life. The show reveals the tension between their fascination with his language and their attraction to his dirty laundry in that the opera's best moments appear in the juxtaposition of Ruskin's riveting words to a wildly dramatic version of his private troubles.

While *The Countess* reveals the calamitous wedding night retrospectively, only in Effie's halting confession of misery to her older friend Lady Eastlake, *Modern Painters* symbolically renders the failed nuptials in the second scene, "Truth," where it portrays Ruskin's idealization of women as the reason for his marriage's collapse. The scene opens with the wedding dinner, showing Effie and her parents eating with the Ruskins. The singers create a cacophony that Ruskin ends by simply ringing his glass: he rises alone to toast Effie as his future wife, as though oblivious to the commotion. [24] The strings here intensify the sweetness and romance of his gesture. He sings: "I dreamt of a woman like an angel / who brought peace into my home, / In her presence all division disappeared" (11). Ruskin's words in the libretto recall "Of Queens' Gardens" (18.122). Of course, that essay was in fact written seventeen years later with Rose, not Effie, in mind.[25]

This toast is the segue to Ruskin and Effie's wedding night. In their bedroom, the young couple tells each other what they expect from life together: she a round of costume balls and gallery openings; he a rigorous work schedule. Ironically, historically and in the opera, both get exactly what in this duet they say they want. What they don't get is a physical relationship. As Effie pleads with him to come to bed, Ruskin reads aloud from a book, intoning lyrically to Effie of a beautiful woman:

> She lies on her pillow, a hound at her feet
> Her arms folded softly over her breast
> Her dress is simple, of medieval style,
> with flowing drapery, marble white.
> Around her head a fillet of flowers. (12)

However, this blossom-crowned beauty lying on a pillow is not Effie, and she knows it. In fact, although the audience never discovers her identity, Ruskin's pretty song describes a statue on a tomb; the woman's white pillow is marble; she sleeps in her grave. The book he reads from is his own *Modern Painters*, which describes the funeral effigy.[26] Ruskin does not even look at Effie in her nightgown as he recalls this deathly figure—probably a good thing, since Ruskin has suffered enough bad press sexually without adding necrophilia to the list. Instead, the bridegroom reads himself to sleep, fully clothed, serenading his lovely homage to the cold sculpture of a long-dead Renaissance woman, while the living wife covers her face on their unhappy bridal bed.

In *The Countess* Ruskin describes the same sculpture, this time to Millais, emphasizing more fleshly details: "One day we will go to Lucca, and I'll show you della Quercia's sculpture of Ilaria di Caretto. You will not believe the perfect sweetness of her lips and closed eyes, or the way her dress folds closely beneath the curve of her breasts" (12). Both playwright and librettist see in this passage, based on an 1845 letter to Ruskin's father, a key to Ruskin's debilitating idealization of women. Hoelterhoff suggests that Ruskin envisions abstracted beauty, whereas Murphy views it in palpably physical terms. He considers Ruskin's focus on the sculpture analogous to problems men still have with unrealistic expectations about women's bodies: Murphy mentioned in interview that today men are taught to want tall, thin models rather than alabaster effigies, but the idea is the same.[27]

This almost anatomical interpretation of Ruskin's idealization of women certainly works both biographically and dramatically as a way to understand Ruskin's disillusionment with his wife once he saw her naked. However, while the opera and the play try to work out Ruskin's private woes by pinning his ideal of womanhood to a marble statue, the empowering effect of his gender mythology on Victorian women (other than Effie) goes unnoticed. When Ruskin writes about housewives' queenship in "Of Queens' Gardens," he concerns himself with redefining and enlarging the domestic sphere so that women will take on greater responsibility outside the home. Seth Koven and others have shown how Victorian feminists found Ruskin's ideas useful. Likewise, when Ruskin advances a progressive education for girls, he promotes their equal schooling with boys. Contrary to what the play and opera depict, the historical Ruskin's ideal for the identity "woman" concerned what women should do rather than how they should look.[28]

The final scene in *Modern Painters,* "Obedience," stages a lecture famously described by A. E. Housman. Ruskin takes a beautiful landscape by J. M. W. Turner, depicting an English scene from before it was polluted by heavy industrialization, and paints ugly modern additions—including smoke, factories, railroads, and prisons—onto the glass that covers the painting, completely disfiguring its beauty. Housman describes this lecture as brilliant and its effect on students at Oxford as electrifying, but the opera presents it as the ravings of a mad seer failing to convince a crowd of jeering workers (contrary to the historical Ruskin's overwhelmingly positive reception by working-class readers).[29] The libretto's method of describing alternately the wretched state of the environment and the appalling condition of the workers' lives—lifting passages from *The Crown of Wild Olive, The Storm-Cloud of the Nineteenth Century,* and *Unto this Last*—underscores Ruskin's link between a just society and a healthy ecology. Yet Ruskin's song turns into an incantatory mumbling as he goes from singing repeatedly, "There is no wealth but life," to chanting "Blackened sun, blighted grass, blinded man" (31), signifying his final insanity. [30]

In both the first and the last scenes, Ruskin futilely addresses working men, first to prevent their demolishing a beautiful building, later to educate them about art and ecology. In each case, the workers dismiss Ruskin as insane, just as the press really had rejected Ruskin's social activism as the preaching of "a mad governess" (17.xxviii). The opera follows suit, depicting a feminized Ruskin. The practical, burly workmen with hammers and menacing voices come across as masculine compared to the aesthetic, moralistic, idealistic, and poetic Ruskin, weak and ineffective. Likewise, in comparison to the opera's virile Millais, who imagines himself as a medieval knight on horseback in armor rescuing Effie, who then fathers eight children during his enthusiastically consummated marriage with Ruskin's neglected bride, the opera emasculates Ruskin. Even in comparison to the lively Effie, who verbally castrates her former husband by shrieking her revenge, Ruskin is feminized. The emasculation is made explicit in the spoken line "He is impotent," cut from the opera before its premiere because the audience tittered.[31]

The ultimate potency in this opera resides in Ruskin's words. The best moment in the opera is the very last. The Santa Fe Opera House is outdoors; the audience sits in the open air at night in the high desert. The lights of Los Alamos shimmer like fireflies in the distant background behind the stage, while a women's chorus quietly chants one of Ruskin's most famous lines about Turner: "It is the living light which sleeps but never dies" (3.308). But now it is the light of Ruskin's language that never dies, as we hear him cry out the famous firefly passage from the end of his autobiography *Praeterita:*

How they shone!
As I entered the town through the gleaming gate
bright, silver hued
and I felt inside me
a light more intense than the stars. . . . (32)

The stage darkens around Ruskin; light in the center brightens, and suddenly he is gone, dropped off the back of the stage, like Tosca. While the opera's focus on sexual dysfunction obscures subtle gender subversion in Ruskin's prose, nevertheless, these rich passages reinvest Ruskin with the power of his own vigorous imagery. The feminized man—now stripped of any meaningful gender—has become most potent as the disembodied spoken word, reverberating on the empty stage bathed in white light.

Ruskin and Wilde in the Underworld

Stoppard's brilliant and very funny play *The Invention of Love*, about A. E. Housman's youth at Oxford, includes both Ruskin and Wilde as characters. Directed by Richard Eyre, *The Invention of Love* opened at the National Theatre in London on September 25, 1997 and moved to the West End's Haymarket Theatre shortly afterwards. It premiered in the United States in 2000 at the American Conservatory Theater in San Francisco, and arrived on Broadway at the Lyceum Theater, March 29, 2001; it has had numerous productions since.[32] Not a realistic play, *The Invention of Love* takes place in Hades with flashbacks to Oxford. Its characters are dead or are remembered in their college days by the dying Housman; two actors play the protagonist, allowing the old Housman to react to, comment on, and even to converse with his younger self.[33] Stoppard's play chronicles the old Housman's realization that perhaps he should have had the courage to declare openly his love for the young heterosexual Moses Jackson at Oxford for whom he wrote poetry, instead of burying himself in the classicism that formed the bulk of his life's work.

Covertly introduced in the play's opening seconds by an allusion to one of his Oxford lectures, Ruskin drifts on and off stage, playing croquet with fellow don and aesthete Walter Pater. Both wear angel wings as they discourse decoratively on art, life, and society. Unlike the patriarchal tyrant of *The Countess* or the pitiable, impotent pedophile of *Modern Painters,* this Ruskin is hilariously pretentious, declaring, "I have announced the meaning of life in my lectures" (15).[34] Referring to his utopian social project of St. George's Guild, Stoppard's Ruskin cares more about his undergraduate student's prettiness than any principles of social justice. Ruskin says:

> I had my students up at dawn building a flower-bordered road across a
> swamp. . . . There was an Irish exquisite, a great slab of a youth with white
> hands and long poetical hair who said he was glad to say he had never seen

a shovel, but I . . . taught that work with one's hands is the beginning of virtue. Then I went sketching to Venice and the road sank into the swamp. My protegé rose at noon to smoke cigarettes and read French novels, and Oxford reverted to a cockney watering-place for learning to row. (15)

While the historical Ruskin really did set his students to road-building and really did make the crack about Oxford as a place for learning to row (22.274), Stoppard's Ruskin is a clever maker of empty aphorisms. He resembles a Gilbert and Sullivan parody of Oscar Wilde more than the passionate moralist critics recognize[35]; indeed the character of Bunthorne from their operetta *Patience* also makes a cameo appearance in this play, appropriately before the "real" Wilde shows up. Very different from *The Countess* or *Modern Painters*, this depiction of Ruskin leaves out women completely; instead of fearing women or repressing desire for them, he displaces onto art an attraction for the "Irish Exquisite" we recognize as Wilde. But Ruskin's utility in Stoppard's play is not that far off finally from *The Countess* and *Modern Painters*. Ruskin acts the warped and faded aesthete, too wrapped up in rigid theories of beauty or impractical social experiments to pay attention to what genuinely matters, which in the dead or dying Housman's estimation is sex after all. Moreover, *The Invention of Love* portrays Ruskin as puritanical and hypocritical. In an even more sinister note, in the National Theatre production, the actor playing Ruskin also plays the M.P. Labouchere, whose earlier legislation against acts of "gross indecency" between men resulted in Wilde's conviction and imprisonment.

The historical Wilde, who overlapped with Housman at college, also studied with both Ruskin and Pater, remaining friends with them afterwards (Ellmann 47–52). Not only did Wilde and Ruskin go to the theater together, but also they were sufficiently intimate that Oscar and his wife, Constance, asked Ruskin to be godfather to their son Vyvyan. Ruskin declined, saying he was too old, as indeed in 1886, at the age of sixty-seven and only a few years away from complete disability, he was (Ellmann 266; Amor 61). In the play, Stoppard's desiccated Ruskin becomes a backboard against which we bounce our own superiority. In contrast, Stoppard assigns Wilde a much more positive role, making the flamboyant wit into a model both for Housman and for the audience. At the end of the play, Wilde at last appears in person. He has been talked about—perfectly appropriate to Wildean practice—all throughout the play. He arrives to be ferried across the Styx. With instructions to pick up "a scholar and a poet," Charon has been waiting since the very first scene for a second passenger, despite Housman's emphatic assurances that no second passenger would show up, sure that he is both the scholar and the poet. Wilde's appearance in Hades vindicates the ferryman and suggests that Housman is more scholar than poet, more repressed than liberated, more closeted than out. In the set of binaries implicit here, Wilde's claim to identity as poet is at one with his identity as gay.

Wilde talks glibly about art and what he has learned from Ruskin. He declares, "I banged Ruskin's and Pater's heads together, and from the moral severity of one and the aesthetic soul of the other I made a philosophy that can look the twentieth-century in the eye" (96).[36] But Wilde's foundational modernism in art and aesthetics is conflated with his bravery in loving Lord Alfred Douglas, known as Bosie. Although in college and for many years afterward until 1886 the historical Wilde had sexual relations only with women (Ellman 277),[37] most of the characters in *The Invention of Love* and indeed the play itself equate the aesthetic long-haired Wilde's plum- colored breaches with practices that they variously call "spooniness" (40), "beastliness" (7), or "buggery" (17). As we shall see in a moment with *Gross Indecency*, this requires us not only to read backward from our twentieth/twenty-first century vantage point in which a gay identity category already exists but also to assume that all the sex Wilde had in the years before his first homosexual experience with Robbie Ross at the age of thirty-three somehow did not count.[38] In other words, in this play even the undergraduate Wilde symbolizes daring in same-sex love as much as new ideas in art. As Stoppard's Wilde says to Housman of both love and poetry: "Better a fallen rocket than never a burst of light" (96).

The Invention of Love conjures Ruskin only to dismiss him as impotent (94), as making virtue into a vice (93), as too removed from real feeling to be of any use at all. In contrast, Oscar Wilde appears as the example of what Housman could have done, had he the courage to choose illicit love and its poetry over scholarship. Ruskin, along with Pater and Jowett, represents the latter, the sublimation of sexuality into erudition and dry aesthetics. Again Ruskin—even for Stoppard—serves to establish through opposition postmodern identities as sexually and socially liberated; Stoppard's Wilde, on the other hand, articulates his own contribution explicitly: "The blaze of my immolation threw its light into every corner of the land where uncounted young men sat each in his own darkness. I awoke the imagination of the century" (96) to the identity of the homosexual.[39]

WILDE'S TRIALS

Gross Indecency: The Three Trials of Oscar Wilde, written and directed by Moisés Kaufman, premiered with great success off Broadway at the Greenwich House theater in 1997, transferring to the larger Minetta Lane Theater a few months

later. By 1998 it had opened in Plymouth, England and by 1999 was playing in London at the Gielgud Theatre. It has enjoyed brisk performance
regionally ever since. More conventionally biographical than the dream-vision
netherworld landscape of *The Invention of Love,* both *Gross Indecency* and
The Judas Kiss concentrate on the period of Wilde's life from his court trials to his final break with Bosie. Despite moments of humor provided by
quotations of Wilde's own or inventions of Wilde-like wit, *Gross Indecency*
and *The Judas Kiss* are tragedies, enacting what in retrospect we know is
Wilde's doom as we are "ushered into a narrative" of destruction that Joseph
Bristow describes as "almost as relentless as *Oedipus Rex*" (1995, 24).[40]

By far the more rigorous and interesting play, *Gross Indecency* dramatically presents records from Wilde's three trials (from H. Montgomery Hyde's
compilation *The Three Trials of Oscar Wilde*)[41] interspersed with other Victorian
documents, such as letters from all the principals, Wilde's lectures and other
writing, newspaper accounts, and the later autobiographies of Bosie and Frank
Harris. Abandoning the fourth wall, *Gross Indecency* nevertheless promotes
a sense of documentary realism. However, as with Ruskin, Wilde's significance as a writer and as a philosopher of art becomes almost irrelevant; what
emerges from this focus on his fall, guaranteed by a slip in admitting that
he avoided kissing a particular boy "because he was, unfortunately,
extremely ugly" (57), is that Wilde's real importance lies in his narrative of
martyrdom for the right to homosexuality. What is so interesting about this
reification of Wilde as gay before that identity existed historically is that
Wilde's actual sexuality and his sense of self were far more slippery and thus,
one could argue, both more queer and more postmodern than these plays
suggest. As S. I. Salamensky points out, the historical Wilde's "sheer per-
formativeness," his flippant, verbose, and consciously artificial "behaviors
enthusiastically stressed their own theatrical quality" (578). Wilde's personal
theatricality highlights the instability of identity, but current theatrical representations squash it. As Alan Sinfeld explains, "it is hard to regard Wilde
as other than the apogee of gay experience and expression"; nevertheless,
his being always already gay is a historical anachronism (2) . But *The Invention
of Love, Gross Indecency,* and *The Judas Kiss* reinforce the notion that
Wilde's boundary-breaking aesthetic pose and his flamboyant persona
were consubstantial with his homosexuality. These plays do not recognize
that to some degree flamboyance as a signifier of homosexuality began as
an imitation of Oscar and can not be read backwards as a sign of Wilde's
gay identity. Even Wilde's later defense of Uranian love's nobility does not
come with a statement of exclusivity. Wilde argued for freedom to explore
beauty and sensation wherever he found it: in sexual terms, that meant with

female prostitutes in college; in ardent marriage to his wife Constance; in his introduction to same-sex experiences by his friend Robbie Ross; through his besotted love affair with Bosie; and in entertaining dalliance with the "rent boys" who proved his downfall. The identity labels based on sexuality that these plays depend upon and solidify do not quite fit either the details of Wilde's life or his definition of life as art.

Gross Indecency recognizes and dismisses the idea that Wilde might more accurately be labeled by the current use of the word *queer*, with its connotations of indeterminacy and disruption, rather than *gay* or *homosexual*. The play does so primarily by incorporating an interview between the author (played by Kaufman in the original production) and scholar Marvin Taylor, based on the real-life scholar Marvin Taylor, curator at the Fales Collection at NYU, who stands in for other Wilde scholars and queer theorists, such as Joseph Bristow, Ed Cohen, Jonathan Dollimore, and Alan Sinfield. Kaufman's Taylor comes off as ridiculous in arguing for a Foucauldian historicization of the term *homosexuality*.

> Taylor: [W]hat happens in the trial is [Wilde] comes head on up against legal discourse, and perhaps I would even say legal-medical discourse. And he begins to lose to this sort of patriarchal medical discourse that makes him appear to be a homosexual, as opposed to . . . hum . . . someone who has desire for other men.
>
> Moises: Are you saying that Wilde didn't really think of himself as "homosexual"?
>
> Taylor: . . . It is after the Wilde trials that people began identifying themselves as a specific type of person based on the their attraction to people of the same sex. See, it created the modern homosexual as a social subject. . . . You know Foucault talks about how it was impossible for men in the Victorian era to think of themselves as gay or homosexual because that construction didn't exist. (76)

Michael Schiavi reports that in the off-Broadway production "the baffled Kaufman squinted, to the audiences' hysterical laughter, at Taylor's stumbling depiction of Wilde as 'a disruption of all kinds of things, of class, of gender, of hum sexuality, hum'" (410). The attitude of the play toward these distinctions is best summed up by Tony Kushner in his "Afterword" to *Gross Indecency*. While declaring admiration for the "whole splendid Queer Theoretical Company" (138), including Marvin Taylor (137), Kushner comments that "Wilde was destroyed at an early age by reactionaries, conservatives, liberals, and homophobes (and I know, I know, you can't call them 'homophobes' because there are no 'homosexuals' and blah blah blah)" (139). So finally, even for people who know that Wilde's usefulness as a model for homosexual identity is the product of anachronism, this anachronism makes him most precious for gay liberation. To the notion that such a limiting reduction of Wilde's life, work, and persona ultimately diminishes the elasticity of Wilde's performed existence, which could actually open up the possibility of even more ways of being than we now recognize, the response is "blah blah blah."

Gross Indecency presents Wilde's fall primarily through staged but historically viable documentary evidence, offering—despite its Brechtian anti-realist presentation—an even greater sense of authenticity than the realistic drama of *The Countess*. Audiences leaving a production of *Gross Indecency* feel (rightly) that they have learned something about Wilde's life. But mostly what they learn is that Wilde suffered for being gay.

APOTHEOSIS

The Judas Kiss, by David Hare, intensifies Wilde's suffering to Christian martyrdom. Directed (like *The Invention of Love*) by Richard Eyre, *The Judas Kiss* opened with Liam Neeson playing Oscar Wilde in 1998 at the Playhouse in London, earning mixed reviews. It moved to Broadway's Broadhurst Theater a month later, with the London cast. Like *The Countess, The Invention of Love,* and *Gross Indecency,* it too continues in production regionally. Echoing *De Profundis,* this play presents Wilde as a Christian martyr. In the first act, Wilde sacrifices himself for Bosie by staying in England at Bosie's request to continue the fight against Bosie's father, the Marquess of Queensbury, when he could have fled the country before criminal prosecution. Again in the second act, after release from prison, Bosie (carrying on with other lovers) betrays Wilde by abandoning him for money in the form of an allowance from his family. Because this straightforward realistic drama does not present the trials themselves, there is no staged shocking courtroom lie by Wilde that he did not have sex with men, and of course no climactic revelation that he had. There are no celebrated witticisms on the stand. Instead, there is the story of Wilde's catatrophic obsession with a spoiled, aristocratic Adonis, and Bosie's caddish disregard for Wilde's best interest.

The Judas Kiss allows for even less ambiguity regarding Wilde's gay identity than *Gross Indecency.* Wilde refers to himself outright as an invert (18), a pederast (76), and one who loves boys (87). No Marvin Taylor character presents a queer analysis of Wilde's biography. With none of the aesthetic posing from *The Invention of Love* or imitating in lecture the parody of himself created by Gilbert and Sullivan, Hare's Wilde disastrously throws away his reputation, career, friends, freedom, and family for love of a manipulative, unworthy user. When Wilde's friend Robbie urges Wilde to save himself from prison and ignominy by fleeing from London in defiance of Bosie's wishes, Wilde responds:

> I have acted out of love. I have defended this love. . . . The redeeming fact
> of my life. . . . It is what I have left. . . . All else has now been taken away.
> So now would you take even that from me. You would tell me I have been
> deceived and used in all this? . . . If the love between us is not as I think
> it, I shall have suffered to no purpose at all. (49–50)

For Hare, Wilde's suffering for love actuates his existence.

Their private affection gives Wilde purpose, but for Hare's Bosie the point of their relationship is to proclaim their gay identity. Bosie accuses Wilde of cowardice and duplicity in having not proclaimed his homosexuality on the stand:

> Lying in public! . . . You could have defended Greek love! How will his-
> tory judge you? . . . You will be known for ever as the man who was
> ashamed to admit his own nature! . . . When a better time comes, when
> this kind of love is accepted and understood, then you will be condemned
> because you took the coward's way. (100–101)

Although the play sides with Wilde in sacrificing himself for love and highlights Bosie's self- centered hypocrisy in leaving Wilde, the charge of his denying his true or core self remains. Bosie's expression of the play's concern with Wilde's lie only makes sense if Wilde has an intrinsic rather than socially constructed identity. By the end of the play, Wilde has sacrificed himself not just to free Bosie but as a Christ figure whose self-sacrifice frees succeeding generations to be true to their own natures. But *The Judas Kiss's* apotheosis of Wilde eradicates any indeterminacy in his identity, crystallizing him as essentially and exclusively gay.

CONCLUSION

The Oscar Wildes of *The Invention of Love, Gross Indecency: The Three Trials of Oscar Wilde,* and *The Judas Kiss* participate in the vision of Wilde as a gay icon for contemporary audiences to admire, to feel outrage on his behalf, and to sympathize with, to model themselves after, and to feel finally relief that no matter how bad their own coming-out scenarios might be, Wilde's will always be worse.[42] All depend on the audience's identifying Wilde as homosexual, which, while understandable and even valuable, is a narrower construction than either history or Wilde himself would acknowledge. For *Gross Indecency,* Wilde is a brilliant, hubristic victim; for *The Judas Kiss,* he is an eloquent, self-destructive martyr; but in both cases he is the quintessential gay man, struggling for a place to survive in a homophobic culture. Even *The Invention of Love* ultimately restricts his significance to a more essential expression of self than to a performed one. These Oscar Wildes operate primarily to maintain him as a glittering figurehead of gay identity for twenty-first-century audiences.

The John Ruskins of *The Countess, Modern Painters,* and *The Invention of Love* operate primarily to establish the turn-of-the-millennium spectators' superiority to the supposedly frigid (and homophobic) Victorians, despite the fact that the historical record shows that the Victorians often do not fit these stereotypes of sexual repression. Victorian attitudes toward sexuality were not as monolithic and very often not as puritanical as the rebellious and dismissive Modernists claimed about the previous generation. Beginning at least with Stephen Marcus's *The Other Victorians* and going on through Porter and Hall's *The Facts of Life* to a long list of books and articles, researchers have drawn a picture of a diverse set of attitudes toward sex.[43] Ultimately, the sympathetic opera *Modern Painters* uses Ruskin's own words against him, making him pitiable. *The Countess* not only indicts Ruskin but also necessarily renders the stage Effie less complex than the historical Effie's correspondence reveals. For *Modern Painters,* Ruskin is a tragic, brilliant madman; for *The Countess* he is an eloquent, manipulative tyrant; but in both cases he is a quintessential Victorian prude, too wrapped up in ideal beauty to recognize it in the flesh. Although Murphy believes his drama reveals to play-goers that they do the same thing, neither show holds a mirror to its public. Instead, the audience reacts with relief that no matter how bad their relationships are, at least they (probably) consummated their own marriages. The audiences disapprove of Ruskin's failure to appreciate Effie, confirming their complacency about their own enlightenment regarding sex and women's right both to a loving, respectful relationship without psychological abuse and to physical pleasure within that relationship. So in neither case do these theatrical representations awaken audiences to their own faults. Rather they function to validate audiences in their self-satisfaction and to reinforce current identity categories as natural and fixed.

The historical Ruskin and Wilde died over a century ago, within months of each other. They each left a tremendous legacy of extraordinary writing, serious ideas, and both documented and incalculable influences. Both have also sparked a growing proliferation of Ruskins and Wildes as literary characters, not only in *The Countess, Modern Painters, The Invention of Love, Gross Indecency: The Three Trials of Oscar Wilde,* and *The Judas Kiss* but also in a variety of films, novels, radio plays, and other kinds of representation. As time goes by, there will be more. What purpose do theatrical Ruskins and Wildes perform? What cultural work do they accomplish? How do they contribute to the construction of current identities? What does Ruskin- or Wilde-as-character represent?[44] In a sense, any theatrical adaptation of autobiographical material diminishes the historical subject and will always say as much or more about the adaptor's culture than that of the figures represented on stage. *The Countess, Modern Painters,* and *Gross Indecency* demonstrate how fragile the selves created in letters and autobiography are, how inevitably words change out of context. Even the most sensitive, nuanced attempt reduces a full life to a few hours' span, choosing what is dramatic, powerful, symbolic, or entertaining to succeed or fail as a work of art, not as a somehow genuine translation to stage of the historical person's lived experience. Even the so-called historical Ruskin or historical Wilde is inaccessible, available to us only as a textual artifact that we read rather than meet. Such texts stand ready to be interpreted and re-created for us by critics, scholars, autobiographers, novelists, playwrights, directors, actors, audiences, and readers. With each iteration, a new Ruskin or new Wilde appears. While we use these figures to confirm the seeming solidity of our current identity categories, the repetition and performativity of each incarnation ultimately undermines the security of these labels. Recognizing the artifice of each performance reveals to us the instability and constructedness of our own identities more surely than it reconstructs a Ruskin or Wilde long past.

"Scene from 'Jack in the Box' at the Drury Lane Theatre." *The Illustrated London News* 64 (January 10,1874): 28.

Conclusion
Queering Ruskin

Throughout this book I have touched repeatedly on the issue of Ruskin's sexuality. As I conclude my argument that Ruskin's writing shows a reluctant recognition of identities as performed rather than innate, I would like to address the enigma of his sexuality directly. At the beginning of the twenty-first century in the western world, sexuality and identity have become almost synonymous. People commonly are labeled or label themselves in conversation by sexuality: "I'm straight," " . . . a lesbian," "gay," "bi-," "queer," or, most recently, "metrosexual," all variations on a theme of sexual polarity. Amazon.com lists literally hundreds of books on sexual identity, while the homo/hetero opposition so dominates our thinking that no other possibilities enter America's consciousness as it watches *Queer Eye for the Straight Guy.* Even bisexuality is perceived more as an oscillation between homo and hetero than its own subject position.[1] What Ruskin's apparently unusual sexuality offers us now is a vehicle to talk about how completely we circumscribe and limit our identities within the current homo-/hetero-/bi-sexual triad. Foucault and many other sex historians have proven that the identities of homosexual and heterosexual are late nineteenth-century discursive inventions[2]; Derrida and deconstruction have taught us to distrust the hierarchies inherent in such definitions through linguistic bipolarity. Both Ruskin's writing and his biography afford an opportunity to enlarge this limiting discourse of dichotomies. While occasionally critics suggest that Ruskin may have been homosexual without realizing it, most have not really known what to make of Ruskin's unsatisfied desire, other than to snicker or to diagnose a pathology.[3] And so I say the *enigma* of Ruskin's sexuality because, even though some recent books and articles have speculatively and pejoratively labeled Ruskin a pedophile, in fact we know virtually nothing of his sex life other than that he had none, at least not with his wife of six years.

The recent scholars and critics using the term *pedophile* to describe Ruskin employ it even though they agree that we have no hint of molestation (Hilton 2000, 438; Robson 40). However, *pedophile* does not simply mean "one who loves children" and has never been analogous to *Anglophile* or *bibliophile,* suggesting instead predatory sexual feelings or actions.[4] The most concrete detail that might seem to confirm this charge of pedophilia is that Ruskin proposed marriage to the very slender eighteen-year-old Rose La Touche when he was forty-seven; they had met eight years earlier when he became friends with her family. He became increasingly fond of her in intervening years.[5] While today such a mismatched (if not quite May–December) courtship may provoke raised eyebrows and snorts of disgust, it was not that unusual in 1866. The eighteen-year-old Rose postponed giving a definitive answer to Ruskin's proposal for three years, until she would reach the age of twenty-one (when legally she could marry whomever she pleased), apparently not because of her own youth or Ruskin's middle age, but because, as an evangelical Christian whose father had been converted and baptized by the famous Mr. Spurgeon, she—and her parents—disapproved of Ruskin's religious doubts. Nevertheless, by way of encouragement, Rose sent her lover "a copy of Elizabeth Sheppard's *Charles Auchester* (1855), a novel in which teenage, musical heroines are wooed by much older men" (Hilton 2000, 100). Never approving a match for their daughter with the infidel Ruskin, the La Touches only broke off the delayed engagement entirely when they received a damning letter from Ruskin's ex-wife (probably charging that he was impotent),[6] not because they felt that the mid-life Ruskin's having begun to fall in love with their teenage daughter some time in the few previous years was wrong or sick or particularly inappropriate due to their age difference.

It is of course Effie's description of their wedding night that has provoked the most speculation about Ruskin's desires or his scandalous lack of them. In a famous letter written after the fact to defend her own course of action in leaving the unconsummated marriage after six years, Effie states that Ruskin declared on their first night together that, when he saw her naked, he was disgusted with her person (Lutyens 1967, 156); later Ruskkn agreed himself that he had found her not formed to excite desire (Lutyens 1967, 191). So critics and scholars, playwrights, librettists, and anyone who has ever heard the tale since, have wondered exactly what form *would* excite his desire. Once they hear about his tragic love of Rosie, the most frequently suggested figure is that of the prepubescent girl.

Ruskin's commitment to teaching at Winnington also adds fuel to this fire, although again there is no evidentiary whisper of molestation, or even of his ever having made a student there feel uncomfortable. Many of the Winnington students maintained long friendships with Ruskin after he stopped lecturing at the school (Hilton 2000, 133). The principle evidence of pedophilia Catherine Robson offers in *Men in Wonderland* is textual analysis of the imagery Ruskin uses to describe the girls at the progressive school, which she sees as manifesting fantasies "that would appear to confirm everyone's worst fears about Ruskin's delight in the beauty of little girls" (40). She points to passages in his prose describing little girls made up, as she describes it, of "endless gazing and coquettish conversations; kisses, laps and wriggling; the breathless excitement of the playroom; little fingers and buttons; most of all, perhaps the wetness of those eyes" (40). Robson's summary of Ruskin's language regarding his friendships with the Winnington girls brims with sexuality, but I am not sure that it is Ruskin's. The last comment that Robson describes is intended to indicate Ruskin's erotic view of the girls' "wet eyes, round-open," "eyes all wet with feeling" (qtd Robson 4); yet these lines appear in a letter Ruskin writes to his octogenarian mother describing the Winnington students as they listened to music. While we cannot know Ruskin's unconscious thoughts, clearly he himself did not expect his elderly parent to interpret his description sexually. More importantly, if such wet eyes were evidence of his particular sexual attraction to girl-children, they should only appear in reference to young girls; yet Ruskin uses this description in other contexts. For example, in the same group of letters, he refers to Alfred Tennyson's "half wet half open sparkling eyes" when the poet was also visiting the school (*Winnington Letters* 150). No one has yet insinuated Ruskin's attraction to the aging poet laureate. I can offer many more examples of what Robson evocatively calls the "world of soft and flexible moistness" (40) beyond his descriptions of little girls. The term *pedophile*, in our common understanding based on daily newspaper revelations of physical and psychological violations by "pedophile priests," coaches, teachers, scout leaders, and so on, surely involves more than vivid prose in a lushly descriptive style.[7]

Whatever Ruskin's sexuality was or was not, it did not involve molesting children.[8] Nevertheless, for a number of readers, Ruskin's obvious pleasure in the company of active, playful, intellectually eager girls bears no construction other than that of sexual perversity. The question is, why? The scenario in which children delight in dressing Ruskin, already fully clothed, in a backwards overcoat (the small fingers and buttons remarked upon above) becomes sinister for Robson in a way it probably would not have if we had never known that his marriage to a robustly adult woman remained uncon-summated. It is this lack of sexual activity that provokes us. As shocking as the reason for Ruskin's annulment was to the Victorians, the scandal of no sex is so incomprehensible to us now that it requires a pejorative term. All entertaining speculation aside, we will never really know why Ruskin rejected Effie on their wedding night and avoided physical involvement with her during the rest of their marriage. More uncomfortably, we will never know exactly how young Rose was when Ruskin first fell in love with her,[9] since he wrote the apotheosis of Rose-as-child that appears in his auto-biography long after he had proposed to her, long after her death as a men-tally ill young woman of twenty-six, and even after he had himself slipped into periods of insanity in which he confused her with St. Ursula. Indeed, we do not even know if, for Ruskin, being in love involved sexual feelings at all. All we know is that his love life does not fit any patterns we are famil-iar with now, when we expect people to be either heterosexual or homo-sexual, or to complete the dialectic, bisexual. Ruskin, who never had sex with anybody (as far as we know), disrupts this neat paradigm.

I won't spend more time defending Ruskin from this charge for which there is no support and of which his contemporaries felt no hint; my real point in raising the issue is that the concern over what to call him stems from our very contemporary need to label people according to their sexu-ality. To the extent that such labels might promote acceptance and under-standing of self and others, they are surely a good thing. But why do we feel the need to ascertain and to judge Ruskin's sexuality? Why do we need to define it in order to define him? How, ultimately, is that useful? In the theatrical representations discussed in chapter 4, Tom Stoppard, Greg Murphy, David Lang, and Manuela Holterhoff see Ruskin as someone who deflects the sexual onto the aesthetic, and for each of them this makes him tragically unfulfilled, even sick. While such characterization makes for satisfying entertainment in the theater, it misses the truly radical possibil-ities inherent in an aberration of such interest. Ruskin's sexuality supplies "resistance to regimes of the normal," Michael Warner's definition of queer (xxvi). Ruskin's missing desire becomes a perversion that subverts; in Jonathan Dollimore's terms, it is a "transgressive agency," "a perverse dynamic [that] denotes certain instabilities and contradictions within dominant structures" to the point of "sexual dissidence" (33). In the sense of queer as looking aslant or as any "disruptive desire" (Hall 2003, 16). Ruskin's strange or mysterious sexuality highlights what is missing in our current paradigm and presses us to admit that we have reified into a fixed identity that which is basically a performed one.

In a sense, for contemporary readers Ruskin's lack of sexual performance is a lack of identity performance. The fact that Ruskin does not fit
into the sexual identities that we acknowledge now, and indeed caused a
scandal of inactivity in his own day, gives us an opportunity to consider
what is wrong with the our whole mode of classification.[10] Although we
may think of postmodern identities as more fluid and more generous than
previous eras', the oddity of Ruskin's case exposes that our seeming welter
of possibility is in fact sharply limited after all. So, despite the promise of
this chapter's title, rather than queering Ruskin, I want to suggest that
Ruskin queers us.

Not only does the cipher of Ruskin's sexuality subvert rigid notions of
identity, but also and more importantly, so does the uncomfortable focus
on performed identity in his writing about theater, science, and education.
This nineteenth-century thinker offers twenty-first-century readers a radical take on the instability of epistemological and ontological categories as
he grapples with his own anxiety about how they shift. I don't want to
argue a cause-and-effect relationship, that Ruskin's transgressive sexuality
prompted him to undermine identity categories. But his usefulness today
stems in part from his rupturing our neatly bipolar sexual paradigms just
as he dislocated Victorian notions of a core identity based on essence
rather than performance. Theater provides the best venue for Ruskin to
express his concern with the self because it manifests the malleability of
identities as they are performed on stage. For Ruskin, theater provides
entertainment and escape; it also offers pedagogical examples to imitate;
more importantly, it is a great art form requiring skill and talent that
demand appreciation from an aesthetically attuned and sympathetic audience. As popular culture, theater supplies a wealth of illustrations for
Ruskin to use to make points of all kinds in his lectures and books. More
importantly, transformation scenes in pantomime create a universe of fantasy metamorphosis that permits the manifestation on stage of a truer reality than that which exists off stage. In this heightened ontological state, the
actors and the audience exist more intensely than anything in the brutal
world outside the theater, always in such terrible need of repair. But
unnervingly for Ruskin, theater also routinely provides examples of the
permeability of boundaries he recognizes as porous but would just as soon
see as unbreachable. Ali Baba, his forty thieves, and their forty friends
played by girls ungirling themselves by smoking cigars; a Japanese juggler
re-creating his English audience by balancing on a pole unnaturally, like a
monkey; a young girl's dancing like a snake or an insect: these examples all
flirt with the evaporation of divisions between gender, race, nationality, and

species. While Ruskin vehemently wants such borders to be permanent and intrinsic, his discomfort over their depiction on stage as fleeting and performed, along with his own despairing descriptions of the shifting margins of existence throughout his writing, show how strongly he recognizes the instability of all categories of identity and knowledge.

Nowhere is this more apparent than in Ruskin's writing about science. While grappling with his reactions to Darwin's theory of evolution through natural selection, coming to understand its validity while wishing it were not so, Ruskin imagines a science based on myth in which metamorphosis occurs through symbolic rather than competitive value. He uses examples drawn from the theater repeatedly to provide the only vehicle to express adequately the performative quality of all existence. The shape-shifting that turns one species into another and teaches evolution to Darwin tells Ruskin nothing of species' origin but only of meaningful correspondences between them as each signifies something else in a natural language that Ruskin imagines luminously apparent to everyone who learns to read it. This kind of observation distinguishes Ruskin's science as a gentle, passive, meticulous scrutiny that constitutes the identity of a feminized scientist, who not only performs in this non-competitive and non-exploitative manner in scientific research, but who also reacts to the performance of nature as a good audience should, with an astute and sympathetic reception. Ruskin feminizes science more directly by encouraging women to become scientists, by encouraging men to accept women as scientists, by writing science textbooks for girls, by teaching girls and women a variety of sciences, by quoting non-traditional authorities they would recognize and feel comfortable with, and finally by reorganizing Linnaeus's taxonomy according to girls' names from Shakespeare's plays, suggesting that in a sense the flowers play their part in nature's spectacle. By identifying women ever more closely with the subject they study, Ruskin breaks down the barriers between observer and observed, between scientist and specimen. He subverts all ontological and epistemological classifications as even non-human species are identified by how they act rather than how they look, and as science merges with ethics. By focusing on the significance of an aesthetic manifestation of form in the moment rather than a search for origin as revealed by form over time, Ruskin erases the conventional boundary between science and art.

The maturation of children into adults through education is another kind of unsettling metamorphosis that fascinates Ruskin. Ruskin tells us that clouds, flowers, and children change before our eyes, that they exist as they are only for a moment, literally. Knowing that children will in large part become what their parents teach them to be, Ruskin writes urging a more progressive plan of education for girls and puts his ideas into effect when lecturing at the Winnington school. In demanding equal education for girls, Ruskin erases gender from student identity, a surprising move in the famous essay "Of Queens' Gardens," often seen as the quintessential statement of Victorian claustrophobic idealizing of women and mythologizing their separate sphere. Even more radically, in *Ethics of the Dust* Ruskin dramatizes a world in which, far from being innate, identity is performed. In that book, Ruskin interrogates the meaning of the word "self" and suggests that even inanimate things play themselves in a universal spectacle that observers enjoy and learn from. In using the dialogue form for these lectures, Ruskin abdicates the role that the Old Lecturer would seem to have on the platform stage. By decentering his own authority as lecturer, Ruskin subverts the traditional hierarchy in education and theater, splintering the paired identities of teacher/student, performer/audience, lecturer/listener, and so on. As the girls learn mineralogy, mythology, and ethics, they also learn that, like crystals, their core or essential selves only appear to be stable; really they are a confluence, fixed into a particular pattern by a moment in time. Identified with living crystals, the girls demonstrate in these playlets that distinctions between animal and mineral, between human and rock, are as vague as those between species, between nations, and between genders that we have seen Ruskin explore in his writing on theater and on science.

Ruskin's inventive wildness evaporates completely from the theatrical performances of Ruskin's life that the late twentieth century has brought us, which ignore his radicalism in order to depict him as tragically emaciated in love, at best displacing erotics onto aesthetics, at worst deformed in his desire for an ideal woman to the point of rejecting and restricting real ones. The simmering dislocations of our seeming reality that attract and disturb Ruskin disappear from these depictions of Ruskin as Other, the repressed Victorian prude against which we, in most stereotypical fashion, can construct our own contemporary identities as progressive, liberated, healthy, and sane. This is standard fare for the current but erroneous image of Victorian sexuality, as noted by many scholars,[11] but Ruskin's case seems particularly egregious considering the gap between his importance for Victorian culture and his popular perception now. These depictions of Ruskin are in direct contrast to depictions of his contemporary Oscar Wilde, whose function in concurrent plays is as the premiere model of gay identity. Ironically, one could argue that the preponderance of Wilde's life experience is (anachronistically) more heterosexual than Ruskin's: unlike

Ruskin, Wilde passionately and pleasurably consummated his nuptials, fathered two children with his satisfied bride, remained married twice as long, and reacted with agony (rather than Ruskin's relief) when his wife left him (Hunt 235; Ellmann 486). Obviously my point is not to re-label Wilde as straight, but to emphasize that acknowledging Ruskin's unknowable sexuality as outside our present set of identity categories throws the instability of our other seemingly settled categories into greater relief. Excellent theater in their own right, these fin-de-millennium productions construct a Ruskin and a Wilde for today's spectators that masks the very aspects of their insights that are most postmodern: in Ruskin's case, his vision of the self that—to his own fascinated distress—is as permeable, fluid, and performed as any current gender theorist's.

Our postmodern identities defined through sexual orientation would be very foreign and indeed distasteful to Ruskin, particularly since whatever his sexuality was would not fit into our current paradigm. But if post-structuralist gender theories, particularly those of Judith Butler, have lasting impact, then Ruskin's concern over the fluidity of gender (as well as nation, race and species) on stage and enacted in science and education help expand our understanding of gender identity as performed. Examples of identity performance rattle Ruskin; he records his reactions in purple prose that has resonated across centuries. Ruskin's sexuality rattles us, and we record our discomfort in puerile ridicule that obscures his profound utility.

One way in which Ruskin is genuinely useful as a theorist today is in terms of something one might call ethical aesthetics. Another way to talk about this is that Ruskin's approach—like current cultural studies approaches—requires social justice. Elin Diamond points out that "cultural studies seeks to link the humanities, social sciences, arts and political economy" (1996, 6); this is precisely what Ruskin does. Yet Ruskin values beauty in itself, however difficult that is to define. From a postmodern perspective that inherits both an "art for art's sake" mentality that celebrates the art object divorced from its context and a historicist perspective that recognizes ways in which notions of beauty are the result of social construction, Ruskin's insistence on the identity of aesthetics and social justice must give us pause. Ruskin's theories of theater, performance, and pantomime truth resonate with his theories of art, architecture, and political economy, intriguing us not because he has the answers, but because he raises questions that still haunt us.[12] He is a formalist who nonetheless insists that architecture built under circumstances that exploit the worker is necessarily inferior and degraded art. He is a passionate social critic whose language and preoccupation with beauty not only imply a detached and escapist aestheticism but also surely help institute it. More than a litany of paradoxes, this set of complications suggests that Ruskin—as much as Friedrich Nietzche, Karl Marx, Wilde, or Brecht—grapples with issues of aesthetics, ideology, identity, and social conscience that confront us now. Ruskin's resistance to easy answers can never reconcile ideal beauty with the reality of class relations, aesthetics with sexuality, self with construction of self. Nevertheless, he shows how a serious mind recognizes that in the pleasures and anxieties of theater reside a continually transforming power, that in the destabilizing effect of performance lies the potential for the realignment of beauty and justice.

NOTES

INTRODUCTION

1. The original production of *The Invention of Love* won the Evening Standard Theatre Award, 1997.

2. In 1995 the Santa Fe Opera premiered a widely reviewed opera about Ruskin called *Modern Painters* with music by David Lang and libretto by Manuela Hoelterhoff.

3. In his autobiography, Gandhi describes how reading Ruskin's *Unto This Last* caused in him "an instantaneous and practical transfomation" (299). His determination to live the principles he found in this book resulted in his immediately founding the Phoenix Settlement based on its concepts, which he carried back with him to India many years later (298–310).

4. Most prominently, Kate Millett in *Sexual Politics,* but also many other excellent critics, including Deirdre David.

5. An indication of interest in Ruskin and gender is Yale's edition of *Sesame and Lilies* (2002) in its "Rethinking the Western Tradition" series, which reprints Ruskin's important lecture on women's roles and girls' education, "Of Queens' Gardens," as well as new criticism on it. Several other excellent pieces on Ruskin and women's education have appeared recently, such as in Shuman's *Pedagogical Economies* (2000), Green's *Educating Women* (2001), Birch's volume of essays *Ruskin and Gender* (2002), and Robson's *Men in Wonderland* (2003); however, none takes a performance approach. My own *Ruskin's Mythic Queen* (1998) concentrates on Ruskin's writing about women and mythology rather than broader identity performance.

6. In addition to *Sesame and Lilies,* see *The Queen of the Air* (about the Greek goddess Athena) and *Ethics of the Dust* (about the Egyptian goddess Neith).

7. These include John Keats, Elizabeth Barrett Browning, Dante Gabriel Rossetti, George Eliot, Max Müller, Andrew Lang, and Jane Ellen Harrison.

8. I argue that uses of myth in twentieth-century feminist theory and gender studies continue in Ruskin's vein. Mine was the first book-length study on Ruskin and gender; it remains the only monograph on that topic to date.

9. This story created a stir in both *The Guardian* and *The New York Times*. See Warrell 2003. My thanks to Pallavi Rastogi for pointing out the *Times* article and to the VICTORIA listserve, moderated by Patrick Leary, for the piece in the *The Guardian.*

10. Hereafter, all citations of Ruskin will be from the the standard library edition of Ruskin's works in thirty-nine volumes, Cook and Wedderburn edition (1903-12), unless otherwise indicated. Parenthetical citations will include only the volume and page, separated by a period.

11. Ruskin's fascination with the theater, which he attended avidly and wrote about often in works on other subjects, is perhaps most usefully understood as part of his attraction to the heightened reality he derives from all forms of critical experience. That is, for Ruskin the whole universe plays itself for us to enjoy and to learn from; as an appreciative audience, we analyze and interpret. Nothing really exists unless it is performed and observed.

12. Thanks to Dan Novak for bringing this chapter in Kate Flint's book to my attention.

13. See Weltman's *Ruskin's Mythic Queen* for detailed analysis of the identity between girls and crystals in the *Ethics of the Dust* (124–48).

14. He contradicts his depiction of a toyless childhood in the very same text, in which he attributes his having developed a good architectural sense to the benefits of a large, elaborate set of building blocks.

15. Perhaps Ruskin was inviting comparison with John Keats, who wanted his gravestone to read only "Here lies one whose name was writ in water."

16. Biblical quotations come from the Authorized King James version.

17. Metaphorically so: Reuben slept with Bilhah, his concubine stepmother, not with his blood mother, Leah.

18. He alludes in letters to a habit of masturbating (Hilton 2000, 135–36; Simpson 1982, 33) by saying that he shares Rousseau's weakness, which was well known.

19. See Dollimore's *Sexual Dissidence* and Dellamora's *Victorian Sexual Dissidence.*

20. See Gagnier's *Subjectivities: A History of Self-Representation in Britain, 1832–1920* for a seminal treatment of subjectivity in regards to Victorian autobiography, including Ruskin's *Praeterita.* As Gagnier explains, the "post-structural conception of subjectivity claims that the I, the apparent seat of consciousness, is not the integral center of thought but a contradictory, discursive category constituted by ideological discourse itself (10).

21. Each of these terms comes freighted with decades of complicated, multivalent usage. Their distinctive nuances are important intellectually and even politically, but I have chosen words that behave the most flexibly, absorbing connotations from more specialized terms while retaining the resonance of plain English. But no matter which of these terms I use, I operate under the post-Foucauldian and post-Derridaean assumption that our identities or subjectivities are socially constructed, that is, that we are who we are because language and discourse constitute us within an overarching framework of possibility.

22. *Bodies that Matter* stirs up the sex/gender distinction to argue for the linguistic and performative construction of the sexes as well as genders (since there is

no access to the notion of biological sex except through discourse, which inevitably shapes our only way of thinking about it). The construction of seemingly natural divisions of gender (and sex) is "a temporal process" of establishing and destabilizing norms through reiteration:

> As a sedimented effect of a reiterative or ritual practice, sex acquires its naturalized effect, and, yet, it is also by virtue of this reiteration that gaps and fissures are opened up as the constitutive instabilities in such constructions, as that which escapes or exceeds the norm, as that which cannot be wholly defined or fixed by the repetitive labor of that norm. (Butler 2003, 10)

Even more stringent a statement of the effect of reiterated performance to create and to subvert identity than in *Gender Trouble*, *Bodies that Matter* pushes past naturalized gender polarity to subvert perceptions of biological difference through the lens of performance as a kind of discourse.

23. This calls for me to address what I mean by *performance, performativity,* and *theatricality.* These three words are a fashionable part of critical discourse in the first decade of the twenty-first century, and their histories are even more complicated than *identity, subjectivity,* and *self.* Erika Fischer-Lichte defines *theatricality* in severely semiotic terms: actors are entirely replaceable by other actors in their parts, making the actors signs that represent other cultural signs outside the performance, so that theatrical signs are "always signs of signs"; the experience of theatricality provides consciousness of this doubling (88). In "The Politics of Discourse: Performativity Meets Theatricality," Janelle Reinelt defines *theatricality* somewhat differently, seeing more divergence between the text-based experiences of spectators in a theater-like setting suggested by the term *theatricality* and the particular instances of bodies engaged in temporal action suggested by the term *performance,* only to complicate the distinction. W. B. Worthen in "Drama, Performativity and Performance" also usefully synthesizes the multiple threads of discussion about performativity. Beginning with linguistic theorist J. L. Austin's definition in *How to Do Things with Words* of a performative speech-act as one that in itself performs an action (as in the oft-quoted example of a judge pronouncing a couple to be married), Worthen travels through John Searle to speech-act theory's appropriation by post-structuralist theorists, such as Eve Kosofksy Sedgwick, who (influenced by Claude Lévi-Strauss and Jacques Derrida) join Judith Butler in her idea from *Gender Trouble* and *Bodies that Matter* that gender is constituted through reiterated performance of gendered acts. In *Performance and Performativity,* Andrew Parker and Eve Sedgwick pull together diverse theatrical and philosophical uses of *performativity,* pointing toward their amalgamation in performance studies (1995, 2–6). Lynn Voskuil provides a useful critique in both her essay and book entitled *Acting Naturally.*

24. In *Dandies and Desert Saints: Styles of Victorian Masculinity,* James Eli Adams argues that Carlyle, Arnold, Newman, Pater, and Wilde depict "intellectual vocations as affirmations of masculine identity" (2). He does not include Ruskin. Instead, Adams reads Ruskin's definition of gentlemanliness as due to heredity, bodily breeding, and physically innate qualities, citing passages from

Modern Painters V (7.343–45) to prove it (167–68). Yet, as Adams points out, the key characteristic of gentlemanliness for Ruskin is "touch faculty," or the power of responding with great sensitivity (like a mimosa plant, which curls away at a touch, as Ruskin explains in "Of Kings' Treasuries"). Curiously, Ruskin sees this characteristic best cultivated in women, but wants to promote it among men. Thus, Ruskin won't work for Adams's list not because Ruskin defines identity as innate but rather because Ruskin redefines masculinity as feminine.

25. Intellectual history usually credits Pater, in his celebrated "Conclusion to *The Renaissance*," with the Victorian articulation of such Heraclitan flux, but Ruskin has already done it obliquely over and over in his writing about art, architecture, education, science, and culture. However, Ruskin is deeply disturbed by the disorienting temporality he describes, whereas Pater appears both to revel in it and to offer an antidote—the aesthetic mode of appreciation.

26. This is like Hegel's notion of self-consciousness that "never exists in isolation" (Hall 2003, 51).

27. See also Kucich and Sadoff.

28. See Donald Hall's *Queer Theories* for an excellent introduction to these ideas.

CHAPTER ONE

1. Despite the puppet show's immense popularity, Ruskin particularly disliked the violence of Punch and Judy. The entertainment pervaded Victorian culture generally, and Ruskin's life was no exception. In *Praeterita* Ruskin tells of how when he was a small child, his Croyden aunt pitied his supposedly toyless existence and gave him a beautiful Punch and Judy set. Though his mother thanked the aunt, as soon as the relatives had left, she removed it (35.20). Nevertheless, the image of Punch and Judy permeates Ruskin's work and even his dreams; he describes one in which the Judy puppet "seemed to bruise under the blows, so as to make the whole as horrible and nasty as possible" (*Diaries* 2.684). On a curious biographical note, Ruskin refers to himself as Punch and his cousin Joan as Judy (*Winnington Letters* 705); one of his real-life Winnington school friends, Lily, who writes him for many years, also refers to Joan as Judy (*Winnington Letters* 694).

The traditional puppet show's plot is violent and misogynist: Millett reacts with understandable disgust to the way in *Sesame and Lilies* Ruskin misrepresents Bill Sykes's brutal murder of Nancy in *Oliver Twist* as a mutual battery; Ruskin compares it to Punch and Judy's beating each other before Punch kills Judy (Millett 100). Though space does not allow analysis of Punch and Judy here, the puppets' significance for Ruskin deserves further treatment.

2. See David Reide for a discussion of the self in Arnold's poetry.

3. See Meisel for a fascinating look at stage "realizations" of well-known art works.

4. Throughout his life, Ruskin's mother objected to the theater, having "the strictest Puritan prejudice against the stage" (35.176). His father, however, liked it (he even performed in amateur theatricals in his youth), and frequently took

Ruskin as a child. As an adult, Ruskin often went despite his mother's dislike for it, but only if she gave her permission—which she must have given routinely (19.xxxvii note). For a discussion of Ruskin's memory regarding his mother's admiration of his father's remarkable beauty as he performed in "high, black feathers," including its gender ambivalence, see Birch, "Fathers and Sons" (148–49).

5. Ruskin's diaries prove his voracious theater attendance, but rarely give much description of the plays, operas, or pantomimes he has seen, usually recording only the name of the entertainment or theater or principal actor, with an occasional brief note, such as "delicious acting" (*Diaries* 2.707) or "rubbish" (*Diaries* 3.964) or "saw the vilest thing last night ever put on stage in my hearing or sight" (*Diaries* 3.990). He mentions actors Charles Macready, the Bancrofts, Madge Kendall, Ellen Terry, Henry Irving, and many others by name. His letters also bring in Rachel: he dislikes her even more than Ellen Terry, whom he compares unfavorably to Mrs. Kendall in a way that suggests that Ellen Terry's un-ladylike actions compromise her (*Diaries* 3.693), though he admits Terry is an excellent actress (*Diaries* 3.1044).

Another clue to Ruskin's theater-going habits resides in the letters of his many friends. For example, Oscar Wilde reports having gone with Ruskin to a performance of *The Merchant of Venice* with Henry Irving as Shylock on September 28, 1879. After the play, Wilde went on to a ball given by John and Effie Millais. "How odd it is," Wilde remarks on the juxtaposition of events: the "Millais ball" celebrated the marriage of the daughter of Effie Gray and John Everett Millais's obviously consummated marriage. The oddity of going from the play with Ruskin, whose six-year marriage with Effie was never consummated, to a ball given by Ruskin's former wife and former protegée struck Wilde even 23 years after the Ruskins' annulment (*The Complete Letters of Oscar Wilde*, 84–85).

6. There has been very little published criticism on Ruskin and the theater other than my own previous essays; no article like Gatens's or Correa's on music, for example. There is one essay by Tally on Ruskin's impact on scenic design. Because Kate Newey and Jeffrey Richards are working on a major multi-year project at Lancaster University's Ruskin Program called "Ruskinian Theatre: the Aesthetics of the Late Nineteenth-Century Popular Stage," we should expect more publications soon on Ruskin's influence on Victorian theater and beyond. In his paper "Ruskin and the Theater," Richards points out the extent of Ruskin's interaction with Henry Irving. He extends that research in his paper "John Ruskin, Wilson Barrett, and the Toga Play." Both should see print before long.

Shakespeare's influence on Ruskin has merited discussion by numerous critics, such as Auerbach in *Woman and the Demon*. Most of Ruskin's sustained analyses of Shakespeare in his published *Works* center on the literary texts rather than on the performance experience. But in letters and diaries, Ruskin often briefly remarks on a particular actor or actress in a Shakespearean role (37.28, 30.341, 34.545, 37.303) or on an aspect of a production (*Diaries* 2.760).

7. See also Parker and Sedgwick.

8. For a detailed explanation of how Ruskin simultaneously establishes and subverts gender dichotomy in the 1860s, see Weltman's *Ruskin's Mythic Queen*, which analyzes his three most significant texts on women and myth: "Of Queens' Gardens," the *Ethics of the Dust*, and *The Queen of the Air*. Especially through his

notion of queenship and his admiration for the goddess Athena, Ruskin blurs the gender boundaries he appears to uphold.

9. See Booth's *Theatre in the Victorian Age* for a clear, brief account of stock characters and lines of business. I am indebted to Jennifer Jones Cavenaugh for pointing out to me that while Victorian pantomime may blur gender boundaries, Victorian stock characters only strengthen types.

10. This indictment is particularly damning for actresses, since women are already associated traditionally with lying and mutability.

11. For Wilde's idea of life imitating art, see his essays "The Critic as Artist" and "The Decay of Lying."

12. See Ruskin's *The Queen of the Air* (19.358–60) for several examples of the tension between his acknowledgment of the accuracy of Darwin's work and his disgust with scientific interest in origin at the expense of symbolic meaning.

13. Ruskin often uses theater, which exemplifies what excites popular imagination, to chastise the public for some moral failing. For instance, in *Modern Painters* IV, Ruskin describes his distress over the audience's pleased reaction to horror, as in the actresses putting on the death mask (6.397), and in *Ariadne Florentina*, Ruskin describes an Italian play about boiling children as an example of people's love of death and horror (22.410). He also believes that immoral intent invalidates skill, resulting in bad art: in *The Eagle's Nest* he describes a dance depicting Hell at the Gaiety Theater in this context (22.133), as we shall see in chapter 2. It contrasts to the positive dream of an opera set in hell in his diary (*Diaries* 3.783).

14. See Lutyens (1965, 106): the opera premiered in Vienna in 1842; its definitive production opened in Paris, followed by London also in 1842. Ruskin also records having seen *Linda* in Milan in his diary entry for August 1, 1862 (*Diaries* 2.566).

15. Ruskin wants as always to move them to despise the pollution and loss of jobs brought on by an increasingly industrialized culture, and to make changes that improve conditions in the environment and the work place. He hopes that since the audience adores the performance, they can be roused to value the workers and the land. He makes the same point when writing about the picturesque in *Modern Painters* (7.268–69). See Landow for a discussion of Ruskin's concern about the aesthetics of poverty (235–36).

16. Later in *Fors,* Ruskin makes a related comment, pointing out that the money that two young women whom he sees at the opera spent on tickets to operas so that they could hear good singing might have been better spent teaching the poor to sing (25.269). His choice of young women for this example suggests several things about his attitude toward women: he assumes that their more highly cultivated feelings are more responsive (as he hopes in "Of Queens' Gardens"); he wants them to act as moral guides to men in their example of charity and self-denial; finally, he implies that the young women attend the opera out of a frivolous attempt to pass unfilled time, whereas men attending the opera seek a legitimate mode of relaxation in reward for hard work.

17. He makes the same point in several different places (18.97), most notably decrying the "mimicry compassion" opera arouses in us, "wasting the pity and love" we feel in a pleasurable response to the theater instead of on repairing social ills (29.269).

18. Auerbach goes farther and links theatricality itself with Woman: "this demonic, elusive spirit of performance . . . is female" (1990, 12); "the spirit of play is perceived by patriarchal culture as demonically female" (1990, 118n).

19. Ruskin's secular parable here reminds us of the irony of appropriating the tragic circumstances of Alpine peasants for our own pleasure. Metropolitan theater-goers still recognize this feeling: for example, those attending a production of *Les Misérables* when it first opened on Broadway in 1987 (before the current Disneyfication of Times Square) surely picked their way with some discomfort around local homeless people before handing over their then exorbitant $60.00 tickets to watch the simulacra of French homeless people sing beautifully for two and a half hours on a Manhattan stage. Twenty years later, fans paying $100.00 a seat for *Rent* may feel similar twinges of conscience. Ruskin begins by complimenting the "good and kind people, poetically minded" (6.390) in the audience, careful to include himself in first person plural, inviting his readers to imagine themselves, ourselves, there, before nudging us all toward a guilty recognition of our own hypocrisy.

20. See Hilton (1985, 254–57) and Hunt (262–65) for Ruskin's unconversion experience.

21. Non-British readers will want to know that British pantomimes are not silent, mimed performances, but rather spectacular song-and-dance, pun-filled entertainments most typically associated with the Christmas season, borrowing from music hall shows, interacting with the audience, drawing on conventional bits, employing innovative stage machinery and lighting effects, and using popular comedians from other stage genres. Pantomime is often affectionately referred to as "panto."

22. Here Ruskin ignores the material lives of the actors as working men, women, and children. He is not always unaware of their needs. In *Praeterita* he tells of how when he was a young man, his mother, concerned that he had squandered 100 pounds "on grapes, partridges, and the opera," gave him five pounds "to make peace with Heaven" in a donation to churches. Instead, he gave it to an "overworked ballerina in Turin" because she "did her work well always; and looked nice,—near the footlights" (35.498). But he seems surprisingly unaware of performers as laborers. Elsewhere in *Fors* Ruskin adjures young women not to become postal workers instead of taking care of children or sewing (27.536), but he never offers a like injunction against acting as one of the five hundred extras in a pantomime. Others did take note of children's stage labor. For example, in 1867 *The Illustrated London News* reports that "hundreds of poor families" "yearly depend on this incidental gain . . . of a few shillings" when they "let their children be hired" as imps or fairies in Christmas pantomimes (December 7, 51.608). In contrast, Ruskin accepts amusement from the "Arcadias of Pantomime" (27.256) with surprisingly little thought of how little the huge pantomime casts earn, or how dangerous their working conditions had become with gas flames licking at diaphanous costumes on a crowded stage. Later, in the early 1880s, Ruskin learned more about the lives of performing children through his friendship with the young Webling sisters, whose public poetry recitations he esteemed (34.545–46). He entertained them in his home (*Diaries* 3.999) and corresponded with them (Hilton 2000, 428). For more

information about this relationship, see Webling. My thanks go to Dinah Birch for making this and many other connections for me.

23. In *London Labour and the London Poor,* Henry Mayhew interviews street performers, including Punch and Judy men. But while Ruskin identifies the performers inside the theater with his notion of a heightened and more beautiful reality, his relationship with Punch and Judy street performance is far more conflicted. He both relished it as entertainment and despised it because of its violence. See note 2 for more about Ruskin's feelings about Punch and Judy.

24. Dickens's own fascination with, involvement in, and influence on the theater has been well researched. Among others, see MacKay, Glavin, and Vlock

25. For another example, see note 13.

26. It also may seem to resemble Aristotle's notion that mimesis is a distillation of the real, but for Ruskin theatrical truth is not merely imitative (3.103); it is in some sense originary.

27. The fairy-tale ending Ruskin imagines is, predictably, both radical and conservative. He points out that "in all dramatic presentations of Little Red Riding Hood, everybody disapproves the carnivorous propensity of the Wolf. . . . But once outside the theater, they declare the whole human race to be universally carnivorous—and are ready to eat up any quantity of Red Riding Hoods, body and soul, if they can make money by them" (28.53). And yet while he readily points to a solution that would protect the poor from the wolfish hunger of capitalism, he does not do as well in regards to gender politics: he envisions a world in which "nobody advises Cinderella to write novels instead of doing her washing" (28.53). Nevertheless, Rachel Dickinson interprets this passage as empowering women by emphasizing that Cinderella has a choice; what impresses Ruskin is that her choice is usefulness.

28. The *Ethics of the Dust* has 1866 on its title page, but actually came off the press in December of 1865.

29. For information on the popularity of Victorian pantomime across classes, see Booth. Ironically, Ruskin's love of theater generally and fairy tale pantomime particularly becomes lost in his posthumous status as a dull aesthete. A 1908 reviewer of the pantomime *Pinkie and the Fairies* envies children's ability to see fairies while grownups are doomed to talk of Turner and quote Ruskin (Davis 2006).

30. The huge numbers here are not exaggerated, although the sense of proliferation is the result of Ruskin's humor. Booth gives the number of thieves and their followers in the 1886 production of *Ali Baba and The Forty Thieves* at nearly five hundred (35).

31. Cook and Wedderburn point out six separate passages sprinkled throughout the *Works* in which Ruskin denounces tobacco as a curse (17.334n). It would surely horrify Ruskin to know that from the 1890s to the 1950s, popular John Ruskin cigars were manufactured and sold widely in America. The box sported at times a pink-cheeked, genial portrait, at times a gaunter, more Cubist likeness of the cigar's namesake. The double irony of a cigar named for Ruskin is that not only is it a vile tobacco product, but also it was a very cheap cigar, using inferior tobacco and poor quality paper. See Dearden (128) for additional information.

32. See "Of Queens' Gardens" (18.109–144) for Ruskin's fullest explanation of women's role as moral guide of men.

33. Although several male Victorian critics express anxiety about actresses playing male roles (for example, Archer decried an 1894 all-female production of *As You Like It*), Powell analyzes their discomfort either as over the actresses' usurpation of the male playwright's intention or as over the artistic insignificance of the cross-dressing (28).

34. For a psychoanalytic interpretation (and a concise history) of transvestism in Victorian pantomime, see David Meyer. See also Laurence Senelick.

35. Although the spectacle of women performing with cigars provokes Ruskin, women performing jobs more practically associated with men sometimes prompts his admiration. For example, in *Academy Notes* he admitted that Lady Elizabeth Butler's much sought-after paintings of military scenes completely disproved his earlier mistaken notion that women can't paint battles (14.308). See Marsh (1994) and Nunn for more information about Ruskin's recognition and encouragement of women artists. He also admired the skill of female iron workers who succeed precisely where he previously thought women would fail (29.173–75). My thanks to George Landow for bringing this point to my attention.

36. He readily carried himself back, however, indulging in the show at least twice, according to entries in his diary. Tim Hilton speculates that this was only in hopes of catching a glimpse of Rose, who was visiting London at that time (2000, 117).

37. In Letters IX and X, Ruskin includes a brief mention of a performance of the can-can in Paris that evokes his most extreme reaction of all, calling it the "Chain of the devil" and the "Cancan of Hell" (17.359). He describes it as "perfect dancing, as far as finish and accuracy of art and fullness of animal power and fire are concerned," but he rejects the can-can as unmitigated evil, with "the object of the dance throughout being to express in every gesture the wildest fury of insolence and vicious passions possible to human creatures" (17.358).

38. The serpent metaphor and the images of vibration here prefigure Ruskin's famous description of the serpent in *The Queen of the Air,* where the snake (along with the bird) symbolizes the goddess Athena. As he gives her more and more power (not only wisdom and war, but also air, metaphor, and finally language), this most masculine of goddesses becomes for Ruskin the ideal woman. See Weltman, *Ruskin's Mythic Queen* (149–65).

39. For additional discussion of serpent imagery in Victorian culture, see Auerbach's *Woman and the Demon* and Dijkstra.

40. Ruskin's concern with taste, audience, and class might well bring up the question of how Ruskin compares and contrasts with Pierre Bourdieu; for consideration of Bourdieu and the Victorians, see Gagnier (1991).

41. That this is a digression is clear: not only do Cook and Wedderburn leave it out of their introductory outline, but also Ruskin himself admits in Letter XI that he has "allowed" himself "to be led into that talk on theaters" (17.368).

42. In addition to the theater dreams discussed in this chapter, such as the Punch and Judy show, the young girl with the Arabian keys, and the opera set in hell, Ruskin records dreaming about the Christy Minstrels, dance, theaters with

dwarves, anxiety about performing his own lectures (*Diaries* 2.690, 3.867, 3.1075, 2.688), and other moments.

43. For an analysis of the simianization of the Other in Victorian literature, see Elsie Michie.

44. The dreamed keys also mean much more than this, recalling keys mentioned throughout Ruskin's oeuvre. One example is his well known close reading of "Lycidas" in *Sesame and Lilies:* there one key unlocks heaven; the other, prison (18.75). This dream may also reveal Ruskin's anxiety about evolution and declining religious faith. Equally significant here is the key of *Fors Clavigera,* one meaning of which Ruskin explains as Fortitude with the key to the "gate of Art and Promise" (27.xx). See also Caws for a psychoanalytic, biographical reading of this dream, focusing on Ruskin's relationship with his father.

45. Many books detail Ruskin's failed romance with Rose La Touche. See Hilton (2000) and Hunt (276–374).

46. For a study of the relationship between aesthetics, ethics, and economics in Wilde as well as Mill and Ruskin that deals precisely with the categories of the good, the true, and the beautiful, see Gagnier's *The Insatiability of Human Wants.* Nunokawa also mentions Wilde's reconciliation of ethics and aesthetics (3).

Chapter Two

1. See Mill's "Inaugural Address at St. Andrews" (1867), in *Collected Works,* Newman's *Idea of a University* (1852), in *The Works of Cardinal Newman,* and Arnold's "Literature and Science" (1888) in *Complete Prose Works.* See Gagnier (2000) for the differences between Mill, Ruskin, Morris, and Wilde on Victorian notions of aesthetics, ethics, and economics.

2. He urges readers to take the same humble approach to books in *Sesame and Lilies* (18.63–64).

3. Spear characterizes Ruskin's late science as "deliberately archaic and Linnaean in conscious opposition to Darwinism" (51). Rosenberg goes further and calls these late works of natural history "deliberately unscientific" "pseudoscience" (181). Ruskin provides plenty of support for this position, especially in the bitterness of his attacks on the ideas of Darwin and Tyndall, but Ruskin's attitude toward science is more complex than these comments suggest. Robert Hewison explains Ruskin's science as contemplative (177). Fitch explores Ruskin's science as expressions of his mythology. Fitch details Ruskin's increasing rage against the "scientific mob" (28.532) as he seeks through his works on Natural History a "general system for the interpretation of the sacred everywhere" (599) and makes a "deliberately anti-scientific effort to read and reclassify natural forms as living myths" (601). Birch also sees Ruskin's science as a mythic alternative to materialism (1981, 173–94). Likewise emphasizing the mythic elements of Ruskin's science, Sawyer claims that Ruskin is not so much anti-science as he is distinguishing "between good science and bad science, that is, between two competing myths": these are, in Ruskin's terms, "savoir vivre" and "savior mourir" (1985, 270). Sawyer points out that Ruskin's science is a precursor of the ecology movement (1985, 272). Likewise, Kirchhoff analyzes Ruskin's ambivalence

toward science and the radicalism of his effort to create a system that allows the student to know nature without dominating it (1977). See also O'Gorman (1999). All these positions have influenced my own, but none explores the constitutive role gender plays in Ruskin's science.

4. See Mellor (305–307), Easlea, and Russett.

5. In *The Queen of the Air,* Ruskin puts the natural hieroglyhic code "wholly under the rule of Athena" (19.345), his ideal of womanhood and the most masculine Greek goddess whose incorporation of phallic symbols in her Medusan shield blurs the gender dichotomy Ruskin elsewhere upholds. Ruskin makes signification itself feminine by identifying what he calls Athena's formative power as that which weaves the linguistic connection between every hieroglyphic signifier and its signified. Ruskin identifies Athena's formative power as the Holy Spirit. In "Ruskin and the Matriarchal Logos," Sawyer points out that Athena becomes the Law, "Logos as present, full, and female" (140). I argue that as Logos, Athena does not simply reign over the "'Words' of God," she is actually the Word itself (*Ruskin's Mythic Queen* 161–62). Furthermore, Ruskin argues that for the Greeks, Athena literally is the air, including "the air carrying vibration of sound" (19.328). He figures sound as the serpentine sine (or sign) wave, carrying speech (*Ruskin's Mythic Queen* 163). Please see chapters 6 and 7 of *Ruskin's Mythic Queen* for the complete argument.

6. Anne Mellor offers quotations with comparable imagery from Isaac Barrow, Robert Boyle, and Henry Oldenberg. For nineteenth-century examples, see Keller (56–72) and Easlea.

7. For readers unable to visit the museum, an excellent virtual tour is available at their website: http://www.thegarret.org.uk/

8. See Kirkup and Keller (73); Haraway (292); Paxton (171–73); Fausto-Sterling (179–87); Russett *passim;* Tuana *passim.*

9. See Tuana (35–50) for a clear overview of this issue.

10. Indeed that notion goes back at least as far as Aristotle (Schiebinger 55).

11. See Jed Mayer for more on Ruskin's response to vivisection.

12. Ruskin records in his diary: "the dreadful *Frou-Frou.* (The best view of Venice I ever saw on stage.) Gives me much to think of." He complains the next day that he is still ill from it (*Diaries* 2.719). In a celebrated 1880 production also at the Gaiety Theatre, Sarah Bernhardt portrayed the unfortunate Gilberte.

13. The word comes down to us through later use of the name Frou-Frou in the operetta *The Merry Widow* and the musical comedy *The Gay Parisienne,* etc., and pictorial representations of a frou-frou skirt in theatrical posters.

14. Ruskin does not so far feminize science as to imagine its giving life: the nineteenth century construes that as monstrous usurpation, as in *Frankenstein.* For two salient readings of *Frankenstein* as feminist critique of nineteenth-century science, see Robin Roberts (1–40) and Mellor.

15. See Birch's "Ruskin's Authorities."

16. Schiebinger points out that botany was considered the most appropriate science for ladies in the nineteenth century, citing several prominent examples of women botanists (36).

17. See Millett, Sonstroem, Gilbert and Gubar, Auerbach (1982), Helsinger et al., Birch's "Ruskin's 'Womanly Mind,'" Nord (1982), and Weltman (1998). For

gender analyses, see Sawyer's "Ruskin and the Matriarchal Logos," Dellamora (116–29), and Emerson (207–28).

18. For McClintock, "The ultimate descriptive task, for both artists and scientists, is to 'ensoul' what one sees, to attribute to it the life one shares with it; one learns by identification" (Keller 1983, 204).

19. See Shuman for a powerful analysis not only of Ruskin's but also of several other important Victorians' attitudes toward competitive examination.

20. The two men enjoyed cordial personal relations, both loving the beauty of the Lake District (25.xlvi). For important analyses of the relationship between Ruskin's science and aesthetics as they relate to Darwin, see Jonathan Smith (20–33) and George Levine (forthcoming 2008).

21. That the sexual aspects of both these arguments should be the very one that Ruskin dislikes should not surprise us. Yet Ruskin couches his rejection of sexuality in birds and plants as an aesthetic rather than prudish repugnance.

22. Although the trout may not seem a likely image to link with domesticity, in the recent opera *Modern Painters,* which is based on Ruskin's life, an ensemble piece about stewed trout foreshadows the failure of John and Effie's marriage. See chapter 4 for more on this opera.

23. See Kristeva's "Woman's Time" for the classic exploration of this issue.

24. Ruskin specifically identifies the capacity for change as feminine, labeling it unflatteringly "caprice" later in *Proserpina* (25.485). "Caprice" becomes sinister as a characteristic of serpentine vines, which snake their way up poles and wind around tree trunks, choking them. Ruskin identifies the honeysuckle (despite its pretty flowers and rich scent) strictly as a parasite (25.527), declaring that "a serpent is a honeysuckle, with a head put on" (26.306). Ruskin stresses the capricious femininity of these plants: "The reason for twining is a very feminine one—that it likes to twine" (25.485). He had more gallantly turned caprice into a feminine virtue in "Of Queens' Gardens," where he explains his quoting Verdi's *La donna è mobile* to be a compliment to women's adaptability in helping others: women "must be wise . . . with the passionate gentleness of an infinitely variable, because infinitely applicable, modesty of service—the true changefullness of women" (18.123).

25. Darwin also personifies nature as feminine; however, his quite effective but conventional rhetorical device is an analogy that allows him to explain natural selection in familiar terms of breeders' artificial selection of traits. He does not mean that nature selects as an intelligent agent. In fact, he dismisses the notion of agency implied in his personifying nature, explaining that he only uses such metaphors for brevity and convenience (Beer 69).

26. Ruskin uses Shakespeare to discuss the relationship of art to science before *Proserpina.* In *The Eagle's Nest,* Ruskin invokes the Bard not for his heroines' names but for the man himself. After briefly quoting *A Midsummer Night's Dream* for "a faultless and complete epitome of the laws of mimetic art" (22.152) to express the idea that the best art is but a shadow, he turns the tables on his favorite dramatist. Having examined what Shakespeare would say "as a teacher of science and art," he asks what we can learn from Shakespeare "as a subject of science and art" (22.154). This is meant to be fun for his students: first he enumerates the chemical compounds that would constitute the poet, then how many

vertebrae, then considers "that he differs from the other animals of the ape species by being more delicately prehensile in the fingers, and less perfectly prehensile in the toes." Moving from chemistry and anatomy to natural history, Ruskin discusses more individual aspects of England's greatest writer: "the color of his eyes and hair, his habits of life, his temper, and his predilection for poaching" (22.154). Of course his point is that such a reductive approach to the study of Shakespeare is hardly satisfying. Finally he arrives at his conclusion that the more art involved in a particular branch of science, the more valuable that science is.

27. So in addition to Ruskin's having conceived of an Ethics of the Dust (or of the Mineral), here we have an Ethics of the Vegetable.

28. Ruskin abhors a botanical science that privileges the arrangement of the flowers' least significant parts from an aesthetic perspective, their pistils and stamens, and relegates to less significance what to Ruskin are obviously more important features, their beautiful petals or heady fragrance.

29. Especially in the second volume of *Proserpina,* Ruskin increasingly drifts into autobiography. Apropos of the self-revelatory document he produces, Ruskin asserts that real botany is biography (25.253). He means by this that flowers should be studied like people, "where and how they live and die, their tempers, benevolences, malignities, distresses, and virtues" (20.101). Such personification is at one with Ruskin's approach to all science and myth-making, but the implication remains that through his botany, we can read Ruskin's life. This also implies that just as science is ontological for women, so it is for Ruskin himself. This is not the first time he assigns himself a feminine role; see Birch's essay, "Ruskin's Womanly Nature" as well as my own *Ruskin's Mythic Queen.*

30. For example, Ruskin first describes 12 Orders based on Greek mythological names, then supplements them with 16 more, arriving at 28 orders (25.348–58). In *Hortus Inclusus,* the number is 25 (37.288). Ruskin's inconsistency parodies the inconsistency he objects to humorously in the scientific authorities whose work he revises.

31. In French feminist terms, Ruskin reveals the inadequacy of Lacan's Symbolic order, represented by the language Ruskin inherits from Linnaeus.

32. Another way of seeing "systematic desystemitization" is as an example of "*l'écriture feminine.*" *Proserpina* demonstrates several defining characteristics: fragmentation, instability, irrationality, multiplicity, myth, humor, shifting prose styles, and emphasis on process, flux, and circularity. See both Kristeva, "Woman's Time" and Cixous, "The Laugh of the Medusa."

33. For a fuller explanation of the ways in which Ruskin feminizes language in *The Queen of the Air,* see Weltman (*Ruskin's Mythic Queen* 149–65).

34. For example, each plant has two parts, one above and one below ground: "one part seeks the light; the other hates it. One part feeds on the air, the other in the dust" (25.218). Just as bird and snake represent the eternally opposed elements of air and earth, in plants these elements also coexist without coalescing. Ruskin carries the comparison further, and makes the root into a serpent: "a root contorts itself into more serpent-like writhing than branches can; and when it has once coiled partly around a rock, or stone, it grasps it tight, necessarily, merely by swelling" (25.221). Ruskin's insistence on the double nature of the plant, divided above and below the dirt line, is itself unstable, as he leaps from the dust to the

air, pointing out the resemblance between the earthly root and the clasp of a bird's claw (25.219).

35. Ruskin details the serpent as a symbol of degeneration or devolution at length in *The Queen of the Air*. Evil change manifests itself through the snake, which brings "dissolution in its fangs, and dislocation in its coils" (19.362–63). Athena wields this destructive force as a corollary to her formative power. It is the same power we have already seen in "Of Queens' Gardens," where women are praised for the capacity to change. It is the same power we saw in the water leaves whose variability so delights Ruskin. It is the same power that Ruskin recoils from when he calls it "caprice" in women or in strangling vines. "Serpent nature" and "serpent charm" corrupt flowers in the order he calls "Draconidae" (19.372). For example, the foxglove and snapdragon "decorate themselves by spots, and . . . swollen places in their leaves, as if they had been touched by poison. . . . The spirit of the Draconidae . . . enters like an evil spirit into the buttercup, and turns it into a larkspur" (19.376–77). The serpent quality metamorphizes one originally good species into an evil one, so that in Ruskin's botany snapdragons and gladioli are subverted irises.

36. In *Deucalion*'s "The Iris in the Earth," Ruskin matches the colors of real gems to the colors in heraldry, which traditionally carry moral significance.

37. Similar poor sisters are incarnated as feeble florets in "Of Queens' Gardens" (18.142).

38. For further discussion of metaphor and signification in *Ethics,* see Weltman (*Ruskin's Mythic Queen* 124–27).

39. Another way that Ruskin both feminizes flowers (which previous botanists had already proven to be male, female, and hermaphrodite) and demonstrates their startling kinship across all rational lines of demarcation is his assertion that they are crystals (25.250). He describes the young violet that "glows like painted glass" (25.393), an image he uses earlier with even more striking effect about the poppy—the flower he associated most tightly with Persephone—as painted glass: "it is a flame, and warms the wind like a blown ruby" (25.258). Likewise Athena's bird "glows with air in its flying, like a blown flame: it rests upon the air, subdues it, surpasses it, outraces it;—*is* the air" (19.360), "the rubies of the cloud, that are not the price of Athena, but *are* Athena" (19.361). He has already feminized crystals in *The Ethics of the Dust*. In this set of images, birds, poppies, crystals, and the goddess all come together. Disciplinary categories dissolve—ornithology, mineralogy, and botany are one.

40. Although Ruskin claims in *Deucalion* to ground his science in old-fashioned Natural Theology, the religion he describes is belief in a vague, unnamed "Spiritual Power" (26.334). While the method of Natural Theology depends on revealing resemblances throughout creation to demonstrate the existence of a single creator, Ruskin's mode of noticing similarities among virtually all things tends to be not so much morphological as mythological: such similitude is useless for the argument from design. As Sawyer has suggested, Ruskin's Ruling and Judging Spiritual Power is more Athena's "Matriarchal Logos" than the God of Ruskin's evangelical youth (Sawyer 1990).

Chapter Three

1. It is the second of the three essays in those editions that include "The Mystery of Life and Its Arts" as the third essay in *Sesame and Lilies*. Earlier editions included only paired essays: "Of Kings' Treasuries," which presents the need for men with financial means to establish and endow public libraries, and "Of Queens' Gardens," which argues for an expanded role for women by redefining the domestic sphere to include substantial duties outside the home and for a rigorous girls' education to prepare them for this task. The book was Ruskin's best seller in his own life; Cook and Wedderburn record that it sold over 160,000 copies by 1905 (18.5). Ruskin's most popular work in America, it was often taught in high school well into the first third of the twentieth century (Helsinger et al. 96).

2. In two of the lectures he identifies himself as the author of *Modern Painters*.

3. Shuman here draws from Fuss's *Identification Papers*.

4. "Of Kings' Treasuries" is full of interesting instances of identity performance. It encodes interactive moments of audience reaction, focusing the reader's attention on the essay as a performed lecture. Ruskin furthermore castigates his audience for wanting particular careers because of the identity labels ("my Lord" or "Captain") that go along with them rather than the chance to make a contribution. He also denigrates the theatricality of religion and bemoans that "[t]he justice we do not execute, we mimic in the novel and on the stage; for the beauty we destroy in nature, we substitute the metamorphosis of the pantomime," yet another example for our discussion in chapter 1. Helsinger describes Ruskin's position regarding the submissiveness of the permeable self in terms that resemble Keats's notion of "negative capability," in which an author such as Shakespeare is able to empty himself of identity and live in the characters that are created (2002, 116).

5. Other nineteenth-century authors use the word *subjectivity* in this sense, as did Coleridge and Martineau (*Oxford English Dictionary*); Ruskin uses the word *subjectivity* only once in the complete *Works* (5.204), meaning the opposite of objectivity rather than "identity." He does use "identity" as "self" once in the *Works*, in a letter to the poet W. C. Bennett, thanking him for a book of his poems. In reference to having just read Bennett's poem "Toddling May," Ruskin says, "I am terribly afraid of being quite turned upside down so as to lose my own identity, for you have nearly made me like babies" (36.144). Every other use of the word "identity" is in regards to identifying properly a flower, artist, chemical, etc.

6. Examples span the centuries, from the amused response of the *Victoria* reviewers in 1865 to Jan Marsh's astute analysis in 2002 (153).

7. See Bauer on Ruskin's egalitarian plans for boys and girls in the Utopian St. George's guild schools (85). Peterson argues for Ruskin as "champion of women's . . . educational reform" (102). Nord likewise points out that Ruskin allies himself with "those who wanted to reform women's education" (2002, xxi). She also complicates Ruskin's position by pointing out that "the graceful, educated cultivated woman is also a 'production' of culture, likened to a monument or work of art" (2002, xxii). But, most importantly, she points out that *Sesame and Lilies* proves that for Ruskin "the question of gender—of the natures of femininity and

masculinity—lay at the heart of social reform" (2002, xxiii). See also Birch (2002), Koven, Lloyd, Marsh, Pierce, Shuman, and Weltman (1992) for various analyses of Ruskin's ideas about women's education.

8. Burd makes this point: "Like Plato, he gives first place to physical exercise and second place to intellectual experiences that will develop a woman's natural instincts for justice and love" (1969, 479).

9. Georgiana Burne-Jones believed the Winnington School to be "one of the first in which the girls were taught to play cricket" (Burd 1969, 37). They also bowled hoops, played croquet, blind man's bluff, prisoner's base, and swung on a rope "fifteen feet from a high bank" (Burd 1969, 37); Ruskin (and Ned Burne-Jones) approved and joined in many of these games.

10. Using the same rhetorical strategy as with physical education, Ruskin urges happiness as the path to loveliness. He assumes his auditors already recognize their daughters' virtue, innocence, and charm; his advice will help them preserve those qualities.

11. See Yeates for an alternative and intriguing analysis of how Ruskin views censorship for girls.

12. "Neither Bowdler's, Chambers's, Brandram's, nor Cundell's 'Boudoir' Shakespeare" meets Carroll's standards for expurgation (497).

13. Hagstotz, Phegley, and Yeates select Ruskin's banishing the modern magazine and novel as an example of his restriction of girls ("Keep the modern magazines and novel out of your girl's way," he says in the same essay (18.130)), but he does exactly the same for boys. In *Fiction, Fair and Foul,* he objects not to depictions of sexuality but to representations of a diseased society (34.376). For either male or female readers, Thackery is most damaging "among all writers whatsoever of any people of language" (34.588). The prejudice here is against modern Realism rather than against the mental capacity or moral fiber of women. With the exception of a few favorites, Ruskin characterizes the modern novel as the "gelid putrescence . . . of modern infidel imagination (34.281). Further evidence that this indictment has nothing to do with sexuality or orthodox Christianity is that Byron is high on Ruskin's list of must-reads for all people.

Hilda Hagstotz's influential early study on Ruskin's educational theories, largely sympathetic to Ruskin's position in other areas, oddly misconstrues his suggestions for a girl's course of reading. Hagstotz says that for Ruskin, girls' reading "should be supervised and restricted even more than that of a boy," with "neither books from circulating libraries nor modern magazines and novels to be permitted' (262). This simply is not what Ruskin says. He specifically calls for girls to have the run of their families' libraries, without restriction or censorship. He prefers that girls read intellectually challenging books that may contain things not normally considered fit for young girls by the Victorians:

> Without, however, venturing here on any attempt at decision how much novel reading should be allowed, let me at least clearly assert this,—that whether novels, or poetry, or history be read, they should be chosen, not for their freedom from evil, but from what good they possess. (18.130)

That these last two phrases refer to Ruskin's disdain of censorship or bowdlerization becomes even more apparent when we examine the original wording here: editions one through four read " . . . not for what is out of them, but for what is in them" (18.130).

14. Ruskin likens girls to flowers that need the open air, so parents must not shutter them; to fawns in the field who know the bad weeds from the good better than adults, and whom the occasional nettle will never harm. This is in contrast to boys, who must be chiseled into shape (18.130–31). See Peterson for parallels to Jameson here.

15. This idea provokes Millett to poke fun at Ruskin and accuse him of a misogynist Rousseauian bent. Certainly Rousseau's ideal education for women is deliberately inferior to his ideal education for men, and Ruskin does speak admiringly of Rousseau in private letters of the period (18.lxii). But his admiration is not aimed at Rouseau's plan for the education of Sophie.

16. See Margot Louis's much-needed intervention in the scholarship on nineteenth-century mythography, arguing that "deep religious impulses" toward "greater spiritual diversity" rather than "counter-religious secularization" or an argument that "pagan myth was a distortion of Christianity" animated much of the work" (355). See O'Gorman for Ruskin's Egyptology (2003).

17. Emily Davies, the Victorian advocate of women's education, astutely critiques the Victorian concept of complementary spheres in *The Higher Education of Women* (1866) as an aesthetic theory of human behavior that "gratifies the logical instinct; and many persons, hastily taking for granted that it is the only conception of the relations between men and women which recognises real distinctions, assume it to be the only one which satisfies the craving for harmony and fitness" (13). As Janet Howarth suggests in her introduction, Davies may have been alluding to *Sesame and Lilies* (published the preceding year) when she made this remark; surely it is fitting that Ruskin's theory of human behavior be characterized as an aesthetic one. But Davies specifically mentions Coventry Patmore's ideal, quoting from *Victories of Love* (sequel to *The Angel in the House*), rather than from any of Ruskin's texts on women's role in society. And although Ruskin founded no women's colleges, Davies found him an ally when she sought signatures for the "Memorial respecting Need of Place of Higher Education for Girls," sponsored by Emily Davies and the London Schoolmistresses' Association and presented to the Schools' Inquiry Commission in 1867 (187). As mentioned above, he also lectured women college students at Cambridge, the Whitelands, Cheltenham, and of course Oxford; there he readily spoke at the two women's halls, Somerville and Lady Margaret Hall, and gave additional lectures for "the bonnets."

18. See Poovey (126–63).

19. For a detailed comparison of the two figures, angel and queen, in which I show how much more practically and politically powerful Ruskin's image is than Patmore's, see chapter 6 of my *Ruskin's Mythic Queen*.

20. See Millet and Sonstroem in particular.

21. Later, Rose would hold Ruskin painfully in limbo regarding his marriage proposal to her when she was 18. She asked him to wait three years for her answer, partly in order to be able to respond without parental control at the age of 21, but also partly to consider the discrepancies in their beliefs. The quasi-engagement

ended when Ruskin's ex-wife Effie, now married to Ruskin's protégé, painter John Everett Millais, wrote to Rose's parents, probably stating not only that her never-consummated marriage to Ruskin had been annulled due to his incurable impotence—a condition he denied—but also that she would publicize that reason for the annulment, should Ruskin and Rose become engaged. See Hilton (2000, 135), Koven (176), and Burd (1979, 112–13) for various explanations of what Effie wrote. I will discuss this further in the next chapters.

22. Ruskin did propose different practical life-skill training for boys and girls in the St. George's guild schools on top of their gender-neutral academic subjects, notably domestic arts for the girls and sailing for the boys (22.143).

23. Shuman rightly notes that girls also often read *Sesame and Lilies*. Nevertheless, the audience constructed within the text itself is made of parents.

24. Shuman also points out this statement (176).

25. See Peterson for Ruskin's debt to Anna Jameson regarding this pedagogical view of Shakespeare's heroines (88–94).

26. Some critics discuss Plato's dialogues as plays (see Blondell). Jonas Barish's *The Anti-Theatrical Prejudice* is the seminal study on the history of anti-theatricality and its manifestations in Victorian culture. Ruskin writes approvingly when he finds out that the girls have been studying Plato by listening to a performance of the dialogues "dramatically and feelingly & amusingly read" (*Winnington Letters* 383).

27. See Reinelt.

28. Shuman analyzes this passage as an example of an anti-examination (172).

29. See Weltman (*Ruskin's Mythic Queen* 139–44).

30. Ibid., 170–212.

Chapter Four

1. Michael Schiavi identifies several critics for whom Wilde is a gay martyr (401).

2. An award-winning off-Broadway musical concerning Wilde was also mounted during the period covered by this article: *A Man of No Importance* (2002), based on the 1995 film of the same title, premiered at Lincoln Center Theatre, with music by Stephen Flaherty, lyrics by Lynn Ahrens, and book by Terrence McNally. It ran for three months.

3. See James Dearden, *Facets of Ruskin* (128) for this and many other surprising details of Ruskiniana.

4. Foucault describes the broader cultural phenomenon of which this is a part in "We 'Other Victorians,'" *The History of Sexuality* (6–7).

5. There have been many plays and movies about Wilde. Robert Tanitch lists sixty-one twentieth-century productions depicting Wilde's biography, including within the last ten years the major film *Wilde* (1997) starring Stephen Fry and the quite interesting *The Secret Fall of Constance Wilde* (1997), which precisely coincides with three plays about Wilde that I discuss in this chapter. Michael Schiavi points not only to some of the most famous in the past thirty years: *Feasting with*

Panthers (1974), *Oscar Remembered* (1976), *Lord Alfred's Lover* (1981), *Forbidden Passion* (1976), and *Saint Oscar* (1989), but also to plays too recent for Tanitch's book: *Diversions and Delights* (1999) and *Ever Yours, Oscar* (2000). Even Schiavi does not mention *Aspects of Oscar* (2001) by Barry Day, presented in a staged reading at the NYC Public Library on November 30, 2000, or *In Extremis: A Love Letter* (2000) by Neil Bartlett and directed by Trevor Nunn.

6. Wilde's plays are virtually always in production somewhere. Also, several new plays that draw heavily on Wilde's work have come out in the last few years, including Ravenhill's *Handbag* (1998), which rewrites *The Importance of Being Earnest,* and the dreadful film *A League of Extraordinary Gentlemen* (2003), in which Dorian Gray appears.

7. See Bristow's "'A Complex Multiform Creature': Wilde's Sexual Identities" for a succinct overview of scholarship on the complexity of labeling Wilde's sexuality (195–204). In *De Profundis,* Wilde analyzes how first Bosie's imposition and then his own imprisonment robbed him of the conditions for creating art, the ultimate agony for an artist (especially Wilde 876–79); there also he mourns the greatest loss of his children (900).

8. *The Countess,* also co-produced by Marnee May, opened at The Greenwich Street Theater on March 14, 1999 in an off-off-Broadway showcase; it transferred to The Samuel Beckett Theater off-Broadway on June 8, 1999; it transferred again to the larger mid-town venue of *The Lambs Theater* on May 11, 2000. It ran for 634 performances in all (Beck Lee, press release). Positive reviews include Anita Gates, "Theater Review: A Critic Who Takes His Work Home," *The New York Times,* Tuesday, March 30, 1999 (sec. E, p. 1); Jason Zinoman, "The Countess," *Time Out: New York;* Clive Barnes, "'The Countess' Has Sex-Scandal Appeal," *New York Post* Theater and Dance Reviews; *The New Yorker,* September 20, 1999, p. 14. *Time Out: New York* also named *The Countess* as one of the ten best plays of 1999 (issue 223). *The Countess* was the longest running play to open that year. It played Guilford, England in 2004 and opened at the Criterion Theatre in Picadilly Circus in London's West End on June 7, 2005 to very disappointing reviews in the *Times* (sec. Features, Theatre, p. 22); the *Observer* (iii); and the *Telegraph* (sec. Features, p. 16). *Curtain Up* and *The Stage Online* offered a mixed reaction, while *IndieLondon* responded enthusiastically. The production closed after just one month.

9. Although Gregory Murphy cites first the popular semi-academic book *Parallel Lives* by Phyllis Rose and then *Pre-Raphaelites in Love* by Gay Daly as his original inspiration, the bulk of relevant documents are published in Lutyens's *Millais and the Ruskins.* The most notorious and highly improbable episode in *Parallel Lives* happily does not appear in Murphy's account: *Parallel Lives* contends that the sight of Effie's naked pubis horrified her sheltered bridegroom, whose image of the naked female form supposedly derived from the hairless or at least adroitly covered private parts shown in Renaissance paintings and classical sculpture. In the play, the question of just what Ruskin found repellent about Effie on their wedding night remains a mystery, a solution which succeeds dramatically and holds true historically. Nevertheless, the tale continues to dog Ruskin's reputation. For example, an Arts and Entertainment special on the History of Sex (August 1999) repeats the Freudian "Medusa's Head" explanation, and a lively VICTORIA

listserv debate on the question lasted for weeks in the spring of 2006. However, no evidence supports the story; some refutes it. See Hilton 1985, 114–19; 2000, 135.

10. This mimics nineteenth-century melodrama, in which hissing the villain was part of the entertainment. However, at *The Countess,* the gasps were spontaneous, not relying on a tradition of audience participation. The dialogue and circumstances in this play rely on realistic conventions rather than melodramatic.

11. *New York Times Book Review,* June 4, 2000, sec. 7, p. 4; *The New York Times,* Arts and Leisure, Letters, June 25, 2000, sec. 2, p. 2. See also Lucinda Franks, "A Twisted Victorian Love story that Won't Die Out," *New York Times,* Arts and Leisure, May 28, 2000 (sec. 2, pp. 5 and 18).

12. See both Olney and Mandel.

13. According to Greg Murphy in interview on February 28, 2000. See also Franks 18.

14. For the legal status of Victorian women, see Vicinus, Helsinger et al., and Shanley.

15. For example, Elin Diamond discusses the limits of dramatic realism and mimesis, ultimately indicting them because they reinscribe the dominant culture they depict: "Naturalizing the relation between character and actor, setting and world, realism's project is always ideological, drawing spectators into identifications with its coherent fictions. . . . [R]ealism surreptitiously reinforces (even where it argues with) the social arrangements of the society it claims to mirror" (393). Other feminist theater critics who denounce realism as a genre include Jeanie Forte, Sue-Ellen Case, and Jill Dolan. Many debate this anti-realist position, including Helene Keyssar, J. Ellen Gainor, and Judith Barlow. While I disagree that realist theater inevitably inscribes the ideology it portrays, *The Countess* creates a heroine bound within a patriarchal vision of womanhood.

16. *The Countess* relies on twentieth-century Americans' sense of British Victorians as so proper that spoken dialogue pulled from written forms does not seem stilted—at least, not to a New York audience. London critics of the West End production complain precisely of this, however (Marlowe).

17. Murphy, Interview, February 28, 2000. Murphy is not the only author whose goal is to vindicate Effie. See Lloyd, whose object is "to rescue" Effie from her husband's shadow (1999, 86).

18. The creators made her younger, no doubt, to emphasize overtones of pedophilia that surround discussion of Ruskin's relationship with Rose.

19. Michael Kimmelman, "Music, Love Victorian Style," *Vogue,* August 1995, 144–45; Leighton Kerner, "Critic in extremis," *Village Voice,* August 12, 1985, 68. It was also reviewed by James Oestrich of *The New York Times,* August 7, 1995, sec. C, p. 9; Joshua Kosman of the *San Francisco Chronicle* August 4, 1995, sec. C, p. 1; Mark Swed of the *Los Angeles Times* August 1, 1995; Joseph McClellen of *The Washington Post,* August 1, 1995, sec. E, p. 2; and Raymond Sokolov of the *Wall Street Journal,* July 31, 1995, sec. A, p. 12. For a scholar's perspective, see Helsinger, "Ruskin on Stage II."

20. See Demastes's *Realism and the American Dramatic Tradition.*

21. For example, the opera sets the child Rose's first appearance in 1878, in the midst of artist James Whistler's libel suit against Ruskin, when the critic's men-

tal health was already crumbling; not only is 1878 twenty years after Ruskin and Rose actually met, but also it is three years after the quite grown up Rose had in fact already died.

22. See Levine's *Boundaries of Fiction.*

23. I am indebted to Jennifer Jones Cavenaugh for this point.

24. The cacophony is created by a brilliant scene in which Ruskin's parents, John James Ruskin and Margaret Ruskin, sing a quartet with the young couple Effie and Ruskin about stewed trout, a favorite dish of young John's that his mother serves and wants Effie—who is utterly disgusted—to learn to cook.

25. By having the groom call his womanly ideal an "angel," the libretto confuses Ruskin's idealization of women with Patmore's, which was in fact much more conservative than Ruskin's. For a full explanation of this distinction, see Weltman's *Ruskin's Mythic Queen,* 103–23.

26. The tomb of Ilaria di Caretto, by Jacapo della Quercia, at Lucca. This quotation actually comes from Ruskin's letter to his father on May 6, 1845, reprinted by Cook and Wedderburn as a note to Ruskin's *Modern Painters* (4.122n).

27. Murphy, Interview, New York, February 28, 2000.

28. For sources on how Ruskin contributed to women's advancement, see chapter 3.

29. Besides the testimony of the freshman Labour MPs mentioned in the Introduction, another example of Labour's admiration for Ruskin is that the Trade Unions founded Ruskin College at Oxford in his memory.

30. At times the opera seems a medley of Ruskin's greatest hits (17.105, 34.40).

31. David Lang related this incident to the "Giving Voice to *Modern Painters:* John Ruskin—His Life and Times" Symposium directed by Sharon Aronofsky Weltman, Santa Fe Opera, July 29, 1995. Although the annulment was granted on grounds of incurable impotence, Ruskin denied that he was impotent and claimed that he could prove it (Lutyens 1967, 192).

32. The director of the 1997 world premiere in London in at the National Theatre was Richard Eyre; director of the 2000 American premier at San Francisco's American Conservatory Theater was Carey Perloff; director of New York's 2001 Lincoln Center Theater's Broadway premiere at the Lyceum Theater was Jack O'Brien. Other performances include the Guthrie Theater in Minnesota (2000), Wilma Theater Philadelphia (2000), Court Theatre in Chicago (2000), La Jolla Playhouse (2001), Alley Theatre in Houston (2002), and university performances.

33. A body of scholarly criticism has already appeared on Stoppard's latest play, including Bormeier, Brater, Bull, Hesse, Muller-Muth, Sammells, Schiavi, and Zeifman.

34. In a speech that closely follows Ruskin's text, the subsequent witty dialogue undercuts its rhetorical effect:

> Ruskin: There is a rocky valley between Buxton and Bakewell where once you may have seen at first and last light the Muses dance for Apollo and heard the pan-pipes play. But its rocks were blasted away for the railway, and now every fool in Buxton can be at Bakewell in

half an hour, and every fool in Bakewell at Buxton.
Pater (at croquet): First class return.
Jowett: Mind the gap. (14–15)

Just in case anyone chances to feel moved by Ruskin's aesthetic or ecological concern, Stoppard deflates the moment with funny double-entendres regarding the game of croquet and British railroad journeys. Ruskin's environmentally conscious aesthetics degrade into querulous irascibility.

35. When Stoppard's Ruskin expresses concern about morality, it is not regarding ethical treatment of labor but a diatribe against the "moral degeneracy" and "unnatural behavior . . . under the baleful protection of artistic licence" known as aestheticism (Stoppard 9–10). This is a surprisingly inaccurate interpretation of Ruskin's position as the champion of aestheticism and the Pre-Raphaelites, although it does echo Ruskin's complaint about Whistler.

36. This vision of Wilde's notion of the contrast between Pater and Ruskin echoes Ellmann's (47–52). Yet Wilde always attributed to Ruskin great sympathy rather than severity, and his admiration of Ruskin is aesthetic rather than moral. See, for example, this passage from "The Critic as Artist":

> Who cares whether Mr. Ruskin's views on Turner are sound or not? What does it matter? That mighty and majestic prose of his, so fervid and so fiery-coloured in its noble eloquence, so rich in its elaborate symphonic music, so sure and certain, at its best, in subtle choice of word and epithet, is at least as great a work of art as any of those wonderful sunsets that bleach or rot on their corrupted canvases in England's Gallery; greater indeed, one is apt to think at times, not merely because its equal beauty is more enduring, but on account of the fuller variety of its appeal, soul speaking to soul in those long-cadenced lines, not through form and colour alone, though through these, indeed, completely and without loss, but with intellectual and emotional utterance, with lofty passion and with loftier thought, with imaginative insight, and with poetic aim; greater, I always think, even as Literature is the greater art. (Wilde 1028)

37. See also Sinfeld (5) for a round-up of scholars supporting Wilde's statement to this effect and the opinion of Bartlett, who disagrees.

38. Again, Sinfeld deals with these points more generally (5).

39. Here Stoppard echoes Wilde's comment in *De Profundis* that "I awoke the imagination of my century so that it created myth and legend around me" (Wilde 912–13), in which he refers to his own time, not ours.

40. Often examined together, criticism on these plays includes essays by Ertman, Griffin, Salamensky, and Schiavi.

41. As Ed Cohen points out, the documentary evidence Hyde relies on are not trial transcripts but newspaper accounts of the trials so that the level of mediation here is very high as well (4).

42. Schiavi jokes that the "Wildean narrative . . . is necessarily The Worst Coming-Out Story Ever Told" (403).

43. Victorian women often enjoyed a warm appreciation for physical love, even most famously (and to non-Victorianists often most surprisingly), from Queen Victoria herself. See her private writing about Prince Albert in Helsinger et al. See also Mason's two excellent books on the topic, as well as both Walkowitz and Russett.

44. Tanich's book collecting other representations of Wilde's life appears in note 5 above. Other representations of Ruskin's marriage include the fourteen-minute 1994 film *The Passion of John Ruskin,* directed by Alex Chapple, with Mark McKinney as Ruskin and Neve Campbell as Effie, focusing primarily on the pubic hair issue. Gregory Murphy has also completed a screenplay and entered negotiations for a movie version of *The Countess. Mrs. Ruskin,* a play by Kim Morrissey, directed by Jaqui Somerville, premiered September 12, 2003 at the Warehouse Theatre in Croydon, outside London. Noticed by *Time Out: London* and *The Stage,* it covers much of the same ground as *The Countess,* but focuses more on Ruskin's relationship with his mother; it also dramatizes Tim Hilton's speculation that perhaps the secret horror of Ruskin and Effie's marriage involved Ruskin's masturbating in the marriage bed. *Mrs. Ruskin* includes Effie's nine-year-old sister Sophie as a character, allowing for a plot revolving around pedophilia; the historical Sophie did visit the Ruskins, but there is no historical basis for the scenario depicted here. Ruskin's marital troubles have also appeared in other media: on Sunday, September 8, 1968, BBC's Radio Four transmitted a radio play called *Millais and the Ruskins,* based on Lutyens's book of the same title, written by Thea Holme and covering much the same ground as Murphy's more fully realized drama. This radio play was the sequel to a previous radio dramatization of Lutyens earlier book, *Effie in Venice,* similar to *Millais and the Ruskins* in its use of letters and diary entries to tell her story. In addition, Ruskin's famous skill as a lecturer has prompted actor Paul O'Keeffe to perform recreations of Ruskin's lectures, including an 1853 Edinburgh lecture, the 1858 Cambridge School of Art Address, and the 1854 Bedford lecture "Traffic" (thanks to Stephen Wildman for confirming this information). Besides all these staged versions of Ruskin, every installation of Ruskin's art or of the artists whom Ruskin influenced or championed—and there have been dozens of such exhibits in the last fifteen years—is another version of Ruskin consumed by the contemporary public. Just a few of the most important exhibits have been the major Ruskin show at the Tate Gallery in London in spring 2000, commemorating the centenary of Ruskin's death; likewise the smaller but extremely impressive show at the Pierpont Morgan Library in New York; and another at the Yale British Art Center. In 1995, a large exhibit came to Phoenix and Indianapolis, highlighting Ruskin's championship of women artists. Other major exhibits have appeared in Italy, France, and Japan, with scholarly conferences devoted to Ruskin occurring throughout English-speaking countries, plus Russia, Japan, and Italy. Permanent exhibits and small museums dedicated to displaying Ruskin exist all over the world: each of these presents yet another Ruskin. Finally, every Ruskin scholar, critic, or biographer creates Ruskin anew.

CONCLUSION

1. See Hall and Pramaggiore, *Bisexualities.* Despite the potential queering effect of bisexuality on the hetero/homosexual binary, the term itself poses a problem

in registering its potential to open up this discourse "for it inescapably encodes binarism" (11).

2. See Michel Foucault, *History of Sexuality*, and Lesley Hall, and William Peniston, *Pederasts and Others*.

3. For discussion of Ruskin's homosocial desire, see Bristow 2002 and O'Gorman 1999.

4. The *Oxford English Dictionary* shows the first use of *pedophile* in 1949; its use in the mid-twentieth century seems as connected to predation as now. This initial instance cited is "a sadistic pedophile" (11: 58).

5. Other so-called evidence Hilton cites is the textual sensuality Ruskin uses in his 1865 word-painting from *The Cestus of Aglaia* describing the half-naked ten-year-old "sand-girl" of Turin he had seen in 1853 (1985, 253–354), but even Hilton admits that the passage is "not erotic," but rather that Ruskin sees the girl as a sculpture in a "pictorial setting" (2000, 86–87). Indeed Ruskin's fascination with the remembered visual image of the girl is in the artistic contrasts she presents of light and dark, skin and dirt, stillness and motion. Helsinger elaborates on the serpentine significance of this figure (Helsinger 2002, 134–35).

Unlike Robson, Hilton presents Ruskin's association with the Winnington girls as altogether positive, both for Ruskin, whose interactions there helped him "to define his future role as critic of Victorian society," and for the inhabitants of the school, where "many stories attest to his generosity" (2004, 4). He also points out that half the girls were between sixteen and nineteen years old, many university aged, complicating the whole question of pedophilia regarding his affection for that population of students (2000, 6).

6. See Seth Koven (176) and Burd (1979) for an explanation of this hypothesis. We do not know the exact contents of the letter Effie wrote to Mrs. La Touche and that she in turn showed to her daughter, but we do know that Rose's parents forbade her to write to her quasi-fiancé afterwards, and that Mrs. La Touche specifically refers to having procured copies of the annulment papers in her expression of outrage at Ruskin. The couple continued to communicate through mutual friends, and the obedient Rose circumvented the letter of parental decree by sending her lover symbolic flowers, books, and rose petals, even while avoiding written correspondence. See Hilton for speculations about masturbation rather than impotence as the damaging marital secret that Effie revealed (2000, 135). However, it is of Thomas Carlyle and his wife Jane that Frank Harris tells precisely the same story (210). I am indebted to George Landow for reminding me of that connection.

7. The alliterative phrase "pedophile priests" has been cavalierly bandied about by the press in recent years, particularly in 2002, appearing in papers around the world (such as *New York Times, Washington Post, Pravda, The Times* of London, and the *Cincinnati Post*). I quote this phrase to emphasize just what *pedophile* means in common parlance. I do not mean to suggest in any way that priests are more likely to be pedophiles than any other group, nor do I mean to emphasize the abuses of a few over the excellent pastoral qualities of the many.

8. See James Kincaid's book *Child-Loving: The Erotic Child and Victorian Culture* for discussion of J. M. Barrie and Lewis Carroll. Kincaid does not include John Ruskin in this study on pedophilia in the Victorian imagination.

9. Hilton quotes suggestive letters written when Rosie was fifteen and just before in which Ruskin describes how he feels that he "can no longer make a pet of her" (2000, 50, 53). From context he seems to mean that he can no longer ask her to play childish games, including teasing for (chaste) kisses to cure a headache, as had been their custom. That he loved her devotedly when she was fourteen is without question. What is up in the air is the kind of love he felt and what we can make of his grief and/or confusion over the loss of the child friend as she becomes a woman. But no longer being able to make a pet of her could also mean that this is when Ruskin begins to have particular feelings for Rose that go beyond the friendship described famously in *Praeterita* with the little girl who wrote charming, intellectually precocious letters to her "St. Crumpet"; his own developing desire as well as increasing impropriety would make such play impossible. Again, while a teenager of fifteen or even perhaps fourteen is awfully young, these letters date his attraction (if that's what it was) to a period beyond what Robson implies and even what Hilton indicates. If mere attraction to a teenager were enough to label middle-aged men pedophiles, then a lot of men would be in trouble.

10. The discussion of sexuality and performance (or lack of it) inevitably raises the question of Ruskin's ability to perform sexually. If he were indeed impotent, as Effie claimed in the annulment proceedings and which Ruskin vehemently denied in a letter never presented in court, that surely would have had some impact on his sense of himself as a man; either way, thinking in terms of sexual performance complicates what it means to perform one's identity.

11. In addition to those already mentioned, see James Eli Adams, John Maynard, and Andrew Miller.

12. These should be among the "the big questions" that "have dropped out of Anglo-American philosophy," that interest Elaine Marks, as well as Joe Moran and Donald Hall (qtd Hall 2004, 4).

BIBLIOGRAPHY

Adams, James Eli. *Dandies and Desert Saints: Styles of Victorian Manhood.* Ithaca and London: Cornell University Press, 1995.

———. "Victorian Sexualities." In *A Companion to Victorian Literature and Culture,* ed. Herbert F. Tucker. Oxford: Blackwell, 1999.

Alexander, Edward. "Ruskin and Science." *The Modern Language Review* 64 (1969): 508–21.

Amor, Anne Clark. *Mrs. Oscar Wilde: A Woman of Some Importance.* London: Sidgwick and Jackson, 1983.

Anderson, Norman, and Margene E. Weiss. "Introduction." In *Interspace and Inward Sphere: Essays on the Romantic and Victorian Self.* Macomb, IL: Western Illinois Press, 1978.

Anthony, Peter. *John Ruskin's Labour: A Study of Ruskin's Social Theory.* New York and Cambridge: Cambridge University Press, 1983.

Arnold, Matthew. *Complete Prose Works.* Ann Arbor: University of Michigan Press, 1960–77.

———. *The Poems of Matthew Arnold,* ed. Miriam Allot. London and New York: Longman, 1979.

Arrowsmith, William. "Ruskin's Fireflies." *The Ruskin Polygon: Essays on the Imagination of John Ruskin,* ed. John Dixon Hunt and Faith M. Holland. Manchester, England: Manchester University Press, 1982. 198–235.

Auerbach, Nina. *Woman and the Demon: The Life of a Victorian Myth.* Cambridge, MA and London: Harvard University Press, 1982.

———. *Private Theatricals: The Lives of the Victorians.* Cambridge, MA and London: Harvard University Press, 1990.

Austin, J. L. *How to Do Things with Words.* Cambridge: Harvard University Press, 1962.

Austin, Linda M. *The Practical Ruskin.* Baltimore and London: Johns Hopkins University Press, 1991.

———. "Ruskin and the Ideal Woman." *South Central Review* 4, no. 4 (1987): 28–39.

Ball, Patricia M. *The Science of Aspects: The Changing Role of Fact in the Work of Coleridge, Ruskin, and Hopkins.* London and New York: Athlone Press, 1971.

Barlow, Judith. "Into the Foxhole: Feminism, Realism, and Lillian Hellman." In *Realism and the American Dramatic Tradition.* Tuscaloosa and London: Alabama University Press, 1996.

Barish, Jonas. *The Anti-Theatrical Prejudice.* Berkeley: University of California Press, 1981.

Barnes, Clive. "'The Countess Has Sex-Scandal Appeal," *New York Post* Theater and Dance Reviews. Jan. 21, 2000.

Bauer, Helen Pike. "Ruskin and the Education of Women." *Studies in the Humanities* 12, no. 2 (1985): 74–89.

Beer, Gillian. *Darwin's Plots: Evolutionary Narrative in Darwin, George Elliot, and Nineteenth-Century Fiction.* London: Routledge, 1983.

Bentley, Joyce. *The Importance of Being Constance.* London: R. Hale, 1983.

The Bible: Authorized King James Version with Apocrypha. Oxford: Oxford University Press, 1998.

Birch, Dinah. "*The Ethics of the Dust:* Ruskin's Authorities." *Prose Studies* 12 (1989): 147–58.

———. "Fathers and Sons: Ruskin, John James Ruskin, and Turner." *Nineteenth-Century Contexts* 18, no. 2 (1994): 147–62.

———. "Ruskin and the Science of *Proserpina.*" In *New Approaches to Ruskin: Thirteen Essays,* ed. Robert Hewison. London, Boston, and Henley: Routledge and Kegan Paul, 1981.

———. "Ruskin and Women's Education." In *Ruskin and Gender,* ed. Dinah Birch and Francis O'Gorman. Basingstoke and New York: Palgrave, 2002.

———. *Ruskin's Myths.* Oxford: Clarendon-Oxford University Press, 1988.

———. "Ruskin's 'Womanly Mind.'" *Essays in Criticism* 38, no. 4 (1988): 308–24.

———. "'What Teachers Do You Give Your Girls?': Ruskin and Women's Education." In *Ruskin and Gender.* London: Palgrave, 2002. 121–36.

Blondell, Ruby. *The Play of Character in Plato's Dialogues.* Cambridge: Cambridge University Press, 2002.

Bloom, Harold. "Introduction." In *The Literary Criticism of John Ruskin,* ed. Harold Bloom. Garden City, NY: Anchor, 1965.

Booth, Michael R. *Theatre in the Victorian Age.* Cambridge: Cambridge University Press, 1991.

Borgmeier, Raimund. "'Convergences of different threads': Tom Stoppard's *The Invention of Love.*" *Anglistik & Englischunterricht* 64 (2002): 149–63.

Bradley, J. L. *A Ruskin Chronology.* Basingstoke and New York: Macmillan, 1997.

———, ed. *Ruskin: The Critical Heritage.* London and Boston: Routledge and Kegan Paul, 1984.

Brater, Enoch. "Tom Stoppard's Brit/lit/Crit." In *The Cambridge Companion to Tom Stoppard,* ed. Katherine Kelly. Cambridge: Cambridge University Press, 2001. 203–12.

Bristow, Joseph. "'Any Day that You're a Good Boy': Ruskin's Patronage, Rossetti's Expectations." In *Ruskin and Gender,* ed. Dinah Birch and Francis O'Gorman. Basingstoke and New York: Palgrave, 2002.

———. "'A Complex Multiform Creature': Wilde's Sexual Identities." In *The Cambridge Companion to Oscar Wilde,* ed. Peter Raby. Cambridge: Cambridge University Press, 1997. 195–218.

———. "Coventry Patmore and the Womanly Mission of the Mid-Victorian Poet." In *Sexualities in Victorian Britain,* ed. Andrew H. Miller and James Eli Adams. Bloomington: Indiana University Press, 1996.

———. *Effeminate England: Homoerotic Writing after 1865.* New York: Columbia University Press, 1995.

Brontë, Charlotte. *Jane Eyre.* London and New York: Penguin, 1966.

Bull, John. "Tom Stoppard and Politics," In *The Cambridge Companion to Tom Stoppard,* ed. Katherine Kelly. Cambridge; Cambridge University Press, 2001. 136–53.

Bullen, J. B. "Ruskin, Venice and the Construction of Femininity." *Review of English Studies* 46, no. 184 (1995): 502–20

Butler, Judith. *Gender Trouble: Feminism and the Subversion of Identity.* New York: Routledge, 1990.

———. *Bodies That Matter: On the Discursive Limits of "Sex."* New York and London: Routledge, 1993.

———. *Undoing Gender.* New York: Routledge, 2004.

Burd, Van Akin. "Introduction." In *The Winnington Letters of John Ruskin,* ed. Van Akin Burn. Cambridge, MA: Belknap-Harvard University Press, 1969.

———. *John Ruskin and Rose La Touche: Her Unpublished Diaries of 1861 and 1867.* Oxford: Clarendon Press, 1979.

Burstein, Janet. "Victorian Mythography and the Progress of Intellect." *Victorian Studies* 18, no. 3 (1975): 309–24.

Carlyle, Thomas. *The Works of Thomas Carlyle.* 16 volumes. New York: Collier, 1897.

Calder, Jenni. *Women and Marriage in Victorian Fiction.* London: Thames and Hudson, 1976.

Carroll, Lewis. "Sylvie and Bruno." In *The Complete Illustrated Works of Lewis Carroll,* ed. Edward Guiliano. New York: Avenel Press, 1982.

Cartmell, Deborah, and Imelda Whelan, eds. *Adaptations: From Text to Screen, Screen to Text.* London and New York: Routledge, 1999.

Case, Sue-Ellen. *Feminism and Theater.* New York: Methuen, 1988.

Cate, George Allan, ed. *The Correspondence of Thomas Carlyle and John Ruskin.* Stanford, CA: Stanford University Press, 1982.

———. *John Ruskin: A Reference Guide.* Boston: G. K. Hall, 1988.

Caws, Mary Ann. "Against Completion: Ruskin's Drama of Dream, Lateness, and Loss." In *Sex and Death in Victorian Literature,* ed. Regina Barreca. Bloomington: Indiana University Press, 1990.

Christ, Carol. "Victorian Masculinity and the Angel in the House." In *A Widening Sphere: Changing Roles of Victorian Woman,* ed. Martha Vicinus. Bloomington and London: Indiana University Press, 1977.

Cixous, Hélène. "The Laugh of the Medusa." Trans. Keith Cohen and Paula Cohen. In *Feminisms: An Anthology of Literary Theory and Criticism,* ed. Robin R. Warhol and Diane Price Herndl. New Brunswick: Rutgers University Press, 1991. 334–50.

Clapp, Susannah. "Forest's Gump." *The Observer,* Review Pages. June 12, 2005, 11.

Cohen, ed. *Talk on the Wilde Side: Toward a Geneology of Discourse on Male Sexualites.* New York and London: Routledge, 1993.

Correa, Delia de Sousa. "Goddesses of Industry Desire: Ruskin and Music." In *Ruskin and the Dawn of the Modern,* ed. Dinah Birch. Oxford: Oxford University Press, 1999.

"The Countess." *The New Yorker.* September 20, 1999, 14.

Craik, Roger. "Nightmares of Punch and Judy in Ruskin and M. R. James." *Fantasy Commentator* 9, no. 1 (1996): 12–14.

Daly, Gay. *Pre-Raphaelites in Love.* New York: Tickner and Fields, 1989

Darwin, Charles. *The Descent of Man, and Selection in Relation to Sex.* New York: Collier and Son, 1901.

Darwin, Erasmus. *The Loves of Plants.* Dublin: Moore, 1796.

David, Deirdre. *Intellectual Women and Victorian Patriarchy.* London: MacMillan, 1987.

Davies, Emily. *The Higher Education of Women* (1866). Ed. Janet Howarth. London and Ronceverte: The Hambledon Press, 1988.

Davies, Serena. "Disappointing Portrait of an Unhappy Marriage." *Daily Telegraph.* June 9, 2005. Features, p. 16.

Davis, Tracy C. *Actresses as Working Women: Their Social Identity in Victorian Culture.* London: Routledge, 1991.

_____. "What Are Fairies For?" Paper presented at the North American Victorian Studies Association conference, Purdue University, West Lafayette, IN, September 2006. Forthcoming in *The Performing Society: Nineteenth-Century Theatre's History*, ed. Tracy Davis and Peter Holland. Basingstoke and New York: Palgrave, 2007.

Dearden, James. *Facets of Ruskin*. London: Charles Skelton, 1970.

Dellamora, Richard. *Masculine Desire: The Sexual Politics of Victorian Aestheticism.* Chapel Hill and London: University of North Carolina Press, 1990.

———. *Victorian Sexual Dissidence*. Chicago: University of Chicago Press, 1999.

Demastes, Willam, ed. *Realism and the American Dramatic Tradition*. Tuscaloosa and London: University of Alabama Press, 1996

Diamond, Elin. *Performance and Cultural Politics*. London and New York: Routledge, 1996.

———. "The Violence of 'We': Poiticizing Indentifications." In *Critical Theory and Performance,* ed. Janelle G. Reinelt and Joseph R. Roach. Ann Arbor: University of Michigan Press, 1992: 390–98.

Dickens, Charles. *Hard Times*. Oxford: Oxford University Press, 1989.

———. *Oliver Twist*. Oxford: Oxford University Press, 1966.

Dickinson, Rachel. "Pantomime and the Ideal Woman." Paper presented at the "Victorian Life Writing: Sources and Resources" conference, Lancaster University, July 2005.

Dijkstra, Bram. *Idols of Perversity: Fantasies of Feminine Evil in Fin-de-Siècle Culture*. New York: Oxford University Press, 1986.

Dolan, Jill. *The Feminist Spectator as Critic*. Ann Arbor, MI: UMI Research Press, 1988.

Dollimore, Jonathan. *Sexual Dissidence: Augustine to Wilde, Freud to Foucault*. Oxford: Oxford University Press, 1991.

Dougherty, Charles. "Of Ruskin's Gardens." In *Myth and Symbol: Critical Approaches and Applications,* ed. Bernice Slote. Lincoln: University of Nebraska Press, 1962. 141–51.

Dowling, Linda. *The Vulgarization of Art: The Victorians and Aesthetic Democracy.* Charlottesville: University Press of Virginia, 1996.

Eagleton, Terry. *The Ideology of the Aesthetic*. Oxford: Basil Blackwell, 1990.

Easlea, Brian. *Science and Sexual Oppression: Patriarchy's Confrontation with Women and Nature*. London: Weidenfeld and Nicolson, 1981.

Eliot, George. *Middlemarch*. New York: Penguin, 1972.

———. *The Mill on the Floss*. New York: New American Library, 1981.

Ellmann, Richard. *Oscar Wilde*. New York: Alfred A. Knopf, 1988.

Emerson, Sheila. "The Authorization of Form: Ruskin and the Science of Chaos." In *Chaos and Order: Complex Dynamics in Literature and Science,* ed. N.

Katherine Hayles. Chicago and London: University of Chicago Press, 1991. 149–66.

_____. *John Ruskin: The Genesis of Invention.* London and New York: Cambridge University Press, 1994.

Epstein, Norrie. *The Friendly Dickens.* New York: Penguin, 1998.

Ertman, Martha M. "Oscar Wilde: Paradoxical Poster Child for Both Identity and Post Identity." *Law and Social Inquiry* 25 (winter 2000): 153–83.

Fausto-Sterling, Anne. *Myths of Gender: Biological Theories and Women and Men.* New York: Basic Books, 1985.

Fellows, Jay. *The Falling Distance: The Autobiographical Impulse in John Ruskin.* Baltimore and London: Johns Hopkins University Press, 1975.

Fischer-Lichte, Erika. "From Theatre to Theatricality—How to Construct Reality." *Theatre Research International* 20, no. 2 (1999): 97–105.

———. "Theatricality: A Key Concept in Theatre and Cultural Studies." *Theatre Research International.* 20, no. 2 (1999): 85–118.

Fitch, Raymond. *The Poison Sky: Myth and Apocalypse in Ruskin.* Athens, OH and London: Ohio University Press, 1982.

Fletcher, Kathy. "Planche, Vestris, and the Transvestite Role: Sexuality and Gender in Victorian Popular Theatre." *Nineteenth-Century Theatre* 15, no. 1 (1987): 9–33.

Flint, Kate. *The Victorians and the Visual Imagination.* Cambridge: Cambridge University Press, 2000.

Forte, Jeanie. "Realism, Narrative, and the Feminist Playwright—A Problem of Reception." *Modern Drama* 32, no. 1 (March 1989):115–27.

Foucault, Michel. *The History of Sexuality.* Vol 1. *An Introduction.* Trans. Robert Henley. New York: Vintage Books, 1980.

Franks, Lucinda. "A Twisted Victorian Love Story That Won't Die Out." *New York Times.* May 28, sec. 2, pp. 5 and 18.

Freud, Sigmund. "Medusa's Head." 1940. In *The Complete Psychological Works of Sigmund Freud,* ed. and trans. James Strachey. Vol. 18: 273–74. London: Hogarth, 1955. 24 Vols. 1953–74.

Fuss, Diana. *Essentially Speaking: Feminism, Nature, and Difference.* New York and London: Routledge, 1989.

———. *Identification Papers.* New York: Routledge, 1995.

Gagnier, Regenia. *The Insatiability of Human Wants: Economics and Aesthetics in Market Society.* Chicago and London: University of Chicago Press, 2000.

———. *Subjectivities: A History of Self-Representation in Britain, 1832–1920.* Oxford: Oxford University Press, 1991.

Gainor, J. Ellen. "The Provincetown Players' Experiments with Realism." In *Realism and the American Dramatic Tradition,* ed. William Demasters. Tuscaloosa and London: University of Alabama Press, 1996

Gallagher, Catherine, Joel Fineman, and Neil Hertz, "More about Medusa's Head." *Representations* 14, no. 4 (1983): 55–72.

Gandhi, Mohandas K. *An Autobiography, or the Story of My Experiments with Truth.* Trans. Mahadev Desai. Boston: Beacon Press, 1993.

Gatens, William J. "John Ruskin and Music." In *The Lost Chord: Essays on Victorian Music,* ed. Nicholas Temperly. Bloomington: Indiana University Press, 1989.

Gates, Anita. "Theater Review: A Critic Who Takes His Work Home." *The New York Times.* Tuesday, March 30, 1999 (E1).

Gilbert, Sandra M., and Susan Gubar. *The Madwoman in the Attic: The Woman Writer and the Nineteenth-Century Literary Imagination.* New Haven, CT and London: Yale University Press, 1979; rpt. 1984.

Glavin, John. *After Dickens: Reading, Adaptation and Performance.* Cambridge: Cambridge University Press, 1999.

Glowacka, Dorota, and Stephen Boos. *Between Ethics and Aesthetics: Crossing the Boundaries.* New York: State University of New York Press, 2002.

Green, Laura. *Educating Women: Cultural Conflict and Victorian Literature.* Athens: Ohio University Press, 2001.

Griffin, Ronald. "The Trials of Oscar Wilde: The Intersection between Law and Literature." In *The Importance of Reinventing Oscar: Versions of Wilde during the Last 100 Years,* ed. Uwe Böker, Richard Corballis, and Julie Hubbard. Amsterdam: Rodopi, 2002. 57–66.

Hagstotz, Hilda Boettcher. *The Educational Theories of John Ruskin.* Lincoln: University of Nebraska Press, 1942.

Hall, Donald. *Queer Theories.* New York: Palgrave, 2003.

———. *Subjectivity.* New York and London: Routledge, 2004.

Hall, Donald E., and Maria Pramaggiore. *Representing Bisexualities: Subjects and Cultures of Fluid Desire.* New York: New York University Press, 1996.

Hall, Lesley A. *Sex, Gender, and Social Change in Britain since 1880.* New York: St. Martin's, 2000.

Hare, David. *The Judas Kiss.* New York: Grove Press, 1998.

Harris, Frank. *My Life and Loves.* New York: Grove Press, 1963.

Haraway, Donna. *Primate Visions: Gender, Race, and Nature in the World of Modern Science.* New York and London: Routledge, 1989.

Hayman, John. "Ruskin's *The Queen of Air* and the Appeal of Mythology." *Philological Quarterly* 57, no. 1 (1978): 104–14.

Helsinger, Elizabeth. "Authority, Desire, and the Pleasures of Reading." In *Sesame and Lilies,* ed. Deborah Epstein Nord. New Haven, CT: Yale University Press, 2002.

———. *Ruskin and the Art of the Beholder.* Cambridge, MA and London: Harvard University Press, 1982.

———. "Ruskin on Stage, II: Modern Painters in Santa Fe." *Ruskin Programme Bulletin* 17 (October 1998): 4–6.

Helsinger, Elizabeth, Robin Lauterbach Sheets, and William Veeder. *The Woman Question: Defining Voices, 1837–1883.* Vol. 1 of *The Woman Question, 1837–1883.* 3 vols. New York and London: Garland Publishing, 1983.

Hesse, Beatrix. "Stoppard's Oscar Wilde Travesty and Invention." In *The Importance of Reinventing Oscar: Versions of Wilde during the Last 100 Years,* ed. Uwe Böker, Richard Corballis, and Julie Hubbard. Amsterdam: Rodopi, 2000. 189–95.

Hewison, Robert. *John Ruskin: The Argument of the Eye.* Princeton, NJ: Princeton University Press, 1976.

Higgins, Lesley. "'Chameleon' Words: Gender Inflections in Ruskin's Aesthetic and Sociological Discourses." *The Journal of Pre-Raphaelite Studies* 11 (2002): 5–32.

Hilton, Tim. *John Ruskin: The Early Years 1818–1859.* New Haven, CT and London: Yale University Press, 1985.

———. *John Ruskin: The Later Years.* New Haven and London: Yale University Press, 2000.

Hoelterhoff, Manuela. *Modern Painters: Opera in Two Acts.* David Lang, composer. New York: Red Poppy, 1995.

Homans, Margaret. *Royal Representation: Queen Victoria and British Culture, 1837–1876.* Chicago: University of Chicago Press, 1998.

Housman, A. E. *The Letters of A. E. Housman,* ed. Henry Maas. Cambridge, MA: Harvard University Press, 1971.

Howarth, Janet. "Introduction." In *The Higher Education of Women,* ed. Janet Howarth. London and Roncevert: The Humbledon Press, 1988.

Hunt, John Dixon. *The Wider Sea: A Life of John Ruskin.* New York: Viking Press, 1982.

Hyde, Montgomery. *The Three Trials of Oscar Wilde.* New York: University Books, 1956.

The Illustrated London News. London: The Illustrated London News and Sketch, Ltd. 51–66 (1867–1875).

Irigaray, Luce. *Speculum of the Other Woman.* Trans. Gillian C. Gill. Ithaca, NY: Cornell University Press, 1985.

Jordanova, Ludmilla. *Sexual Visions: Images of Gender in Science and Medicine between the Eighteenth and Twentieth Centuries.* Madison: University of Wisconsin Press, 1989.

Kaufman, Moisés. *Gross Indecency: The Three Trials of Oscar Wilde.* New York: Vintage Books, 1998.

Keller, Evelyn Fox. *A Feeling for the Organism: The Life and Work of Barbara McClintock.* New York: W. H. Freedman and Co., 1983.

———. *Secrets of Life, Secrets of Death: Essays on Language, Gender, and Science.* New York and London: Routledge, 1992.

Kennedy, Maev. "Bonfire of Turner's Erotic Vanities Never Took Place." *The Guardian.* 12/29/04. www.guardian.co.uk/print/,3858,5092904–110427,00.html. 1/5/2005.

Kerner, Leighton. "Critic in extremis." *Village Voice,* August 12, 1985, 68.

Kestner, Joseph A. *Mythology and Misogyny: The Social Discourse of Nineteenth-Century Classical Subject Painting.* Madison: University of Wisconsin Press, 1989.

Keyssar, Helene. *Feminist Theatre and Theory.* New York: St. Martin's, 1996.

Kilroy, Thomas. *The Secret Fall of Constance Wilde.* County Meath, Ireland: Gallery Books, 1997.

Kimmelman, Michael. "Music, Love Victorian Style." *Vogue,* August 1995, 144–45.

Kincaid, James R. *Child-Loving: The Erotic Child and Victorian Culture.* New York and London: Routledge, 1992.

Kirchhoff, Frederick. "A Note on Ruskin's Mythography." *Victorian Newsletter* 50 (1976): 24–7.

———. "A Science against Sciences: Ruskin's Floral Mythology." In *Nature and the Victorian Imagination,* ed. U. C. Knopfflmacher and G. B. Tennyson. Berkeley and London: University of California Press, 1977.

Kirkup, Gill, and Laurie Smith Keller. *Inventing Women: Science, Technology, and Gender.* Cambridge: Polity Press, 1992.

Kissane, James. "Victorian Mythology." *Victorian Studies* 6, no. 1 (1962): 5–28.

Kosman, Joshua. " 'Modern Painters': A Bold New Stroke. David Lang opera premiere at Santa Fe." *San Francisco Chronicle.* August 4, 1995, sec. C, p. 1.

Koven, Seth. "How the Victorians Read Sesame and Lilies." In *Sesame and Lilies,* ed. Deborah Epstein Nord. New Haven, CT : Yale University Press, 2002. 165–204.

Kristeva, Julia. "Woman's Time." In *The Kristeva Reader,* ed. Toril Moi. New York: Columbia University Press, 1986. 187–214.

Kucich, John, and Dianne Sadoff. "Introduction: Histories of the Present." In *Victorian Afterlife: Postmodern Culture Rewrites the Nineteenth-Century.* Minneapolis and London: University of Minnesota Press, 2000.

Kushner, Tony. "Afterword." *Gross Indecency: The Three Trials of Oscar Wilde.* New York: Vintage Books, 1997.

Landow, George P. *The Aesthetic and Critical Theories of John Ruskin.* Princeton, NJ: Princeton University Press, 1971.

Lang, David. Remarks at "Giving Voice to *Modern Painters:* John Ruskin—His Life and Times." Symposium, Santa Fe Opera, July 29, 1995.

Levine, Caroline. "Visual Labor: Ruskin's Radical Realism." *Victorian Literature and Culture* 28, no. 1 (2000): 73–86.

Levine, George. *Boundaries of Fiction: Carlyle, McCauley, Newman.* Princeton, NJ: Princeton University Press, 1968.

———. *Dying to Know: Scientific Epistemology and Narrative in Victorian England.* Chicago: University of Chicago Press, 2002.

———, ed. *One Culture: Essays in Science and Literature.* Madison: University of Wisconsin Press, 1987.

———. *Realistic Imagination: English Fiction from Frankenstein to Lady Chatterley.* Chicago: University of Chicago Press, 1981.

———. "Ruskin, Darwin and the Matter of Matter." *Nineteenth-Century Prose.* Forthcoming 2008.

Litvak, Joseph. *Caught in the Act: Theatricality in the Nineteenth-Century English Novel.* Berkeley: University of California Press, 1992.

Lloyd, Jennifer. "Conflicting Expectations in Nineteenth-Century British Matrimony: The Failed Companionate Marriage of Effie Gray and John Ruskin." *Journal of Women's History* 11, no. 2 (1999): 88–109.

———. "Raising Lilies: Ruskin and Women." *Journal of British Studies.* 34, no. 3 (1995): 325–50.

Louis, Margot. "Gods and Mysteries: The Revival of Paganism and the Remaking of Mythography through the Nineteenth Century." *Victorian Studies* 47, no. 3 (2005): 329–61.

Loveridge, Lizzie. "The Countess." *Curtain Up.* www.curtainup.cot/countess-lond.html

Lutyens, Mary. *Millais and the Ruskins.* New York: Vanguard Press, 1967.

———. *Young Mirs. Ruskin in Venice.* (First published as *Effie in Venice* in England. London: John Marray, 1965). New York: Vanguard, 1966.

Lyall, Sarah. "A Censorship Story Goes Up in Smoke." *New York Times,* January 13, 2005. www.nytimes.com/2005/01/13/arts/design/13rusk.html?ex=1106622092&ei=1&en-457b1/13/2005.

MacKay, Carol Hanbery, ed. *Dramatic Dickens.* New York: St. Martin's, 1989.

Malthus, Thomas. *An Essay on the Principle of Population.* Oxford: Oxford University Press, 1993.

Mandel, Barrett. "Full of Life Now." In *Autobiography: Essays Theoretical and Critical,* ed. James Olney. Princeton, NJ: Princeton University Press, 1980. 49–72.

Marlowe, Sam. "The Countess." *The Times* (UK). June 9, 2005, sec. Features, Theatre, p. 22.

Marcus, Stephen. *The Other Victorians.* New York: Basic Books, 1966.

Marks, Elaine. "Some Final Words: An Interview with Elaine Marks." In *Professions: Conversations on the Future of Literary and Cultural Studies,* ed. Donald E. Hall. Urbana: University of Illinois Press, 2001.

Marsh, Jan. "Of Sesame and Lilies: Education in a Humane Society." In *Sesame and Lilies,* ed. Deborah Epstein Nord. New Haven, CT: Yale University Press, 2002.

————."'Resolve to Be a Great Paintress': Women Artists in Relation to John Ruskin as Critic and Patron." *Nineteenth-Century Contexts* 18, no. 2 (1994): 177–85.

Mason, Michael. *The Making of Victorian Sexual Attitudes.* Oxford: Oxford University Press, 1994.

————. *The Making of Victorian Sexuality.* Oxford: Oxford University Press, 1994.

Matz, Jesse. "Wilde Americana." In *Functions of Victorian Culture at the Present Time,* ed. Christine Krueger. Athens: Ohio University Press, 2002. 67–78.

Mayer, David. "The Sexuality of Pantomime." *Theatre Quarterly* 4, no.13 (1974): 55–64.

Mayer, Jed. "Savoir vivre or savoir mourir?: Ruskin, Vivisection, and Scientific Knowledge." *Nineteenth-Century Prose.* Forthcoming 2008.

Mayhew, Henry. *London Labour and the London Poor.* New York: Dover, 1968.

Maynard, John. *Victorian Discourses on Sexuality and Religion.* Cambridge: Cambridge University Press, 1993.

McLellan, Joseph. "Santa Fe's Powerful 'Paints.'" *The Washington Post.* August 1995, sec. E, p. 2.

Meilac, Henri, and Ludovic Halévy. *Frou-Frou.* Trans. Augustin Daly. New York: Samuel French, 1870.

Meisel, Martin. *Realizations: Narrative, Pictorial, and Theatrical Arts in Nineteenth-Century England.* Princeton, NJ: Princeton University Press, 1983.

Mellor, Anne K. "*Frankenstein:* A Feminist Critique of Science." In *One Culture: Essays in Science and Literature,* ed. George Levine and Alan Ranch. Madison: University of Wisconsin Press, 1987. 287–312.

Michie, Elsie. *Outside the Pale: Cultural Exclusion, Gender Difference, and the Victorian Woman Writer.* Ithaca, NY: Cornell University Press, 1993.

Mill, John Stuart. *Collected Works.* 33 volumes. Toronto: Toronto University Press, 1963.

Miller, Andrew, and James Eli Adams. "Introduction." In *Sexualities in Victorian Britain.* Bloomington: Indiana University Press, 1996.

Miller, J. Hillis. "Catachresis, Prosopopeia, and the Pathetic Fallacy: The Rhetoric of Ruskin." In *Poetry and Epistemology: Turning Points in the History of Poetic Knowledge,* ed. Roland Hagenbüchle. Regensburg, Germany: Putset, 1986. 398–407.

Millett, Kate. *Sexual Politics.* New York: Doubleday, 1968.

Moran, Joe. *Interdisciplinarity.* London: Routledge, 2002

Morgan, Thais E. *Victorian Sages and Cultural Discourse: Renegotiating Gender and Power.* New Brunswick, NJ and London: Rutgers University Press, 1990.

Moy, James. "David Henry Hwang's *M. Butterfly* and Philip Kan Gotanda's *Yankee Dawg You Die:* Repositioning Chinese-American Marginality on the American Stage." In *Critical Theory and Performance,* ed. Janelle Reinelt and Joe Roach. Ann Arbor: University of Michigan Press, 1992. 79–87.

Müller-Muth, Anja. "Writing 'Wilde': The Importance of Re-Presenting Oscar Wilde in Fin-de-Millénaire Drama in English (Stoppard, Hare, Ravenhill)." In *The Importance of Reinventing Oscar: Versions of Wilde during the Last 100 Years,* eds. Uwe Böker, Richard Corballis, and Julie Hubbard. Amsterdam: Rodopi, 2002. 219–27.

Munich, Andrienne Auslander. *Andromeda's Chains: Gender and Interpretation in Victorian Literature and Art.* New York: Columbia University Press, 1989.

Murphy, Gregory. *The Countess.* New York: Dramatists Play Service, 2000.

———. Personal interview. February 28, 2000.

———. "Ruskin's Mysogyny." Letter. *New York Times Book Review.* June 4, 2000, sec. 7, p. 4.

Nadel, Ira Bruce. "Renunciation and the 'Perfect Fredom' of the Victorians." In *Innerspace and the Inward Sphere: Essays on the Romantic and Victorian Self,* ed. Norman A. Anderson and Margene E. Weiss. Macomb, IL: Wesleyan Illinois University Press, 1978.

Newey, Katherine. *Women's Theatre Writing in Victorian Britain.* London: Palgrave, 2005.

Newman, John Henry. *The Works of Cardinal Newman.* 40 volumes. New York: Longmans, 1898–1918.

Nord, Deborah Epstein. "Mill and Ruskin on the Woman Question Revisited." In *Teaching Literature: What Is Needed Now,* ed. James Engell and David Perkins. Cambridge, MA: Harvard University Press, 1988: 73–83.

———, ed. and introduction. *Sesame and Lilies.* Yale University Press, 2002.

Nunn, Pamela Gerrish. "The 'woman question': Ruskin and the Female Artist." In *Ruskin's Artists: Studies in the Victorian Visual Economy,* ed. Robert Hewison. Aldershot and Brookfield, VT: Ashgate, 2000.

Nunokawa, Jeff. *Tame Passions of Wilde: The Styles of Manageable Desire.* Princeton, NJ and Oxford: Princeton University Press, 2003.

Oestreich, James. "Review: Ruskin at Full Cry in a New Form." *New York Times.* August 7, 1995, sec. C, p. 9.

O'Gorman, Francis. *Late Ruskin: New Contexts.* Hants, Aldershot, England and Burlington, VT: Ashgate, 2001.

———. "Ruskin's Science of the 1870s: Science, Education, and the Nation." *Ruskin and the Dawn of the Modern.* Oxford: Oxford University Press, 1999.

———. "'To See the Finger of God in the Dimensions of a Pyramid': A New

Context for Ruskin's *The Ethics of the Dust* (1866)." *Modern Language Review* 98, no. 3 (2003): 563–73.

Olney, James. *Metaphors of Self: The Meaning of Autobiography.* Princeton, NJ: Princeton University Press, 1972.

Parker, Andrew, and Eve Kosofsky Sedgwick, eds. *Performativity and Performance.* New York and London: Routledge, 1995.

Pater, Walter. *Works.* 10 volumes. London: MacMillan, 1913–1920.

Paxton, Nancy. *George Eliot and Herbert Spencer: Feminism, Evolutionism, and the Reconstruction of Gender.* Princeton, NJ: Princeton University Press, 1991.

Peniston, William. *Pederasts and Others: Urban Culture and Sexual Identity in Nineteenth-Century Paris.* New York: Harrington Park Press, 2004.

Peterson, Linda H. "The Feminist Origins of 'Of Queens' Gardens.'" In *Ruskin and Gender,* ed. Dinah Birch and Francis O'Gorman. Basingstoke and New York: Palgrave, 2002. 86–106.

Phegley, Jennifer. *Educating the Proper Woman Reader: Victorian Family Literary Magazines and the Cultural Health of the Nation.* Columbus: Ohio State University Press, 2004.

Pickering, Michael. "Mock Blacks and Racial Mockery: The 'Nigger' Minstrel and British Imperialism." In *Acts of Supremacy: The British Empire and the Stage, 1790–1930,* ed. J. S. Bratton. Manchester and New York: Manchester University Press, 1991. 179–236.

Pierce, Joanna Tapp. "From Garden to Gardener: The Cultivation of Little girls in Caroll's Alice Books and Ruskin's 'Of Queens' Gardens.'" *Women's Studies* 29, no. 6 (October 2000): 741–62.

Plato. *Works.* Tr. Benjamin Jowett. New York: Tudor, 1935.

Porter, Roy, and Lesley Hall. *The Facts of Life: The Creation of Sexual Knowledge in Britain, 1650–1950.* New Haven, CT: Yale University Press, 1995.

Poovey, Mary. *Uneven Developments: The Ideological Work of Gender in Mid-Victorian England.* Chicago: The University of Chicago Press, 1988.

Postlewait, Thomas. "Autobiography and Theatre History." In *Interpreting the Theatrical Past,* ed. Thomas Postlewait and Bruce A. McConachie. Iowa City: University of Iowa Press, 1989.

Powell, Kerry. *Women and the Victorian Theatre.* Cambridge: Cambridge University Press, 1997.

Pratt, Annis. *Dancing with Goddesses: Archetypes, Poetry, and Empowerment.* Bloomington: Indiana University Press, 1994.

Proust, Marcel. *On Reading Ruskin.* Trans. and eds. Jean Autret, William Burford, and Phillip J. Wolfe. New Haven, CT and London: Yale University Press, 1987.

Reide, David G. *Allegories of One's Own Mind: Melancholy in Victorian Poetry,* Columbus: Ohio State University Press, 2005.

Reinelt, Janelle. "The Politics of Discourse: Performativity Meets Theatricality." *SubStance* 31, no. 2–3 (2002): 201–15.

Richards, Jeffrey. "John Ruskin, Wilson Barrett, and the Toga Play." Paper presented at "Victorian Life Writing: Sources and Resources." Lancaster University, Lancaster, England. July 2005.

———. "Ruskin and the Theatre." Paper presented at "John Ruskin: The Brantwood Years." Lancaster University, Lancaster, England. August 2000.

Richardson, Brian. "The Struggle for the Real—Interpretive Conflict, Dramatic Method, and the Paradox of Realism." In *Realism and the American Dramatic Tradition,* ed. William Demastes. Tuscaloosa and London: Alabama University Press, 1996. 1–17.

Roberts, Robin. *A New Species: Gender and Science in Science Fiction.* Urbana and Chicago: University of Illinois Press, 1993.

Robson, Catherine. *Men in Wonderland: The Lost Girlhood of the Victorian Gentleman.* Princeton, NJ: Princeton University Press, 2003.

———. "The Stones of Childhood: Ruskin's Lost Jewels." In *Ruskin and Gender,* ed. Dinah Birch and Francis O'Gorman. London: Palgrave, 2002.

Rose, Phyllis. *Parallel Lives: Five Victorian Marriages.* New York: Knopf, 1984.

Rosenberg, John D. *The Darkening Glass: A Portrait of Ruskin's Genius.* New York: Columbia University Press, 1961.

Ruskin, John. *The Diaries of John Ruskin.* 3 vols. Ed. Joan Evans and John Howard Whitehouse. Oxford: Clarendon Press, 1959.

———. *Fors Clavigera.* Ed. Dinah Birch. Edinburgh: Edinbugh University Press, 2000.

———. *The Winnington Letters of John Ruskin.* Ed. Van Akin Burd. Cambridge, MA: Belknap-Harvard University Press, 1969.

———. *The Works of John Ruskin.* Ed. E. T. Cook and Alexander Wedderburn. London: George Allen. New York: Longmans, Green and Co., 1903–12.

Russett, Cynthia. *Sexual Science: The Victorian Construction of Womanhood.* Cambridge, MA and London: Harvard University Press, 1989.

Salamensky, S. I. "Re-Presenting Oscar Wilde's Trials, Gross Indecency, and Documentary Spectacle." *Theatre Journal* 54, no. 4 (2002): 575–88.

Sammells, Neil. "The Early Stage Plays." In *The Cambridge Companion to Tom Stoppard,* ed. Katherine Kelly. Cambridge: Cambridge University Press, 2001. 104–19.

Sawyer, Paul L. "Ruskin and the Matriarchal Logos." In *Victorian Sages and Cultural Discourse: Renegotiating Gender and Power,* ed. Thaïs Morgan. New Brunswick, NJ and London: Rutgers University Press, 1990. 129–41.

———. "Ruskin and Tyndall: The Poetry of Matter and the Poetry of Spirit." In *Victorian Science and Victorian Values: Literary Perspectives,* ed. James Paradis and Thomas Postlewait. New York: The New York Academy of Sciences, 1981. 217–46.

———. *Ruskin's Poetic Argument: The Design of the Major Works.* Ithaca, NY and London: Cornell University Press, 1985.

Schiavi, Michael. "Wildean War: Politics of Fin-de-Siècle Spectatorship." *Modern Drama* 47 (Fall 2004): 399–422.

Schiebinger, Londa. *Nature's Body: Gender in the Making of Modern Science.* Boston: Beacon Press, 1993.

Sdegno, Emma. "Ruskin's Winnington Deities." In *Athena's Shuttle: Myth, Religion, Ideology from Romanticism to Modernism,* ed. Franco Maracci and Emma Sdegno. Milan: Cisalpino, 2000.

Seaton, Beverly. "Considering the Lilies: Ruskin's 'Proserpina' and Other Victorian Flower Books." *Victorian Studies* 28, no. 2 (1985): 255–82.

Senelick, Laurence. "The Evolution of the Male Impersonator in Nineteenth-Century Popular Stage." *Essays in Theater* 1, no. 1 (1982): 29–44.

Shakespeare, William. *The Complete Works of William Shakespeare.* New York: Pearson Longman, 2004.

Shanley, Mary Lyndon. *Feminism, Marriage, and the Law in Victorian England, 1850–1895.* Princeton, NJ: Princeton University Press, 1989

Showalter, Elaine. *Sexual Anarchy: Gender and Culture at the Fin de Siècle.* London and New York: Penguin, 1990.

Shuman, Cathy. *Pedagogical Economies: The Examination and the Victorian Literary Man.* Stanford, CA: Stanford University Press, 2000.

Siebers, Tobin. *The Mirror of Medusa.* Berkeley: University of California Press, 1983.

Sierz, Alex. "The Countess." *The Stage Online.* June 15, 2005. www.thestage.co.uk/reviews/review.php/8272

Simpson, Marc. "The Dream of the Dragon: Ruskin's Serpent Imagery." In *Ruskin Polygon: Essays on the Imagination of John Ruskin,* ed. Faith M. Holland and John Dixon Hunt. Manchester: Manchester University Press, 1982. 21–43.

Sinfield, Alan. *The Wilde Century: Effeminacy, Oscar Wilde, and the Queer Moment.* New York: Columbia University Press, 1994.

Slinn, E. Warwick. *Victorian Poetry as Cultural Critique: The Politics of Performative Language.* Charlottesville, VA: University of Virginia Press, 2003.

Smith, Jonathan. *Charles Darwin and Victorian Visual Culture.* Cambridge: Cambridge University Press, 2006.

Smith, Lindsay. *Victorian Photography, Painting, and Poetry: The Enigma of Visibility in Ruskin, Morris, and the Pre-Raphaelites.* Cambridge: Cambridge University Press, 1995.

Smith, Peter. "The Ruskins: A Tragedy at Heart." Letter. *The New York Times.* June 25, 2000, sec. 2, p. 2.

Sokol, Raymond. "Opera: *Modern Painters* Premiere." *Wall Street Journal.* July 31, 1995, sec. A, p. 12.

Sonstroem, David. "Millett Versus Ruskin: A Defense of Ruskin's 'Of Queens' Gardens.'" *Victorian Studies* 20, no. 3 (1977): 283–97.

Spear, Jeffrey L. *Dreams of an English Eden: Ruskin and His Tradition in Social Criticism.* New York: Columbia University Press, 1984.

Stern, Rebecca. "Moving Parts and Speaking Parts: Situating Victorian Antitheatricality." *ELH* 65, no. 2 (1998): 423–49.

Stoddart, Judith. *Ruskin's Culture Wars: Fors Cavigera and the Crisis of Victorian Liberalism.* Charlottesville: University of Virginia Press, 1998.

Stoppard, Tom. *The Invention of Love.* New York: Grove Press, 1997.

Sullivan, Arthur, and W. S. Gilbert. *The Complete Plays of Gilbert and Sullivan.* New York: W.W. Norton, 1997.

Tally, Paul M. "Architecture as Craig's Interim Symbol: Ruskin and Other Influences," *Educational Theatre Journal* 19 (1967): 52–60.

Tanitch, Robert. *Oscar Wilde on Stage and Screen.* London: Methuen, 1999.

Tuana, Nancy. *The Less Noble Sex: Scientific, Religious, and Philosophical Conceptions of Woman's Nature.* Bloomington: Indiana University Press, 1993.

Vicinus, Martha. *A Widening Sphere: Changing Roles of Victorian Women.* Bloomington: Indiana University Press, 1977.

Vlock, Deborah. *Dickens, Novel Reading, and the Victorian Popular Theatre.* Cambridge: Cambridge University Press, 1998.

Voskuil, Lynn M. "Acting Naturally: Brontë, Lewes, and the Problem of Gender Performance." *ELH* 62, no. 2 (1995): 409–42.

———. *Acting Naturally: Victorian Theatricality and Authenticity.* Charlottesville, VA: University of Virginia Press, 2004.

Waldrep, Shelton. "The Uses and Misuses of Oscar Wilde." In *Victorian Afterlife: Postmodern Culture Rewrites the Nineteenth-Century,* ed. John Kucich and Dianne Sadoff. Minneapolis and London: University of Minnesota Press, 2000.

Walkowitz, Judith. *City of Dreadful Delight: Narratives of Sexual Danger in Late-Victorian London.* Chicago: University of Chicago Press, 1992

Walsh, Susan A. "Darling Mothers, Devilish Queens: The Divided Woman in Victorian Fantasy." *The Victorian Newsletter* 72 (Fall 1987): 32–36.

Warner, Marina. *Monuments and Maidens: The Allegory of the Female Form.* New York: Athenaeum, 1985.

Warner, Michael. *Fear of a Queer Planet: Queer Politics and Social Theory.* Minneapolis: University of Minnesota Press, 1993.

Warrell, Ian. "A Checklist of Erotic Sketches in the Turner Bequest." *The British Art Journal* 4, no. 1 (2003): 15–46.

———. "Exploring the "dark side": Ruskin and the Problem of Turner's Erotica." *The British Art Journal* 4, no. 1 (2003): 5–14.

Webling, Peggy. *Peggy: the Story of One Score Years and Ten* London: Hutchison & Co, 1924.

Weltman, Sharon. ""Be no more Housewives, but Queens': Queen Victoria in John Ruskin's Domestic Mythology." In *Re-making Queen Victoria,* ed. Margaret Homans and Adrienne Munich. Cambridge and London: Cambridge University Press, 1997.

———. "Gender and the Architectonics of Metaphor: Ruskin's Pathetic Fallacy in *The Ethics of the Dust.*" *Prose Studies* 16, no. 2 (1993): 41–61.

———. "John Ruskin and the Mythlogy of Gender." Ph.D. diss. Rutgers University, 1992.

———. "Myth and Gender in Ruskin's Science." In *Ruskin and the Dawn of the Modern,* ed. Dinah Birch. Oxford: Oxford University Press, 1999. 153–73.

———. "Mythic Language and Gender Subversion: The Case of Ruskin's Athena." *Nineteenth-Century Literature* 52, no. 3 (December 1997): 350–71.

———. "Pantomime Truth and Gender Performance: John Ruskin on Theatre." In *John Ruskin and Gender,* ed. Dinah Birch and Francis O'Gorman. Basingstoke and New York: Palgrave, 2002.

———. *Ruskin's Mythic Queen: Gender Subversion in Victorian Culture.* Athens: Ohio University Press, 1998.

———. "Victorians on Broadway at the Present Time: Ruskin's Life on Stage." In *Functions of Victorian Culture at the Present Time,* ed. Christine Krueger. Athens: Ohio University Press, 2002. 79–94.

Wilde, Oscar. *The Compete Letters of Oscar Wilde.* Ed. Merlin Holland and Rupert Hart-Davis. New York: Henry Holt and Co., 2000.

———. *The Complete Works of Oscar Wilde.* New York: Harper and Row, 1989.

Wilshire, Bruce. *Role Playing and Identity: The Limits of Theatre as Metaphor.* Bloomington: Indiana University Press, 1982.

Woolf, Virginia. "Professions for Women." In *The Death of the Moth and Other Essays.* New York: Harcourt, Brace, and Co., 1942.

Worthen, W. B. "Drama, Performativity, and Performance." *PMLA* 113 (October 1998): 1093–1107.

Yeates, Amelia. ""Keep the Modern Magazine and Novel Out of Your Girl's Way': Ruskin on Women's Reading." *Nineteenth-Century Prose.* Forthcoming 2008.

Zeifman, Hersh. "The Comedy of Eros: Stoppard in Love," In *The Cambridge Companion to Tom Stoppard,* ed. Katherine Kelly. Cambridge: Cambridge University Press, 2001. 185–200.

Zinoman, Jason. "The Countess." *Time Out: New York.* June 24, 1999. Issue 196, p. 11.

INDEX